More praise for Geoffrey R. Stone and *Perilous Times*

"Mr. Stone has written an important, indeed necessary book on freedom."
—Michiko Kakutani, *New York Times*

"We have long needed this book, though perhaps never as badly as we do today. . . . Stone provides a *Profiles of Courage* for the Sept. 11 generation."
—Christopher Capozzola, *Washington Post*

"A compelling account. . . . *Perilous Times* tells a story every American should know."
—Eric Foner, *The Nation*

"This is great, dramatic, and absorbing legal history at its best—beautifully written, highly accessible, and critically important for our time."
—Jonathan Cole

"*Perilous Times* is magisterial, timely, and wise. . . . By placing a spotlight on restrictions of freedom amidst war, Stone has done an extraordinary public service—and produced a classic in the process."
—Cass Sunstein

"Sometimes a book just hits the intellectual spot. . . . As terrorists from abroad pose a continuing and dangerous threat to our safety, we act at our peril if we respond at home without recalling our past history that Stone describes with such clarity."
—Floyd Abrams

"Geoffrey Stone's outstanding book alarms as much as it clarifies. As the current administration flouts the Constitution in genuinely groundbreaking ways, it is also exposing us to dangers hitherto unknown."
—Stephen Holmes, *The New Republic*

"A lively, masterful history—and reminder—of the essential role of the First Amendment during the stresses of war."
—Bob Woodward

# WAR AND LIBERTY

# WAR AND LIBERTY

## AN AMERICAN DILEMMA:
## 1790 TO THE PRESENT

## Geoffrey R. Stone

W. W. Norton & Company
*New York • London*

*War and Liberty* is an abridgement and adaptation of an earlier work,
*Perilous Times: Free Speech in Wartime, From the Sedition Act of 1798
to the War on Terrorism* (W. W. Norton, 2004)

For information about permission to reproduce selections
from this book, write to Permissions, W. W. Norton & Company, Inc.,
500 Fifth Avenue, New York, NY 10110

Manufacturing by Courier Westford
Book design by Rhea Braunstein
Production managers: Amanda Morrison and Anna Oler

Library of Congress Cataloging-in-Publication Data

Stone, Geoffrey R.
War and liberty : an American dilemma : 1790 to the present /
Geoffrey R. Stone.
p. cm.
"War and Liberty" is an abridgement and adaptation of an earlier work,
"Perilous Times : free speech in wartime, from the Sedition Act of 1798
to the war on terrorism. W. W. Norton, 2004."
Includes bibliographical references and index.
ISBN-13: 978-0-393-33004-5 (pbk.)
ISBN-10: 0-393-33004-4 (pbk.)
1. Freedom of speech—United States—History. 2. Civil rights—
United States—History. I. Stone, Geoffrey R. Perilous times. II. Title.
JC591.S76 2007
323.44'30973—dc22                          2006102204

W. W. Norton & Company, Inc.
500 Fifth Avenue, New York, N.Y. 10110
www.wwnorton.com

W. W. Norton & Company Ltd.
Castle House, 75/76 Wells Street, London W1T 3QT

*For my Parents*
*Robert & Shirley Stone*

"I am an American citizen and
I am not at all easy to intimidate. . . ."

—JOHN HOWARD LAWSON,
testifying before the House Committee on
Un-American Activities (1947)

# Contents

❦❦

# Acknowledgments

*War and Liberty* is an abridgement and adaptation of an earlier work, *Perilous Times: Free Speech in Wartime, From the Sedition Act of 1798 to the War on Terrorism* (W. W. Norton, 2004). For that reason, I incorporate by reference the Acknowledgments in that earlier volume. The many people who contributed in so many ways to *Perilous Times* have, of necessity, contributed to *War and Liberty* as well, and I am deeply grateful for their support, their ideas, and their inspiration.

This project received financial support from the University of Chicago Law School's Frank Cicero, Jr. Faculty Fund. In preparing this work, I relied on my superb research assistants at the University of Chicago and New York University, Ross Fulton and Josephine Morse, for their careful scrutiny; my friends Harriet Feinberg, Elenore Freedman, and Selma Eigner for their sage editorial advice; and my wife, Nancy Spector Stone, who more than anyone encouraged this work and was, as ever, an endless source of guidance and support.

PREFACE

# War Fever

❦

THE war on terrorism has posed fundamental questions about the appropriate balance between individual liberty and national security. These questions have been with us from the very founding of the Republic. How we resolve them speaks volumes about the nature and depth of our commitment to the freedoms that define us as a nation.

My goal in *War and Liberty* is to explore with you how well we have—or have not—preserved our constitutional rights under the unique stresses of wartime. My hope is that this inquiry will help *you* make more informed judgments about the vexing issues that confront our nation today. Addressing such matters in a thoughtful and informed manner is, after all, one of the most daunting responsibilities of a citizen of a self-governing society.

WAR EXCITES GREAT FEAR, patriotism, and anxiety. Thousands, perhaps millions, of lives may be at risk. The nation itself may be in peril. If ever there is a time to pull out all the stops, it is surely in wartime. In war, the government may conscript soldiers, commandeer property, control prices, ration food, raise taxes, and freeze wages. May it also limit our liberties?

To make sense of this question, it is necessary first to know what those liberties are. This is not as easy as you might think. Consider the First, Fourth, and Fifth amendments to the Constitution:

> Congress shall make no law . . . abridging the freedom of speech, or of the press. . . .

> The right of the people to be secure in their persons, houses, papers, and effects, against unreasonable searches and seizures, shall not be violated. . . .

> No person shall be . . . deprived of life, liberty, or property, without due process of law. . . .

As Justice Oliver Wendell Holmes illustrated with his oft-quoted "false cry of fire in a crowded theatre," the First Amendment cannot mean what it appears to say. It cannot be that you have a right to say anything you want, at any place, time, and manner of your choosing. To give meaning to the First Amendment, we must define "the freedom of speech, or of the press" that Congress may not "abridge."

Similarly, what is a "search"? Suppose an FBI agent orders your bank to turn over your financial records, or deceives you into telling her things about yourself, or uses a parabolic microphone to overhear from a distance your conversations with a friend in a park. Have you been subjected to a "search" within the meaning of the Fourth Amendment?

And what is "due process of law"? Suppose the U.S. military detains you as a "suspected terrorist." Clearly, you have been deprived of your "liberty." Does "due process of law" mean you have a right to a hearing? To the assistance of an attorney? To a jury trial?

Lawyers, judges, philosophers, political scientists, and historians have filled millions of pages wrestling with these issues. Not only is there no consensus on the answers, but there is scant agreement on how to frame the questions. Some argue that we are bound by the "original intent" of those who wrote these provisions more than two centuries ago. Others assert that we must give contemporary meaning to these provisions in light of changing circumstances and our "evolving standards of decency." My goal in this volume is not to resolve these disputes. It is, rather, to consider with you how we should give meaning to these provisions *in time of war*.

Suppose we agree that a law prohibiting any person to criticize the president abridges "the freedom of speech." Now, suppose the United States is at war. Congress declares that, in order for the nation to defend itself effectively, "Americans must stand united." Congress finds that public denunciations of the commander in chief undermine public morale, encourage the enemy, and discourage enlistment in the military. Would you, as a justice of the Supreme Court, hold unconstitutional a statute prohibiting any person "to criticize the president with the intent to undermine the war effort"?

Or, suppose we agree that wiretapping violates the Fourth Amendment unless it is authorized by a judicially issued search warrant based upon a finding of probable cause. Now, suppose the United States is at war. Faced with threats of espionage, sabotage, and terrorism, the president authorizes the National Security Agency to wiretap any telephone call that "might aid the enemy." As a justice of the Supreme Court, would you hold such "searches" unconstitutional?

Or, suppose we agree that the government cannot constitutionally detain a person because he might at some time in the future commit an unlawful act. Now, suppose the United States is at war. Congress enacts a law authorizing the president to detain "for as long as necessary" any person he "reasonably believes may pose a danger to the national security." As a justice of the Supreme Court, would you hold that this law satisfies the requirements of due process?

These are not idle questions. Throughout our history, the United States has confronted precisely these sorts of dilemmas. At the end of the eighteenth century, when the United States was on the verge of war with France, President John Adams signed into law the Sedition

Act of 1798, which effectively made it a crime for any person to make any statement against the president, the Congress, or the Government of the United States, with the intent to bring them into contempt or disrepute.

Sixty years later, during the Civil War, President Lincoln suspended the writ of habeas corpus* on eight separate occasions. Tens of thousands of Americans were imprisoned by military authorities, without any review by a court of law. During World War I, President Wilson launched an aggressive campaign to squelch any criticism of his wartime policies. The U.S. government prosecuted some 2,000 individuals for expressing their opposition to the war or the draft. Those convicted were often sentenced to terms of ten to twenty years in prison.

During World War II, President Roosevelt ordered the internment of more than 110,000 individuals of Japanese descent, two-thirds of whom were American citizens. Men, women, and children were locked away in detention camps for the better part of three years, for no reason other than their race.

Faced with the threat of Soviet espionage, sabotage, and subversion during the Cold War, the government instituted loyalty programs, legislative investigations, blacklists, and criminal prosecutions to ferret out and punish those suspected of "disloyalty." It was an era scarred by the actions of Senator Joseph McCarthy and the House Un-American Activities Committee.

During the Vietnam War, the Johnson and Nixon administrations initiated surreptitious programs of surveillance and infiltration in order to disrupt and neutralize those who opposed the war, prosecuted dissenters for burning their draft cards and expressing contempt for the American flag, and attempted to prevent the *New York Times* and the *Washington Post* from publishing the Pentagon Papers.

Most recently, during the war on terrorism, President George W. Bush has approved the secret detention of hundreds (perhaps thou-

---

*A petition for a writ of habeas corpus is a request by an individual asking a judge to determine the legality of his detention by the government. Suspending the writ of habeas corpus prohibits judges from reviewing the legality of an individual's detention.

sands) of noncitizens, closed deportation proceedings from public view, authorized the interception of telephone calls and emails without a judicial warrant, and ordered the indefinite detention of American citizens on the basis of secret determinations that they are "unlawful enemy combatants."

Are these measures constitutional? Are such compromises of our peacetime liberties necessary to protect the nation? Certainly, in each of these episodes the United States faced extraordinary dangers. War poses threats that do not exist in peacetime, and there is every reason to think hard about whether we can afford to preserve our liberties in time of war.

But we must also be wary of the perils of war fever. Wartime emotions run high. Spies, saboteurs, and terrorists are seen lurking around every corner, and loyalty is the order of the day. Politicians may play the "fear" card for personal and partisan gain. In such circumstances, the line between reason and repression can be elusive and is often ignored.

Indeed, the United States has had a long and unfortunate history of overreacting to the perceived dangers of wartime. Time and again, we have allowed fear and fury to get the better of us. We have suppressed dissent, detained and deported innocent persons, excessively limited our liberties, and then—later—regretted our actions. *War and Liberty* is about why this happens and how we might break this pattern in the future.

We have made progress over time. But the progress is fitful, uneven, and fragile. In order for us to strike a more thoughtful, more mature balance between liberty and security in our own time, we need a deeper understanding of ourselves and our history. Only if we acknowledge our mistakes and learn from the past can we gain the insight, self-discipline, and wisdom that are necessary for us not to repeat those mistakes over and over again.

CHAPTER I

# The Half War with France
# "The Reign of Witches"

✿✿

THE years between 1789 and 1801 marked a critical turning point in American history. In an atmosphere of fear, suspicion, and intrigue, the United States first faced the challenge of reconciling the Constitution with the perceived necessities of wartime. The political struggles of this era revealed sharp divisions in the nation's nascent understanding of the Constitution and yielded fundamental lessons that have shaped our laws and values to this day.

We tend to romanticize the founding fathers, and they were indeed a remarkable group of visionaries and political thinkers. But they were also subject to petty jealousies, partisan squabbling, and deep distrust, especially of one another. Moreover, they were deeply unsure of the constitutional system they had put in place. It was, after all, an experiment. As they embarked upon an adventure in self-governance, they had no precedents to guide them. And when the issue was war and peace, they bitterly disagreed over how much to risk on an untested idea.

No single foreign event affected the United States more profoundly in the 1790s than the French Revolution. Most Americans initially hailed the new Republic's commitment to *"liberté, fraternité, égalité."* Over the next several years, however, France exploded in religious conflict, economic chaos, and civil war. With the executions in 1793

1

of the French King Louis XVI and his Queen Marie Antoinette, the French Republic spiraled into the Reign of Terror. Fearing the spread of anarchy and revolution, a promonarchist coalition, including England, Spain, Austria, the Netherlands, and Prussia, declared war on France. But by 1798, Napoleon's victories had made France the dominant power in Europe, and a mighty French army was poised to cross the Channel to England.

Across the Atlantic, the United States, eager to maintain its growing international commerce, strained to preserve a precarious neutrality. In its efforts to placate both the British and the French, the United States managed to incur the enmity of both. The British navy seized American ships and impressed American seamen into its service, bringing the United States and England to the brink of war. Desperate to avoid a break with England, President George Washington sent John Jay to London. In 1794, Jay negotiated a treaty that ensured cordial Anglo-American relations. But the Jay Treaty affronted the French, who charged that it betrayed the long-standing Franco-American alliance. France then launched its own campaign against American shipping and declared that any captured American seamen would be treated as pirates. Between June 1796 and June 1797 French corsairs seized 316 ships flying the American colors.

MEANWHILE, SHARP POLITICAL divisions had already begun to fracture the United States. Although the framers of the Constitution had warned against the perils of faction, long-standing disagreements between merchants and farmers, creditors and debtors, and northerners and southerners led to the emergence of formal party structures as early as Washington's first term.

The Federalists, led by Alexander Hamilton and John Adams, and the Republicans, led by Thomas Jefferson and James Madison, differed sharply in their attitudes toward government finance, centralization of authority, and popular government. The Federalists distrusted the ignorance, passions, and prejudices of the common man. Citing the example of the French Revolution, they feared that democracy might lapse into anarchy and called for a powerful governing elite to lead the nation. A central mission of the Federalist Party was to save the nation from the perils of democracy. To the Federalists, the paramount end of government was to protect the rights of property and the stability of society. The Federalist Party drew its support largely from the propertied interests—merchants, bankers, shippers, financiers, and large landowners. It was committed to economic growth and a strong central government.

The Republicans, by contrast, held an ardent faith in popular democracy. They feared tyranny more than anarchy, and valued liberty more than security. They advocated a government directly responsive to the will of the people, without the oversight of a ruling class. Consisting largely of artisans, mechanics, and farmers, the Republican Party distrusted the nation's commercial and financial interests and envisioned a decentralized republic that would stand as an international bulwark of individual liberty.

The division between Federalists and Republicans grew increasingly acrimonious over the crisis in Europe. The Republicans saw the French Revolution as an extension of the American promise of liberty, republicanism, and democracy. The Federalists saw it as a menacing harbinger of licentiousness and a clear and present danger to the established order. The political tension and mutual suspicion soon reached fever pitch. In 1796, in the first contested presidential election, John Adams defeated Thomas Jefferson by a scant three electoral votes. After Adams's election, both Federalists and Republicans feared the breakup of the union.

At a special session of Congress shortly after his inauguration, Adams declared that the United States must "convince France and the world that we are not a degraded people, humiliated under a colonial spirit of fear."[1] Although promising a renewed effort to negotiate with France, he asked Congress to establish a provisional army and to expand the navy in order to protect American commerce and defend the nation against a possible French invasion.

When France arrogantly rebuffed Adams's proposal to negotiate, a wave of patriotic fervor swept the nation. Adams called for emergency defense measures and urged Congress to show "zeal" in its "defence of the national rights."[2] The Federalist-dominated Congress gave the president everything he asked for, and more. It ordered additional warships, appropriated funds to fortify the nation's harbors, expanded the army, authorized the navy to attack French ships, and abrogated all treaties with France. With war seemingly imminent, the man who had won the presidency by only three electoral votes was suddenly a national hero. Whenever he appeared in public, bands played, cannon roared, flags unfurled, and crowds cheered "Huzzah." In this fevered atmosphere, the nation's commitment to civil liberties was quickly rationalized out of existence.

THE ANTAGONISM BETWEEN the Federalists and the Republicans came to a head in the rancorous congressional debates in the spring of 1798 over Adams's proposed defense measures. The Federalists were quick to embrace the president's call to strengthen the nation's defense. The Republicans were skeptical. Fearful that a large military buildup would make war with France inevitable, increase the president's authority, and yoke the United States to England, the Republicans opposed every significant measure put forth by the Federalists. But because the Federalists had working majorities in both houses of Congress, the Federalist proposals were quickly enacted by a (more or less) straight party vote.

These debates reveal important patterns that have been repeated throughout our history in times of real or perceived crisis. The Republicans accused the Federalists of exaggerating the danger and precipitating an unnecessary war. The Federalists responded that if the nation failed to prepare immediately for war it could expect "nothing but bloodshed, slaughter, pillage, and a complete subjection to France."[3] In a manner that would become all too common in

American history, the Federalists questioned whether Republicans loved their country and accused them of seeking to preserve a peace of "vile submission."[4] Congressman Robert Goodloe Harper charged his Republican colleagues with attempting to prepare the people for the complete "destruction of the country,"[5] and President Adams fumed that his political opponents "would sink the glory of our country and prostrate her liberties at the feet of France."[6]

In this crisis, the Federalists saw—and seized—an opportunity to strike a critical blow at the Republicans. By discrediting their political opponents as disloyal, they sought to entrench themselves as the nation's dominant party. Leveraging a moment of high patriotism, they enacted a legislative program designed to cripple, if not destroy, the Republican Party.

A THEME THAT RECURS THROUGHOUT the history of the United States in wartime is the status of aliens. After all, who is more likely to be "disloyal" than a noncitizen—a person with no formal allegiance to the nation? With fears about the French in 1798, the Germans in World War I, the Japanese in World War II, and foreign-born Muslims in the war on terrorism, the United States has long wrestled with the question of whether and to what extent noncitizens have constitutional rights.

To the Federalists, the greatest internal danger facing the nation was the rapidly growing foreign-born population. Between 1790 and 1798, a wave of foreigners entered the United States, especially from France, Ireland, and Germany. The Federalists saw these immigrants, many of whom had fled tyrannical governments, as a nest of potential disloyalty and Republican strength. Federalists like Harrison Gray Otis raged that immigrants would "contaminate the purity . . . of the American character."[7]

The First Congress had authorized immigrants to obtain citizenship after only two years of residence. Because these new citizens tended to flock to the Republican Party, the Federalists lengthened the requirement to five years in 1795. Then, in the spring of 1798, in an atmosphere of rampant nativism, the Federalists extended the residence requirement to fourteen years—the longest in American history.

At the same time, the Federalists enacted two alien acts. The Alien Enemies Act provided that, in the case of a *declared* war, citizens or subjects of an enemy nation residing in the United States could be incarcerated or deported at the direction of the president. Adopted with bipartisan support, this act has remained a permanent part of American wartime policy. Because *enemy aliens* have an allegiance to a nation with which we are at war, it is reasonable, within limits, to view them as potential spies and saboteurs.

But the Federalists did not regard the Alien Enemies Act as sufficient to their needs. They also enacted the Alien Friends Act, which empowered the president to detain and deport *any* noncitizen he deemed dangerous to the United States.[8] Under this legislation, the individual had no right to a hearing, to be informed of the charges against him, or to present evidence on his behalf. The act vested *absolute* power over such persons in the president.

The Republicans protested that no amount of danger could justify assigning such an "arbitrary power to the President."[9] Congressman Albert Gallatin of Pennsylvania warned that if such a law were appropriate for alien friends, a similar law might later be directed at citizens. He emphasized that the Constitution did not limit only to citizens the rights to trial by jury, habeas corpus, and due process of law.

The Federalists responded that the act was critical to the nation's security, because "the times are full of danger and it would be the height of madness not to take every precaution in our power."[10] To the charge that the law violated the Constitution, they replied that the Constitution gave no rights to aliens, for they were not part of "We the People" who had originally adopted the Constitution. James Madison decried the act as a "monster"; Thomas Jefferson labeled it "detestable."[11]

The Alien Friends Act was, indeed, a "monster." To put all noncitizens at the mercy of presidential fiat, with no right to due process or independent judicial review, was a betrayal of the most fundamental principles of the Constitution. The Federalists could have achieved their *legitimate* goals without stripping noncitizens of due process of law. The Alien Friends Act, which expired in 1801, did not do the nation proud.

BUT THAT ACT WAS JUST A START. The centerpiece of the Federalists' legislative agenda was the infamous Sedition Act of 1798. To understand this law, we must appreciate the Federalists' view of "the freedom of speech, or of the press." In short, the Federalists had little faith in free and open debate. As the Federalist Congressman James A. Bayard of Delaware observed, confidence that truth prevails over falsehood is "a fine moral sentiment, but our limited knowledge of events [does not] verify it." The Federalists believed that the common man could easily be manipulated and misled. They warned that even one person could "alarm a whole country with ridiculous fears of government," and that if "the alarm is caught by the weak" it will soon be "spread by the foolish" like a "contagious disease."[12] After witnessing the violent aftershocks of the French Revolution, the Federalists had no doubt of both the power and the danger of public opinion.

To the Federalists, these fears were not mere abstractions. They viewed the Republican press as dishonest, abusive, and irresponsible. Its mission, they charged, was to deceive the public. Alexander Hamilton warned that "no character, however upright, is a match for constantly reiterated attacks." "The public mind," he explained, "fatigued" by the struggle to resist "the calumnies which eternally assail it," eventually embraces "the opinion that a person so often accused cannot be entirely innocent."[13] President Adams complained that the Republican press went to "all lengths of profligacy, falsehood and malignity in defaming our government," and demanded that the "misrepresentations which have misled so many citizens . . . must be discountenanced by authority."[14]

These complaints were not without merit. The most prominent of the Republican newspapers, the *Aurora* in Philadelphia, was edited by Benjamin Franklin Bache, the grandson of Ben Franklin. At a time when scurrilous journalism flourished, Bache was a master. He once described President Adams as "blind, bald, crippled, toothless [and] querulous," and he accused even the revered George Washington of reveling in neomonarchical ceremony, dipping into the public treasury, and incompetent soldiering.[15] When Washington stepped down as president—in part to escape Bache's unrelenting attacks—Bache castigated him as "the source of all the misfortunes of our country."[16]

Venom was not the exclusive province of the Republicans, however. The most prominent Federalist paper, the *Gazette of the United States*, also published in Philadelphia, announced that its mission was to oppose "the raging madness" of Republicanism.[17] Its editor, John Fenno, characterized critics of the Adams administration as "dismal cacklers," "propagators of calumny," and the "worst and basest of men."[18]

To what extent should public officials have to tolerate such abuse? Does "the freedom of speech, or of the press" require that we allow critics to vilify the president and members of Congress with attacks on their character, conduct, and motives?

THE SEDITION ACT OF 1798, enacted by the Federalists over furious Republican opposition, provided:

SEC. 2. . . . That if any person shall write, print, utter or publish . . . any false, scandalous, and malicious writing or writings against the government of the United States, or either house of the Congress of the United States, or the President of the United States, with intent to . . . bring them, . . . into contempt or disrepute; or to excite against them, . . . the hatred of the good people of the United States, . . . then such person . . . shall be punished by a fine not exceeding two thousand dollars, and by imprisonment not exceeding two years.[19]

In its bitter debate over this legislation, Congress first began to explore the meaning of the First Amendment. How, the Republicans asked, could this act *possibly* be constitutional, given that less than a decade earlier the nation had adopted the First Amendment, which promised that "Congress shall make no law . . . abridging the freedom of speech, or of the press"?

Albert Gallatin threw down the gauntlet. The proposed act, he charged, could be understood only as a deliberate and unconstitutional attempt by the Federalists "to perpetuate their authority." He observed that from time immemorial tyrants had used laws against political criticism "to throw a veil on their folly or their crimes." The "proper weapon to combat error," he argued, "is truth."[20] Gallatin maintained that such legislation could be justified in the United States only if it was necessary to save the nation.

The Federalists replied that the act was indeed necessary. Connecticut Congressman John Allen argued that the act was necessary because a treasonable conspiracy of Republican congressmen and editors was attempting to "ruin the Government by publishing the most shameless falsehoods" and inciting the people to "insurrection."[21] To prove this "conspiracy" Allen pointed to several items of "evidence," including a "false" accusation in the *Aurora* that the Adams administration had failed to exhaust all reasonable efforts to negotiate a peaceful settlement with France, a "false" statement in the *Aurora* that it was no longer clear whether there was more "liberty to be enjoyed at Constantinople or Philadelphia," and a "false" assertion in another Republican newspaper that described Adams as a "mock Monarch" who had been "jostled" into office by a combination of "Tories and speculators." The First Amendment, Allen maintained, "was never understood to give the right of publishing [such] falsehoods."[22]

Gallatin responded that "every one" of the statements Allen had quoted included "a mixture of truth and error." He asked whether the Federalists believed they required "the help of force in order to suppress . . . the opinions of those who did not approve all their measures." He also noted the irony that Allen would chastise the *Aurora* for questioning whether there was more freedom in Constantinople than in Philadelphia, while at the same time avowing "principles perfectly calculated to justify" the *Aurora's* query.[23]

With respect to the issue of "falsehood," the Republicans argued that the matter was not as simple as the Federalists maintained. Gallatin acknowledged that under the Sedition Act a defendant would be acquitted if he proved the truth of his statements. But, he observed, the act was directed against "writings of a political nature," and it "was well known" that such writings almost always contain "not only facts but opinions." Certainly, the examples offered by Allen fit this description. How, Gallatin asked, could the *truth* of such statements be proved?

As an illustration, Gallatin posited an individual who maintained that the proposed Sedition Act was unconstitutional. Would a jury, Gallatin asked, "composed of the friends of that Administration," hesitate to declare that "opinion . . . false and scandalous, and its publication malicious?" In the "present temper of the parties," he asked, could the accused convince such a jury "that his opinion was true?"[24]

The Federalists flatly rejected Republican claims that the act violated the First Amendment. The most forceful argument was offered by Congressman Otis, who maintained that every government must have the authority to "preserve and defend itself against injuries and outrages which endanger its existence."[25] Especially in time of war, he insisted, the government must be able to defend itself against malicious attacks. Otis observed that the language of the First Amendment had been borrowed from English law, which allowed prosecutions for seditious libel. He therefore reasoned that it was implausible to contend that the First Amendment prohibited such prosecutions.

The Republicans dismissed this reasoning as "preposterous." Congressman Gallatin called it an "insulting evasion" of the Constitution to tell the people that "we claim no power to abridge the liberty of the press," but "if you publish anything against us, we will punish you for it."[26]

TRUTH BE TOLD, THE FRAMERS of the First Amendment had no common understanding of its meaning. They embraced a broad and largely undefined constitutional principle, not a concrete, well-settled legal doctrine. It was an aspiration, to be given meaning over time. As Benjamin Franklin observed, referring to the First Amendment, "few of us" have any "distinct Ideas of its Nature and Extent."[27] But anyone who thought seriously about the issue had to begin with the crime of seditious libel.

To understand the English law of seditious libel, we must look back more than seven hundred years to a 1275 statute that outlawed "any false news or tales whereby discord . . . may grow between the king and his people." Although the essence of the crime as fixed by the statute of 1275 was the *falsity* of the libel, by the early seventeenth century the English courts had held that the government could punish even *true* libels—that is, even statements that *accurately* charged government officials with misconduct.

An English court explained why this should be so: "If people should not be called to account for possessing the people with an ill opinion of the government, no government can subsist. For it is very necessary for all governments that the people should have a good opinion of it."[28] Seventeenth-century English judges punished as seditious libel any criticism of "any public man" or of any public "law or institution whatever."[29] As a prominent historian has observed, "no single method of restricting the press was as effective as the law of seditious libel."[30]

The Republican view of seditious libel was best stated by James Madison, who argued that whatever the peculiarities of English history it made no sense to construe the First Amendment as embodying the English law of seditious libel. He explained that fundamental differences between the English and American political systems rendered the limited English conception of free speech inappropriate for the United States.

In England, he observed, the rulers—kings and lords—were deemed the "superiors" of the people. In such a system, it was natural to require subjects to treat their rulers with respect and to prohibit them from criticizing their judgments and policies. In the United States, however, "a greater freedom" of criticism is essential, because government officials in the United States are "responsible to their constituents," who have a *right* to bring them "into contempt or disrepute" if they fail "to live up to their trusts."

Madison concluded that whatever might have been the case in England, the Sedition Act violated the First Amendment, because it undermined "the responsibility of public servants and public measures to the people" and embraced the "exploded doctrine 'that the administrators of the Government are the masters, and not the servants, of the people.' "[31]

But the Federalists had the votes. On July 14, 1798, President Adams signed the Sedition Act into law.

THE ENMITY THAT MARKED THE congressional debates of 1798 also infected Federalist enforcement policy. In an era described by Thomas Jefferson as "the reign of witches," the Adams administration issued fourteen indictments under the Sedition Act—all against supporters of the Republican Party. The Federalist strategy was aimed directly at the presidential election of 1800. Its objective was to silence leading Republican newspapers and critics as the contest between Adams and Jefferson drew near. The Adams administration prosecuted four of the five most influential Republican journals, as well as several lesser Republican newspapers. As a result of these prosecutions, two Republican journals folded and several others suspended operations while their editors were in jail.

The first person prosecuted under the Sedition Act was Vermont's controversial Republican congressman, Matthew Lyon. The only former indentured servant ever to serve in Congress, Lyon was an Irish émigré and a hardscrabble frontiersman. He once spit in the eye of a Federalist congressman who had insulted him, resulting in a bloody fight on the floor of the House. Responding to unremitting Federalist attacks, Lyon lashed out at Adams and his administration, declaring that under President Adams "every consideration of the public welfare" had been "swallowed up in a continual grasp for power."[32] In October 1798, Lyon was indicted, tried, and convicted by a Federalist judge and jury on the ground that, in making this statement, he had attempted "to bring the President and government of the United States into contempt."[33] The judge sentenced Congressman Lyon to four months in jail.

The Federalists were overjoyed with Lyon's conviction. The Republicans were outraged. One Republican newspaper hailed Lyon as a martyr who had been imprisoned "directly in the teeth of the Constitution." Thomas Jefferson wrote that federal judges had become "objects of national fear."[34] Undaunted by his plight, Lyon launched a vigorous reelection campaign from jail. For the first time in American history, a candidate for Congress championed his cause from a federal prison. When the ballots were counted, Lyon had won a stunning victory.*

Another victim of the Sedition Act, the journalist Thomas Cooper, published a handbill stating that before Adams assumed the presi-

---

*Several years later, Lyon retired from Congress and moved his family west, where he established a trading business along the Mississippi River. After suffering business reverses, he was appointed to the humble position of U.S. factor to the Cherokee Indians at Spadre Bluffs, Arkansas. He lived in a cabin and slept on bearskins on the floor. He became an advocate for the Indians and persuaded the U.S. government to supply the Cherokees with a cotton gin so they could learn to cultivate their land. In 1822, however, to Lyon's bitter disappointment, the government reneged on its agreement. In his seventy-seventh year, Lyon loaded a flatboat with furs, pelts, and Indian goods and set off from Spadre Bluffs down the Mississippi River to New Orleans. On arriving there, he exchanged these products for the ironware and machinery necessary to establish a cotton gin in Spadre Bluffs. The round trip, which he made in frigid winter conditions, covered more than 3,000 miles. On August 1, 1822, at the age of seventy-seven, Matthew Lyon died at his lonely trading post in Arkansas.

dency the nation had not been "saddled with the expense of a permanent navy, or threatened . . . with the existence of a standing army," and that the nation's credit had not been "reduced so low as to borrow money at eight per cent." For publishing this statement, Cooper was charged under the Sedition Act with publishing "a false, scandalous and malicious attack on the character of the President of the United States, with an intent to excite the hatred and contempt of the people of this country against the man of their choice."

The trial convened in Philadelphia, then the nation's capital. Supreme Court Justice Samuel Chase was the presiding judge. The trial, a major political event, took place during the heat of the 1800 presidential campaign. Cooper maintained that he had "published nothing which truth will not justify," that his assertions were "free from malicious imputation," and that his motives were "honest and fair."[35] He conceded the "necessity of a certain degree of confidence" in the president, but argued that this confidence ought to be earned by the "evidence of benefits conferred," not imposed by "attacks on the freedom of the press." Cooper added that, "in the present state of affairs, the press is open to those who will praise" the president but not to those who dare to criticize him.[36]

The prosecutor exclaimed that Cooper's defense was "one of the most extraordinary" he had ever heard. "It is," he said, "no less than to call into decision whether Thomas Cooper [or] the President of the United States . . . is best qualified to judge whether the measures adopted by our government are calculated to preserve the peace and promote the happiness of America."[37] Stating the Federalist view of self-governance, the prosecutor declared that "those who are qualified and who have been appointed for the purpose" can judge the wisdom of these measures "for the nation." It is not for Cooper "to raise surmises and suspicions of the wisdom and design of measures of this kind, which he cannot know sufficient of to explain, or the people to understand."[38]

Justice Chase's handling of the trial was extraordinary. A passionate Federalist, Chase blocked the defense at every turn. His most memorable improprieties were in his charge to the jury. He informed the jury that "if a man attempts to destroy the confidence of the people in their officers," he saps the very "foundation of the government." He accused Cooper of attempting to "arouse the people against the President so as to influence their minds against him on the next election."[39] The handpicked members of the jury returned a verdict of guilty, and Chase sentenced Cooper to six months in prison.*

Another illustrative prosecution involved James Callender, perhaps the most effective of the Republican journalists. Variously described as "a little reptile" and as "a dirty, little toper with shaved head and greasy jacket,"[40] Callender was often down at the heels. His ability to write with rare verve, however, made him a great asset to the Republicans. In *The Prospect Before Us*, a pamphlet advocating the election of Jefferson in 1800, Callender charged that the "reign of Mr. Adams . . . has been one continued tempest of malignant passions." Callender accused Adams of contriving "a French war, an American navy, a large standing army, an additional load of taxes, and all the other symptoms and consequences of debt and despotism." "Take your choice," Callender concluded, "between Adams, war and beggary, and Jefferson, peace and competency."[41]

Callender was promptly arrested and indicted. His attorneys argued that the Sedition Act should be construed to apply only to false statements of fact and not to statements of political opinion. The latter, they maintained, cannot constitutionally be deemed "false," because they are not susceptible of proof by "direct and positive evidence." Justice Chase, who headed to Virginia in order to preside over Callender's trial, rejected this argument, branding

---

*Several years later, Cooper was appointed a judge in Pennsylvania, where he served without distinction. He was ignominiously removed from office for a stunning array of misconduct, including imprisoning a Quaker who refused for religious reasons to remove his hat in court. Toward the end of his career, Cooper repudiated the natural rights philosophy of Jefferson, became an advocate of the moral and economic virtues of slavery, and fiercely defended the right of the southern states to secede from the Union.

Callender's statements "false" without regard to whether they were couched as "opinions."[42]

It was all over quickly. The jury brought in a verdict of guilty. At sentencing, Chase sternly lectured Callender on the evils of sowing "discord among the people" and asserted that Callender's attack on Adams was "an attack upon the people themselves." He explained that to believe Adams capable of the "atrocities" charged by Callender necessarily implied that the people who had elected him "must be depraved and wicked."[43] He then sentenced Callender to nine months in jail.*

YEARS LATER, RECALLING THE FEAR inspired by the Sedition Act, Thomas Jefferson reflected that "no person who was not a witness to the scenes of that gloomy period, can form any idea of the afflicting persecutions and personal indignities we had to brook."[44] The act had been adopted as a war measure to strengthen the nation in its impending war with France, but had served as a political weapon to strengthen the Federalists in their partisan war with the Republicans. Although Federalist editors and speakers were as guilty as their Republican counterparts in their resort to innuendo, hyperbole, and false statement, not a single Federalist was ever indicted under the act.

As events played out, the war with France never materialized, and Jefferson defeated Adams in the election of 1800. The Sedition Act expired on March 3, 1801, the final day of Adams's term of office. The net effect of the act was to alienate a majority of the American people, give the Republicans a powerful issue around which to rally, and hasten the downfall of the Federalist Party. In this respect, the

---

*Callender used his time in jail to write the second volume of *The Prospect Before Us*, intensifying his attack on Adams, whom he described as a "wretch" and "a repulsive hypocrite." He also went after Justice Chase, calling him a "detestable and detested rascal." When Chase wrote Callender in reply that he planned to beat him after his release from prison, Callender vowed, "[I]n case of attack, I'll shoot him." After regaining his freedom, Callender turned against Jefferson and unleashed upon him the same venom he had earlier directed at Adams. Callender died in 1803 in a drunken seizure when he fell off a ferry and drowned in the James River.

story of the Sedition Act teaches an important lesson for the future: the protection of freedom rests ultimately with *the people themselves.*

A fundamental test for the new nation was whether it could peacefully transfer power from one faction to another. In 1800, the nation tottered on the edge of chaos. Many Americans feared that the election of 1800 would trigger a civil war and the dissolution of the nation. But beneath the abusive rhetoric and venomous invective, it turned out that the Federalists and the Republicans shared a deeper allegiance to the Constitution than even they had suspected.

In his inaugural address in March 1801, President Jefferson was conciliatory. He urged Americans to "reflect that, having banished from our land that religious intolerance under which mankind so long bled and suffered, we have yet gained little if we countenance a political intolerance as despotic, as wicked, and capable of as bitter and bloody persecutions." "Every difference of opinion," he observed, "is not a difference of principle. . . . We are all republicans—we are all federalists."[45] As one of his first official acts of office, Jefferson pardoned all those who had been convicted under the Sedition Act and freed those who were still in jail, noting that he considered the act "to be a nullity as absolute and as palpable as if Congress had ordered us to fall down and worship a golden image."[46]

Forty years later, on July 4, 1840, Congress repaid all of the fines levied under the Sedition Act. A congressional report declared that the Sedition Act had been passed under a "mistaken exercise" of power and was "null and void." The unconstitutionality of the act, the report explained, had been "conclusively settled."[47]

More than a century after Congress's action, the Supreme Court, in its landmark 1964 decision in *New York Times v. Sullivan*,[48] celebrated our "profound national commitment to the principle that debate on public issues should be uninhibited, robust, and wide-open," noting that it may well include "vehement, caustic, and sometimes unpleasantly sharp attacks on government and public officials." The Court added that "this is the lesson to be drawn from the great controversy over the Sedition Act of 1798, which first crystallized a national awareness of the central meaning of the First Amendment." It concluded that, "although the Sedition Act was never tested in this Court, the attack upon its validity has carried the day in the court of history."[49]

WHAT SHOULD WE LEARN from this episode? The threat of imminent war with France fostered a climate of fear, anxiety, and suspicion. Given the recent history of France, which had undermined other governments by promoting domestic subversion, suspicions of disloyalty were inevitable. Such charges were quickly leveled at both aliens and Republicans. In this atmosphere of high anxiety and fevered patriotism, the nation rallied in support of legislation purportedly designed to strengthen the military, ferret out potential subversives, and crush disloyalty. The cautions voiced by Republicans were swept aside as the self-interested protests of a suspect faction. Circumstances were ripe for the aggressive suppression of legitimate dissent.

As this episode teaches, when we act in the heat of war fever, we are prone to overreact against those who question the need for military action. Fear, anger, and an aroused patriotism can undermine sound judgment. The congressional debates in 1798 reveal how easily we can slide from disagreements about policy to accusations of disloyalty. The consequence is not only the suppression of individual dissent but the mutilation of public debate. Moreover, as the events of 1798 illustrate, those in power may exploit a threat to the nation's security to serve their own partisan ends. A time-honored strategy for consolidating power is to inflate the public's fears, inflame its patriotism, and then condemn political opponents as "disloyal." A national crisis (real, fabricated, or imagined) invites this strategy.

The struggle over the Sedition Act should also cause us to question whether we can count on judges and jurors to protect our liberties in moments of high national anxiety. Although the circumstances in 1798 were unique in that the Federalists had appointed *all* sitting federal judges, the conduct of those judges is nonetheless revealing.

Because federal judges are guaranteed life tenure, are professionally trained to be impartial and independent of the elected branches, and understand that they have a special responsibility to enforce the Constitution and laws of the United States in an objective and even-handed manner, they can play an important role in preserving constitutional rights even in the face of social, political, and military pressures.

But even the best and most well intentioned judges cannot separate themselves *entirely* from their own political, social, philosophical, and personal beliefs. Moreover, judges live in the same world as the rest of us and are subject to the same fears, passions, and uncertainties. Thus, in times of national crisis, judges will not always be inclined or even able to preserve our liberties when they are under assault. In a self-governing society, citizens must not sit back passively and expect judges and jurors to make the hard decisions for them. To preserve their liberties, citizens must educate themselves and play an active part in the political process. In the long run, a passive citizenry will be a citizenry without rights.

We should also learn from this episode to be skeptical of confident assurances that courts can readily distinguish "malicious" intent from "legitimate" dissent. Inquiries into a speaker's subjective intent are elusive at best. If a speaker condemns a president as ill informed and incompetent, is his intent "maliciously" to bring the president into contempt or "legitimately" to criticize him for failing in his official responsibilities? As the judgments of jurors in the Sedition Act prosecutions suggest, this is a perilous distinction. Jurors are much more likely to find "malice" when they disagree with a speaker's views. This is too fine a thread on which to rest the constitutional protection of free expression. If citizens know their criticisms can so easily be construed as criminal acts, they are likely to remain silent.

The Sedition Act controversy should also cause us to look askance at government assertions that its "real" reason for punishing dissent in wartime is to protect the national security. Republican criticism of the Adams administration could have dampened enthusiasm for the military buildup and made it more difficult for the government to rally the troops and provision the army. But it could also have changed public opinion about the nature of the French threat and legitimately called the administration's leadership into question. The government's "real" purpose in suppressing such criticism might be to protect the national security, to stifle political opposition, or some combination of the two. Suppressing speech because it is dangerous to the national interest is one thing; suppressing speech because it is dangerous to a partisan interest is something else entirely. The problem is that it is difficult, if not impossible, to tell the difference.

The most important lesson of this episode is that the very concept of a false political *opinion* is unalterably at odds with the First Amendment. In perhaps its single most important sentence on the freedom of speech, the Supreme Court declared in 1974 that "under the First Amendment there is no such thing as a false idea."[50] As the Court explained, "however pernicious an opinion may seem, we depend for its correction not on the conscience" of legislators, judges, or voters "but on the competition of other ideas."[51] In making this judgment, we are balancing two competing risks. On the one hand, there is the risk that, if permitted to consider all ideas, the people will sometimes embrace bad ones. On the other hand, there is the risk that, if given the power to suppress ideas they believe to be "false," the people will sometimes prohibit the consideration of ideas that would better be left open to continued debate and deliberation.

In choosing between these risks, and deciding whether the people, acting through their government, should be able to declare certain ideas "false," we must consider the nature of human nature. As history teaches, people are prone to intolerance. We tend to believe we are "right" and want to silence those who disagree. If we have the authority to act on that inclination, there is every danger we will do so. It is not inherent in human nature to be skeptical, self-doubting, or tolerant. The First Amendment, on this view, cuts against human nature. It demands that we be better than we would be.

The Supreme Court has it right. The danger of repression is

greater than the danger of debate. For our nation to declare that "under the First Amendment there is no such thing as a false idea" is, in effect, to embrace ambivalence, to foster an ongoing reexamination of our beliefs, and to insist upon openness to opinions we might otherwise dismiss. That is one of the most fundamental lessons of the controversy over the Sedition Act of 1798.

# CHAPTER II

# The Civil War
# "The Man Who Holds the Power"

❧

THE Missouri Compromise, Bleeding Kansas, and Harpers Ferry marked the path to Civil War. The presidential election of 1860 was the culmination of nearly a century of sectional conflict. Citizens voted along strict sectional lines, leading to the election of the Republican candidate, Abraham Lincoln, who received only 40 percent of the popular vote. Despite repeated warnings from Southerners that a Republican victory would leave the nation "crimsoned in human gore,"[1] Lincoln did not expect any serious effort to dissolve the Union. The "people of the South," he opined, "have too much of good sense, and good temper, to attempt the ruin of the government."[2]

Six weeks after Lincoln's election, however, amid fireworks, marching bands, and celebratory rallies, South Carolina announced its secession from the Union. Submission to a Republican administration, wrote one South Carolinian, would mean "the loss of liberty, property, home, country—everything that makes life worth having."[3] The other states of the lower South soon followed South Carolina's lead.

The lame-duck administration of President James Buchanan did nothing to counter these developments. In December 1860, in an address to Congress that has aptly been described as one of the most "unfortunate" in U.S. history,[4] Buchanan declared that although secession was unconstitutional, the national government had no power "to coerce a State into submission."[5] Prosecessionist forces seized most of the federal forts in the South, and in early February of the new year, a month before Lincoln's inauguration, South Carolina, Georgia, Florida, Alabama, Mississippi, and Louisiana met in Montgomery, Alabama to establish the Confederate States of America.*

In this critical period of transition, many in the North urged conciliation in order to preserve the Union. Others, like the powerful newspaper editor Horace Greeley, urged the North to let the South "go in peace."[6] Although Lincoln remained firm in opposing the extension of slavery to the territories, he approved a compromise that would have guaranteed slavery in the states in which it then existed "against any future interference by the federal government."[7] Before this proposal could be acted upon, however, Confederate guns opened fire on Fort Sumter in early April 1861. For the next four years, the twenty-three states of the Union and the eleven states of the Confederacy were locked in one of history's most brutal conflicts. Some 620,000 soldiers lost their lives in the Civil War, dwarfing the human cost of any other American conflict.

The Civil War presented Lincoln with a tangled knot of complications, including sharply divided loyalties, fluid and often uncertain military and political boundaries, and easy opportunities for espionage and sabotage. Those problems are common to most civil wars, but Lincoln also faced an additional set of dilemmas because of his need to retain the loyalty of the border states, address the divisive questions of race, slavery, and emancipation, and impose conscription for the first time in the nation's history.

IN ANY CONSTITUTIONAL SYSTEM, THERE exists a tension between the need for government constrained by law and the need for discre-

---

*They were later joined by Virginia, North Carolina, Tennessee, Texas, and Arkansas.

tionary authority to respond to immediate crises. Lincoln faced this tension more acutely than any other president. The most dramatic example involved Lincoln's suspensions of the writ of habeas corpus. This writ, the "Great Writ," was fundamental to the framers of the Constitution and held a hallowed place in American law long before the Civil War. A writ of habeas corpus is a judicial mandate directing a government official to present to the court an individual held in custody so the *court* can determine whether the detention is lawful. The writ is essential to the separation of powers, for it empowers an *independent* branch of the government—the judiciary—to decide whether the executive has detained an individual unlawfully.

Without the writ of habeas corpus, a president could order an individual detained for any reason, or no reason at all, and no court could intervene. The individual would be at the mercy of the executive. The Supreme Court has therefore characterized the writ as a "fundamental instrument for safeguarding individual freedom against arbitrary and lawless" government action.[8] In recognition of the importance of the writ, the Constitution expressly provides in Article I, Section 9, Clause 2, "The privilege of the Writ of Habeas Corpus shall not be suspended, unless when in Cases of Rebellion or Invasion the public Safety may require it." Prior to the Civil War, the federal government had suspended the writ on only a few occasions, and then only in very localized circumstances. During the Civil War, however, Lincoln suspended the writ on eight separate occasions.

UPON ASSUMING OFFICE, LINCOLN was desperate to nurture the precarious loyalty of Delaware, Maryland, Kentucky, and Missouri—the four slave states that had not yet seceded. If these four states left the Union, they would add almost 50 percent to the military manpower of the Confederacy. Maryland was especially vital because it surrounded the nation's capital on three sides (with Virginia on the fourth).

The gravity of the challenge in Maryland was apparent even before Lincoln's inauguration. While en route to Washington, Lincoln had to pass through Baltimore, a port city teeming with secessionist sympathizers. Multiple assassination threats caused Lincoln to cancel a public appearance and sneak though Baltimore "like a thief in the night."[9] Rumors quickly spread that he had donned a Scotch plaid hat and a long military cloak to disguise his appearance. This was not true, but the Democratic press had a field day.

A month later, shortly after the attack on Fort Sumter, the Sixth Massachusetts Volunteers attempted to march through Baltimore in order to reach the nation's capital. A mob of Confederate sympathizers attacked the soldiers, causing 16 deaths and widespread rioting. To prevent additional Union troops from entering the city, the mayor ordered the destruction of all railroad bridges connecting Baltimore with the North. The nation's capital was isolated and gripped by fear. Republicans demanded action. One influential Republican advised Lincoln to "take possession of Baltimore at once." Another urged that, if necessary, Baltimore be "laid in ruin." Lincoln's private secretaries revealed years later that the stress of this crisis put Lincoln in a severe "state of nervous tension."[10]

Because there was scant precedent for the suspension of habeas corpus, Lincoln turned for guidance to Attorney General Edward Bates. Bates, in turn, delegated the assignment to an assistant, who prepared an inconclusive memorandum. The memo cited Joseph Story's *Commentaries on the Constitution*, which assumed that only Congress had the constitutional authority to suspend the writ. This was hardly encouraging, particularly because Congress was not in session and could not be quickly convened. Lincoln decided to act. On April 27, he issued an executive order suspending the writ of habeas corpus in those areas of Maryland in which secessionists might block military access to Washington.

Among those imprisoned by military authorities was John Merryman, who had allegedly burned bridges and destroyed telegraph wires. Merryman immediately filed a petition for a writ of habeas corpus, seeking his release from military detention. The judge assigned to hear his petition was Roger B. Taney, chief justice of the United States.* It was Taney who several years earlier had attempted to end the nation's agony over slavery by holding in the *Dred Scott* decision[11] that Congress had no power to ban slavery in the territories and that members of the African race were not citizens of the United States.

On May 26, 1861, Taney ruled in *Ex parte Merryman*[12] that only Congress was authorized to suspend the writ of habeas corpus and that Lincoln's order was therefore unconstitutional. Indeed, Taney "supposed it to be one of those points of constitutional law upon which there was no difference of opinion." To support his judgment, Taney invoked Chief Justice John Marshall's opinion in *Ex parte Bollman*,[13] Joseph Story's *Commentaries on the Constitution*,[14] and President Jefferson's application to Congress for authority to suspend the writ of habeas corpus when he found it necessary to deal with the Aaron Burr conspiracy. Most telling, though, was the text of the Constitution, which addresses the suspension power in Article I, which sets forth the powers of Congress. In Taney's judgment, the matter was without doubt: "the president has exercised a power which he does not possess under the constitution."[15]

Taney issued a writ of habeas corpus directing General George Cadwalader, who was in charge of Fort McHenry and had custody of Merryman, to appear before him in order to comply with whatever the "Court shall determine."[16] Taney intended this decision to be a decisive rejection of Lincoln's assertion of excessive executive authority. Lincoln's defenders argued that the rebellion involved treasonable activity on so vast a scale that the ordinary criminal process was inadequate to deal with it. They maintained that because exceptional measures were essential, they were necessarily lawful.

Lincoln flatly refused to comply with the chief justice's ruling.

---

* At this time, as in 1798, the justices of the Supreme Court still "rode circuit" and presided over federal cases at the local level.

When the federal marshal arrived at Fort McHenry to serve the writ on Cadwalader, he was denied entrance to the fort. Taney was stymied. Although noting that the marshal technically had legal authority to seize Cadwalader and bring him forcibly before the Court, Taney recognized that the marshal "will be resisted in the discharge of that duty by a force notoriously superior" to his own and, "such being the case, the Court has no power under the law."[17] Taney concluded that all he could do was to "reduce to writing" the reasons under which he had acted and report them to the president, in the hope that he will "perform his constitutional duty to enforce the laws; in other words to enforce the process of this Court."[18] Lincoln ignored Taney's "report." Given the perilous state of the Union in the spring of 1861, it is hardly surprising that there was no widespread public opposition either to Lincoln's suspension of the writ or to his flagrant disregard of Taney's order.

AS THE WAR PROGRESSED, MATTERS grew worse. Both the Emancipation Proclamation and the nation's first draft law generated bitter opposition. From the very beginning of the war, Lincoln had insisted that his only goal was to preserve the Union. If a state could secede at will whenever it disagreed with the majority, there could be no lasting Union, no lasting democracy, and the great American experiment would fail. This, rather than slavery, was the issue that motivated most northerners. As the conflict wore on, however, Republicans came increasingly to view the fate of the nation as tied to the fate of slavery. As Representative George Julian of Indiana declared in January 1862, "the mere suppression of the rebellion will be an empty mockery of our sufferings and sacrifices, if slavery shall be spared."[19] On September 22, 1862, Lincoln finally announced the Emancipation Proclamation, which he defended as a military measure to help bring the war to a close. The proclamation warned that unless the rebel states returned to the Union by January 1, 1863, their slaves would "be then, thenceforward, and forever free."[20]

The antiwar Democrats, or Copperheads,* protested the Proclamation. In their view, it fundamentally transformed the nature of the war. Its goal was no longer to restore the Union but to destroy the South. Congressman Samuel Cox of Ohio warned that soldiers would not fight "if the result shall be the flight and movement of the black race by millions northward."[21] Many Union soldiers shared this view. One volunteer wrote his fiancée, "It is not for the emancipation of the African race I fight. I want nothing to do with the negro. I want them as far from me as is possible to conceive."[22] The Copperheads made this their central issue in the 1862 elections and scored substantial gains at both the federal and local levels.

The difficulty of raising an army posed another challenge. The attack on Fort Sumter galvanized the North. On April 15, 1861, Lincoln called 75,000 militiamen into service to quash the rebellion. As a wave of patriotism swept across the North, volunteers raced forward to join the army and claim their share of glory. A year later, however, after a succession of military defeats, Lincoln called for an additional 300,000 volunteers. This time, there was no rush to the battlements. As the casualty lists lengthened and the grim realities of combat set in, many states had to resort to conscription to meet their quotas. Democratic newspapers warned that the draft "would force white working men to fight for the freedom of blacks who would come north and take away their jobs."[23]

The draft triggered violent resistance. Mobs murdered two enrollment officers in Indiana, and the army had to send troops into Pennsylvania, Wisconsin, Ohio, and Indiana to restore order. Secretary of War Edwin Stanton imprisoned hundreds of alleged draft resisters without benefit of trial. Protest groups marched under banners declaring WE WON'T FIGHT TO FREE THE NIGGER.[24] The government's heavy-handed efforts to enforce conscription outraged many citi-

---

*The term "copperhead" was originally coined as an epithet to liken the Democrats to the venomous snake. Over time, however, the Democrats proudly accepted the label and began wearing badges that resembled copper pennies.

zens. Soldiers conducted house-to-house searches and brutally broke up antidraft demonstrations.

Ever more violent protests exploded across the North in the cruelly hot summer of 1863. Mobs killed several enrollment officers, and antidraft, antiblack violence erupted in Boston, Newark, Albany, Chicago, and Milwaukee. In July, four days of rioting in New York City left 105 people dead. Led by Irish immigrants, the riot was the worst in American history. Rioters burned a black orphanage, destroyed black homes, and lynched blacks on lampposts.

In the face of continuing disorder, Lincoln's most extreme order suspending the writ of habeas corpus applied *nationwide* and declared that "all persons . . . guilty of any disloyal practice . . . shall be subject to martial law."[25] Lincoln placed Secretary of State William Seward in charge of what we would today call "homeland security," authorizing him to order the arrest of any person suspected of disloyalty. Seward commented to the British minister, "I can touch a bell on my right hand and order the arrest of a citizen in Ohio. I can touch the bell again and order the imprisonment of a citizen of New York, and no power on earth but that of the President can release them. Can the Queen of England, in her dominions, say as much?" These arrests "spread fear and hate" among those who opposed the administration's policies.[26]

How did Lincoln justify his suspensions of habeas corpus? Recall that the Constitution provides that the "privilege of the Writ of Habeas Corpus shall not be suspended, unless when in Cases of Rebellion or Invasion the public Safety may require it." Lincoln defended his initial suspension order in a special address to Congress on July 4, 1861. He maintained that the Constitution was "silent" on whether suspension of the writ was a presidential or a congressional power, and that in any event the "war power" and the president's constitutional role as "commander in chief" placed upon him the responsibility to defend the nation against imminent destruction. He asserted that Chief Justice Taney's interpretation of the Constitution would allow "all the laws, *but one*, to go unexecuted, and the government itself go to pieces, lest that one be violated." This, he argued, was implausible. Acknowledging that it was uncertain whether his actions were "strictly legal or not," Lincoln insisted they were justified because they had been taken in circumstances of strict "public necessity."[27]

Two years later, Lincoln elaborated on this rationale. He recalled that when he first assumed office secessionist "sympathizers pervaded all departments of the Government." Although he revered the "rights of individuals," he had reluctantly come to the conclusion that "strong measures" were "indispensable to the public safety."[28] He explained that he had decided to suspend the writ of habeas corpus in April 1861 because the ordinary civil courts in Maryland could not deal with the crisis:[29]

> Civil courts are organized chiefly for trials of individuals . . . in quiet times, and on charges of crimes well defined in the law. . . . Ours is a case of rebellion . . . and the [suspension clause] . . . plainly attests the understanding of those who made the Constitution, that ordinary courts of justice are inadequate . . . in such cases.

Lincoln insisted that "when Rebellion or Invasion comes, the . . . commander-in-chief . . . is the man who holds the power, and bears the responsibility" of making the decision.[30]

As a matter of strict construction of the Constitution, Taney was right. The Constitution grants Congress, not the president, the power to suspend the writ of habeas corpus. The English had long struggled to shift the power to suspend the writ to Parliament, and the framers' deep suspicion of unchecked executive power made it implausible that they would have given "the president the exclusive, final word about his own power to deprive citizens of their liberty without legal process."[31]

On the other hand, what was Lincoln to do? In April 1861, the nation's capital was in imminent jeopardy, Union troops were blocked by mobs in Baltimore, local officials and courts were unable or unwilling to control the situation, and Congress was not in session. In 1861, there was no way Lincoln could have convened Congress quickly enough to enable it to deal with the emergency. In such circumstances, may the president act "unconstitutionally"?

Interestingly, Congress proved much less concerned about its prerogatives than Chief Justice Taney. Congress silently deferred to the president and then, in 1863, enacted legislation ratifying his actions and authorizing future suspensions of the writ. Lincoln was thereafter free to exercise this power at will.

It is unknown precisely how many civilians were imprisoned by military authorities during the Civil War. Estimates range from 13,000 to 38,000. Most of the arrests were for alleged draft evasion, trading with the enemy, bridge burning, and other forms of sabotage. Some individuals, however, were arrested merely for expressing their political beliefs. Usually, they were men of obscurity whose outbursts hardly threatened the war effort. For example, David Lyon of Illinois was arrested for saying that "anyone who enlists is a God Damn fool," William Palmer of Ohio for writing that "not fifty soldiers will fight to free Negroes," and Jacob Wright of New Jersey for declaring that anyone who enlists is "no better than a goddamned nigger." These arrests were usually initiated at low levels of authority. The detainees typically were released within several weeks, after taking an oath of allegiance to the Union.[32]

Lincoln generally learned of these arrests, if at all, only after the fact. He was almost always displeased. He believed that such speakers posed no threat to the Union, and complained that such arrests needlessly polarized the public. By 1863, Lincoln had grown weary of these incidents. On May 17, he made clear that "unless the *necessity*" for such arrests is "*manifest* and *urgent*," they "should cease."[33] His exasperation is best captured by his reaction to General John Schofield's arrest of a newspaper editor in St. Louis. Lincoln wrote Schofield, "Please spare me the trouble this is likely to bring."[34] But Lincoln did not act decisively to prohibit such arrests. He chose instead to defer to his military commanders, and allowed the arrests for seditious speech to continue.

THE MOST DRAMATIC CONFRONTATION over free speech during the Civil War arose out of a speech in Mount Vernon, Ohio. In March 1863, Lincoln appointed General Ambrose Burnside to serve as the Union commander of the Department of Ohio. Burnside soon grew concerned that local newspapers were filled with "treasonable expressions" and that "large public meetings were held, at which our Government authorities and our gallant soldiers in the field were openly and loudly denounced for their efforts to suppress the rebellion."[35] A man of impulsive character, Burnside issued General Order No. 38, which announced (among other things) that "the habit of declaring sympathies for the enemy will not be allowed in this Department."[36]

Clement Vallandigham, a former Ohio congressman, was one of the national leaders of the Copperheads. He vigorously opposed the war, the draft, the military arrest of civilians, the suspensions of habeas corpus, and the Emancipation Proclamation. On May 1, 1863, he decided to challenge General Order No. 38. In a spirited two-hour address before a huge throng, estimated at between 15,000 and 20,000, Vallandigham characterized the war as "wicked, cruel, and unnecessary,"[37] asserted that the right to criticize the government was protected by the First Amendment, and urged citizens to use " 'the ballot-box' to hurl 'King Lincoln' from his throne."[38] The speech brought rousing cheers from the crowd.

General Burnside ordered Union soldiers to arrest Vallandigham at his home in the dead of night. The former congressman was brought before a five-member military commission and charged with "declaring disloyal sentiments and opinions with the object and purpose of weakening the power of the government in its efforts to suppress an unlawful rebellion."[39] The commission found Vallandigham guilty and recommended his imprisonment in "close confinement" for the duration of the war. Vallandigham immediately filed a petition for a writ of habeas corpus in federal court. He argued that he had been denied his constitutional right to due process of law. The judge dismissed Vallandigham's petition, reasoning that in the face of a rebellion the president "is invested with very high powers" and "is only amenable for an abuse of his authority by impeachment."[40]

Certainly, a speech like Vallandigham's would have been punished under the Sedition Act of 1798. On its face, his address was not much different from the speeches and publications of Matthew Lyon, James Callender, and Thomas Cooper. But hadn't Jefferson's election in 1800, the demise of the Federalists, and the rejection of the English doctrine of seditious libel transformed the American constitutional landscape?

Newspapers across the nation championed Vallandigham's cause. The *Albany Argus* charged that his arrest was a "crime against the Constitution." The *Detroit Free Press* declared sarcastically that if speakers may be jailed "because they are opposed to the war," then the polls may be closed, or voters excluded from them, for the same reason. If it is disloyal to make a speech against the war, "it is doubly disloyal to vote for men who are opposed to it."[41] There were mass demonstrations protesting Vallandigham's confinement in almost every major Northern city.

A month after Vallandigham's arrest, the Ohio Democratic Convention nominated him for governor. The convention adopted a resolution maintaining that rights guaranteed to the people "are their rights in time of war as well as in times of peace," and charged that Lincoln had effectively reintroduced the Sedition Act of 1798, but without the authority of an act of Congress to support him.[42]

Even some Republicans were critical. The Republican *New York Tribune* noted that the Constitution does "not recognize . . . unpatriotic speeches as grounds of infliction," and the *New York Evening Post* declared that "no governments and no authorities are to be held as above criticism." Republican Senator Lyman Trumbull denounced Burnside's action, noting that "we are fighting for the . . . preservation of the Constitution, and all the liberties it guarantees to every citizen."[43] One of the most impressive features of this controversy was that many Republicans joined Democrats in condemning this suppression of dissent. This was a far cry from the rampant partisanship of the Sedition Act debate, and a promising development in the maturation of American democracy.

LINCOLN WAS SURPRISED AND EMBARRASSED by Burnside's arrest of Vallandigham. According to John Nicolay and John Hay, Lincoln's secretaries, if the president had "been consulted before any proceedings were initiated," he "would not have permitted them."[44] Vallandigham was not the type of agitator Lincoln expected the military to arrest. The president's security policy was aimed at draft dodgers, deserters, and bridge burners, not leaders of the national Democratic Party. Vallandigham's arrest compelled Lincoln to consider just how far he was prepared to go in allowing the suppression of dissent.*

Though vexed with Burnside, Lincoln did not want to undermine his general. He therefore sought a middle ground. He ordered Burnside to commute Vallandigham's sentence from imprisonment to banishment to the Confederacy. He defended this decision by arguing that the purpose of imprisoning Vallandigham was not to punish him but to prevent him from causing further injury to the military. Exile was a more humane and "less disagreeable" means of "securing the same prevention."[45]

The president's solution may have been brilliant in theory, but it did not defuse the situation. Democratic editors launched blistering attacks against Lincoln, deploying such phrases as "Caesar," "usurper," "demagogue," "tyrant," and "dictator." The *Dubuque Herald* declared that "a crime has been committed" against the "right to

---

*The Vallandigham incident must have been particularly poignant for Lincoln. In 1848, as a young congressman, Lincoln had sharply challenged President Polk over the Mexican War. Lincoln accused the president of being "completely bewildered" and of having not even a "conception" of how or when the war would end. Lincoln's constituents accused him of disloyalty and charged that he had betrayed the thousands of young men who had fought bravely for their country. The press denounced his "dastardly and treasonable assault upon President Polk" and tagged him the "second Benedict Arnold." Although Lincoln had hoped to run for reelection, this incident dashed his hopes.

think." The *Detroit Free Press* protested that Vallandigham had been exiled "for no crime known to law."[46] The Republican press chimed in as well. The *New York Independent* criticized the president's "great mistake," the *Anti-Slavery Standard* chastised his "blunder," and the *New York Sun* observed that "the Union can survive the assaults" of the South but "cannot long exist without free speech."[47] According to Nicolay and Hay, no other act of the administration was "so strongly criticized" or generated "so deep and so wide-spread" a feeling of opposition among the general public.[48]

Democrats staged mass protest meetings in almost every Northern city. The most important was held in Albany on May 16, 1863. The leaders asked whether the Civil War was being waged to restore the Union or "to destroy free institutions" and drafted ten resolutions against the Lincoln administration. The "Albany Resolves" demanded that Lincoln respect the liberties of the people and charged that Vallandigham had been unconstitutionally exiled for criticizing the administration.[49]

The Albany Resolves afforded Lincoln an opportunity to explain his position. He prepared a carefully crafted reply for public dissemination. His goal was to quell the rising tide of public outrage. His response provides us with rare insight into his views of free speech in wartime. At the outset, Lincoln made an important concession:

> It is asserted . . . that Mr. Vallandigham was . . . seized and tried "for no other reason than words addressed to a public meeting, in criticism of the . . . Administration, and in condemnation of the Military orders of the General." Now, if there be no mistake about this; . . . if there was no other reason for the arrest, then I concede that the arrest was wrong.[50]

Why, then, was it lawful to arrest and banish Vallandigham?

> [T]he arrest, as I understand, was made for a very different reason. . . . [H]is arrest was made because he was laboring, with

some effect, to prevent the raising of troops; to encourage desertions from the army; and to leave the Rebellion without an adequate military force to suppress it.[51]

Lincoln therefore argued that Vallandigham had been arrested not for criticizing the administration but for attempting to obstruct the military. But how did Lincoln *know* that Vallandigham was "laboring" to "encourage desertions" rather than attempting to persuade citizens to vote him out of office? Moreover, why should the government punish Vallandigham, who was only *speaking*? Why not leave the speaker free and punish only those who actually desert? Lincoln answered:

> Long experience has shown that armies cannot be maintained unless desertions shall be punished by the severe penalty of death. . . . Must I shoot a simple-minded soldier boy who deserts, while I must not touch a hair of a wily agitator who induces him to desert? . . . I think that in such a case to silence the agitator, and save the boy is not only constitutional, but withal a great mercy.[52]

Is this a satisfactory response? Note that the "simple-minded soldier boy" might desert even if the speaker merely criticizes the war and does *not* "labor" to "encourage desertions." How are critics of the war to know when they might be in jeopardy?

At almost the exact moment when Lincoln was circulating his reply to the Albany Resolves, Ohio Democrats approved their own resolutions condemning the banishment of Vallandigham. In particular, they argued that Vallandigham had never advocated unlawful resistance or violence. On June 26, Lincoln published his reply to these new resolutions, expanding upon his earlier analysis:

> I certainly do not *know* that Mr. V. has specifically, and by direct language, advised against enlistments, and in favor of deser-

tion. . . . [But we] all know that combinations, armed in some instances, to resist the arrest of deserters, began several months ago. . . . I solemnly declare my belief that this hindrance, of the military, including maiming and murder, is due to the course in which Mr. V. has been engaged, in a greater degree than . . . to any other one man.

These things have been . . . known to all, and of course known to Mr. V. . . . When it is known that the whole burthen of his speeches has been to stir up men against the prossecution [sic] of the war, and that in the midst of resistance to it, he has not been known, in any instance, to counsel *against* such resistance, it is next to impossible to repel the inference that he has counselled directly in favor of it.[53]

In Lincoln's view, Vallandigham could properly be punished not because he had criticized the war but because he had attempted, with substantial success, to persuade men to desert. How did Lincoln *know* Vallandigham's intent? As Lincoln conceded, he had no proof that Vallandigham had "specifically, and by direct language, advised against enlistments, and in favor of desertion." Thus, Lincoln relied on *circumstantial* evidence to condemn Vallandigham. Because the harm caused by Vallandigham's speeches was "known to Mr. V.," and because Mr. V. "has not been known . . . to counsel *against* such resistance," Lincoln inferred that Vallandigham must have intended to incite unlawful resistance. Vallandigham was free to criticize the war, but only if he made clear to his listeners that they should not violate the law. This was an ingenious argument, but it had no fair application to Mr. V., who consistently counseled *against* unlawful resistance, a fact of which the president was presumably unaware.

Whatever the deficiencies in Lincoln's analysis, his responses to the Albany and Ohio resolutions reflected a serious and subtle effort to think through complex First Amendment questions. The debates over the Sedition Act of 1798 were often eloquent, but they never approached this level of intellectual rigor. These letters show Lincoln not only as a brilliant politician and rhetorician, but as an impressive constitutional lawyer as well.*

THROUGHOUT THE CIVIL WAR, the government made sporadic efforts to limit the "secessionist" press, especially in the border states. According to one estimate, as many as three hundred Democratic newspapers were shut down by military authorities, at least for a brief period, for expressing sympathy with the enemy. In other instances, Union soldiers and "loyal" citizens, outraged by the utterances of Democratic journals, attacked their offices and editors. On one occasion, for example, the editor of the *Essex County Democrat* was dragged from his home, covered with a coat of tar and feathers, and ridden through town on a rail.

Despite such incidents, the antiadministration press was generally given wide latitude. The *New York Daily News* characterized Lincoln as "that compound of cunning, heartlessness and folly" the people "now execrate in the person of their Chief Magistrate."[54] The *New York Evening Express* published a scathing attack on the draft, describing conscription as a "horror" and as an "accursed slavery." The *Chicago Times* derided General Burnside as "the jumping-jack of the principal butchers and assassins."[55] *Harper's Weekly* collected a list of the invectives that had been used in the press to castigate the president, including "despot," "liar," "usurper," "thief," "monster," "perjurer," "ignoramus," "swindler,"

---

*And what of Mr. V.? He was outraged at Lincoln's accusation that he had attempted to encourage desertion and had failed to counsel obedience to lawful authority. Ironically, he was not welcome in the Confederacy, because he still considered himself a loyal citizen of the Union. He soon escaped from the South, made his way to Canada, and ran unsuccessfully from there for governor of Ohio. He returned to the United States in 1864 and played a pivotal role in the Democratic National Convention that nominated General George McClellan for president. After the war, he resumed his highly successful legal career. He died on June 17, 1871, at the age of fifty-one, while getting ready for a murder trial. Mr. V. accidentally shot himself to death in his hotel room while preparing to demonstrate in court how his client's alleged victim could accidentally have shot himself to death.

"tyrant," "fiend," "butcher," and "pirate." Lincoln was the most excoriated president in American history.

Lincoln did not enjoy these attacks. But he kept them in perspective. One anecdote is revealing. After he announced the Emancipation Proclamation, Lincoln was subjected to a torrent of ugly calumny. According to the *Springfield* (Mass.) *Republican*, someone sent the president a stack of negative editorials. Lincoln later told a friend, "[H]aving an hour to spare on Sunday I read this batch of editorials, and when I was through reading I asked myself, 'Abraham Lincoln, are you a man *or a dog?*' " Although the editorials were "bitter in their criticisms upon him," Lincoln "smiled very pleasantly as he spoke of them, though it was evident that they made a decided impression upon his mind."[56]

SHORTLY AFTER THE CIVIL WAR, the Supreme Court finally considered the constitutionality of Lincoln's use of military tribunals to try civilians. Military authorities in Indiana had seized Lambdin Milligan for allegedly conspiring to aid the Confederacy. He was tried by a military tribunal, convicted, and sentenced to death. In *Ex parte Milligan*,[57] the Court held that the government could not constitutionally use military tribunals to try civilians, even in time of war or insurrection, if the civil courts were open and functioning, as they were in Indiana. To justify such action, the Court added, "necessity must be actual and present; the invasion real, such as effectually closes the courts and deposes the civil administration."[58] The Court emphasized that the Constitution applies "equally in war and in peace." Indeed, "no doctrine, involving more pernicious consequences, was ever invented by the wit of man than that any of its provisions can be suspended during any of the great exigencies of government."[59]

These are ringing words. But are they realistic? It is much easier to utter such phrases after a struggle has passed than while it is ongoing. Would the Court have said the same thing in 1863? Lincoln could not escape being, as he put it, "the man who holds the power." In his devotion to keeping "the country whole so that democracy could not be said to have failed,"[60] he charted a course that melded his sense of the practical with his commitment to the law. He claimed for himself—as president—powers both unprecedented and extraordinary, but he took care to root his assertions of authority in the Constitution. Even at the darkest moments, Lincoln openly addressed these questions and always insisted that "the Constitution mattered."[61]

CHAPTER III

# World War I
# "Disloyalty Must Be Crushed Out of Existence"

❦❦

THE carnage was horrifying. In the spring offensives of 1915, England and France lost 240,000 men and Germany 140,000, with no net change in position. The following summer, the British suffered 60,000 casualties on *a single day* in the battle of the Somme. Between the outbreak of war in Europe and the decision of the United States to enter the conflict in the spring of 1917, there was continuing debate about the nation's best course of action.

Most Americans believed that the war in Europe did not implicate vital interests of the United States. What finally drew the United States into the war was the German submarine blockade. Unlike the British, who could deny Germany essential supplies by laying mine-fields in its narrow shipping routes, the Germans had to resort to sub-marine warfare to cut off shipping to England and France, which had broad access to the sea. These blockades infuriated the neutrals, who maintained that they were entitled under international law to trade freely with all belligerents.

Although Americans valued the "freedom of the seas," most did not find it a sufficiently compelling reason to spill American blood on the battlefields of Europe. The more sensible course was to stand aside, forgo trade with the belligerents, and let the storm pass. Nonetheless, in the winter of 1917, after German submarines sank three American vessels, Woodrow Wilson—who had won reelection the preceding fall on the slogan that he had "kept America out of war"—sought a declaration of war. Echoing John Adams in 1798, he proclaimed that the United States could not "choose the path of submission and suffer the most sacred rights of our nation and our people to be ignored or violated."[1]

The voices of dissent were immediate. On April 4, during Congress's debate over the war resolution, Republican Senator George Norris of Nebraska stated that "we are about to put the dollar sign upon the American flag."[2] Like Norris, many Americans saw the conflict not as a war to make the world "safe for democracy," but as a war to make the world safe for munitions manufacturers and armaments traders. Wilson's proposal to reinstitute the draft also triggered bitter attacks. Senator James A. Reed of Missouri, recalling the draft riots during the Civil War, warned that reinstitution of the draft would have the nation's streets running red with blood.

Unlike Abraham Lincoln, Wilson was a man with little tolerance for criticism. In seeking a declaration of war, he cautioned that "if there should be disloyalty, it will be dealt with with a firm hand of stern repression."[3] Disloyal individuals, he explained, "had sacrificed their right to civil liberties."[4] In these and similar pronouncements, he set the tone for what was to follow. Wilson understood that if dissent were allowed to fester it could undermine the nation's morale and make it more difficult to prosecute the war. Disgruntled and disillusioned citizens are less willing to serve in the military, contribute their financial resources, and support the war politically. A distinguished historian and constitutional scholar, Wilson knew that war is not merely a battle of armies but a contest of wills, and that defeat could come from collapse of the home front as readily as from failure in the trenches.*

---

*It is ironic that Wilson took so strident a position on this issue. Only four years before his election to the U.S. presidency, while serving as president of Princeton University, he published his influential *Constitutional Government in the United States*, in which he staked out a quite different position. Wilson observed, "We are so accustomed to agitation, to absolutely free, outspoken argument for change, to an unrestrained criticism of men and measures . . .

A critical question during World War I was whether the government could constitutionally prohibit opposition to the war. For the first time in our history, this question implicated not only the president and the Congress, but the Supreme Court as well, for it was during World War I that the Court first attempted to make sense of the First Amendment. In a series of decisions in the spring and fall of 1919, the Court fretted over "fire in a crowded theater," wrestled with "clear and present danger," and established dismal precedents that took the nation half a century to overcome. Yet it was in these seminal decisions that we can locate the origins of the First Amendment as we know it today.

AMERICANS OF GERMAN ANCESTRY made up almost 25 percent of the population in 1917. They did not relish the prospect of war between the United States and Germany. The awkwardness of their position was made painfully evident shortly after the sinking of the *Lusitania* in 1915, when some German-Americans echoed the German government's claim that the liner was carrying arms to Britain. (The *Lusitania* was indeed carrying 173 tons of munitions.) President Wilson furiously replied that "there are citizens of the United States, born under other flags, . . . who have poured the poison of disloyalty into the very arteries of our national life." Such "disloyalty," he added, "must be crushed" out of existence.[5]

Internationalists and pacifists also opposed our entry into the war. Jane Addams, the founder of Hull House and the 1931 recipient of the Nobel Peace Prize, and Crystal Eastman, a radical feminist and founder of the *Liberator* magazine, for example, despised war as an archaic and immoral means of resolving international disputes. In 1915, Addams warned an overflow audience in Carnegie Hall that

---

that to us it seems a normal, harmless part of the familiar processes of popular government." Such freedom, he added, is "of the essence of a constitutional system."

Just as Lincoln's view of inherent presidential power shifted significantly between the Mexican and Civil wars, Wilson's view of the legitimate role of "agitation" in a democracy changed dramatically after he assumed the presidency.

war feeds upon itself, for as a war progresses, deaths mount, hatreds deepen, and the need for vengeance grows. She called for immediate mediation to bring the conflict to a close.

The Socialists also protested America's declaration of war. The Socialist Party had demonstrated its political clout in 1912 when its candidate for president, Eugene V. Debs, received almost a million votes—6 percent of all votes cast in that election. With a sharper edge than the pacifists, the Socialists argued that war was a capitalist tool contrived by industrialists to boost armament sales and enforce social order, while bringing only misery, demoralization, and death to the working class.

Anarchists also opposed American participation in World War I. Mostly recent European immigrants, the anarchists were more radical—and more militant—than the Socialists. The Socialists wanted to seize the state's power; the anarchists wanted to eliminate the state. Alexander Berkman, an anarchist leader, told a mass rally in New York City, "When the time comes we will not stop short of bloodshed to gain our ends."[6] Berkman's colleague, Emma Goldman, known in the press as the High Priestess of Anarchism, was the most prominent anarchist of her generation. Goldman defined anarchism as "the philosophy of a new social order based on liberty unrestricted by manmade law—the theory that all forms of government rest on violence, and are therefore wrong and harmful, as well as unnecessary."[7]

Goldman vehemently opposed American participation in World War I. Her essay entitled "The Promoters of the War Mania," published in *Mother Earth** in March 1917, just three months before she and Berkman were arrested for obstructing the draft, is illustrative of her response to the call for American involvement:

At this critical moment it becomes imperative for every liberty-loving person to voice a fiery protest against the participation of

---

* *Mother Earth* was an anarchist monthly published by Berkman and Goldman. It included works by such authors as Maxim Gorky, Leo Tolstoy, Eugene O'Neill, Peter Kropotkin, Margaret Sanger, and Ben Hecht.

this country in the European mass murder. [It] is unthinkable that the American people should really want war. During the last thirty months they have had ample opportunity to watch the frightful carnage in the warring countries. . . .

We are told that the "freedom of the seas" is at stake and that "American honor" demands that we protect that precious freedom. What a farce! . . . The only ones that have benefited by the "freedom of the seas" are the exploiters, the dealers in munition and food supplies. . . . Out of international carnage they have made billions. . . .

Militarism and reaction are now more rampant in Europe than ever before. Conscription and censorship have destroyed every vestige of liberty. . . . The same is bound to take place in America should the dogs of war be let loose here. . . .[8]

FOR 120 YEARS, FROM THE EXPIRATION of the Sedition Act of 1798 until America's entry into World War I, the United States had no federal legislation against seditious expression. The lessons of 1798 had carried the nation through the War of 1812, the Mexican War, the Civil War, and the Spanish-American War. But by World War I, those lessons had been forgotten.

Less than three weeks after it voted a declaration of war, Congress began debate on what would become the Espionage Act of 1917. Although directed primarily at such matters as espionage and the protection of military secrets, the bill included three sections directly relevant to free speech in wartime. For the sake of convenience, I shall refer to them as the "press censorship" provision, the "disaffection" provision, and the "nonmailability" provision. An understanding of the debate over these three provisions is essential to understanding what went wrong in the United States over the next eighteen months.

As presented to Congress, the "press censorship" provision would have made it unlawful for any person in time of war to publish any information that the president declared to be "of such character that it is or might be useful to the enemy."[9] The "disaffection" provision would have made it unlawful for any person willfully to "cause or attempt to cause disaffection in the military or naval forces of the United States."[10] The "nonmailability" provision would have granted the postmaster general authority to exclude from the mails any writing or publication that violated "any of the provisions of this act" or was otherwise "of a treasonable or anarchistic character."[11]

The *press censorship provision* provoked the most heated discussion. The Wilson administration's support of this section triggered a firestorm of protest from the press, which objected that it would give the president the final authority to decide whether the press could publish information about the conduct of the war. The American Newspaper Publishers' Association, for example, protested that this provision "strikes at the fundamental rights of the people, not only assailing their freedom of speech, but also seeking to deprive them of the means of forming intelligent opinion." The association added that "in war, especially, the press should be free, vigilant, and unfettered."[12]

When the press censorship provision was presented to the House, Representative Edwin Webb of North Carolina sternly reminded the press that, "in time of war, while men are giving up their sons," the press should be willing to give up its right to publish what the president "thinks would be hurtful to the United States and helpful to the enemy."[13] Echoing this view, Senator Lee Overman of North Carolina argued that "the good of society is superior to the right of the press to publish what it pleases," and "if the activities of newspapers were a hindrance in the prosecution of the war, their curtailment would not be unconstitutional."[14]

Opposition to the provision was fierce. Senator Hiram Johnson of California reminded his colleagues that "the preservation of free speech" is of "transcendent importance."[15] Representative Fiorello LaGuardia of New York characterized the provision as a "vicious precedent,"[16] and Representative William Wood of Indiana warned that it could become "an instrument of tyranny."[17] Describing the provision as "un-American," Representative Martin B. Madden of Illinois protested that "while we are fighting to establish the democracy of the world, we ought not to do the thing that will establish autocracy in America."[18]

When it began to appear that the press censorship provision would go down to defeat, President Wilson made a direct appeal to Congress, stating that the "authority to exercise censorship over the press . . . is absolutely necessary to the public safety."[19] Members of Congress were unmoved. Representative Ira Hersey of Maine complained that "we, the Congress of the United States," are now "importuned by the executive . . . to place in the hands of the President unlawful powers, to grant to him the . . . authority to take away from the citizen the protection of the Constitution."[20] On May 31, 1917, the House defeated the provision by a vote of 184 to 144, effectively ending consideration of the "press censorship" provision for the duration of the war.

The *nonmailability provision* also generated controversy. Several members of Congress objected to granting the postmaster general such broad authority to exclude political material from the mail. Senator Charles Thomas of Colorado, for example, argued that this provision would enable postmasters to exclude "legitimate" as well as illegitimate publications and would produce "a far greater evil than the evil which is sought to be prevented."[21] Representative Meyer London of New York declared the provision a "menace to freedom," adding that "there is nothing more oppressive . . . than a democracy gone mad."[22] There was particular concern about the words "treasonable" and "anarchistic." Senator Johnson objected that this provision would be subject to the whim of whoever "happens to be high in the Post Office Department."[23]

After vigorous debate, Congress amended the "nonmailability" provision to replace the phrase "treasonable or anarchistic character" with the much narrower phrase "containing any matter advocating or urging treason, insurrection or forcible resistance to any law of the United States."[24] It is noteworthy that as a result of this

amendment only *express advocacy* of unlawful conduct could fall
within the catchall clause of the provision. As we shall see, this will
become a critical concept in later debates about the meaning of both
the Espionage Act and the First Amendment.

The *disaffection provision*, which turned out to be the most important part of the bill, received less attention. But even this provision
was amended in a significant manner. The potential difficulties with
this provision were made clear in hearings before the House Committee on the Judiciary. Gilbert Roe, a civil liberties lawyer who represented the Free Speech League, testified that this provision was even
more troubling than the Sedition Act of 1798. He explained that the
1798 act at least purported to recognize the defense of truth. Under
the "disaffection" provision, however, truth was no defense. Every
effort to discuss or criticize the war could be "brought under the ban."
To illustrate the magnitude of the problem, Roe noted that "the people
. . . retain their right at the next election to return to Congress Senators and Representatives . . . who are opposed to the continuation of
the war." How, he asked, is any voter "to form an intelligent opinion"
on this question "unless there is the fullest discussion permitted of
every phase of the war, its origin, its manner of prosecution, and its
manner of termination?" Without such free discussion, he argued,
the very essence of the democratic process would be impaired.[25]

In light of these concerns, the Judiciary Committee found the term
"disaffection" to be "too broad," "too elastic," and "too indefinite."[26]
In order to narrow and clarify the provision, it replaced the phrase
"cause or attempt to cause disaffection" with "cause or attempt to
cause insubordination, disloyalty, mutiny, or refusal of duty."[27] Representative Webb explained that "to make it a crime to create disaffection" in the military "might subject a perfectly innocent person to
punishment." A mother, for example, might write her son to "tell
him the sad conditions back home." Webb insisted that this amendment would "protect the honest man," but "get the dishonest fellow
who deliberately undertakes to spread disloyalty."[28]

After nine weeks of grueling debate, Congress enacted the Espionage Act of 1917, as amended. Violations were punishable by prison terms of up to twenty years. As the congressional debate suggests, the legislation, as enacted, was not a broadside attack on all criticism of the war. It was, rather, a carefully considered enactment designed to deal with specific military concerns.

But what would the act mean in practice? Would passing out antiwar leaflets be regarded as a willful "attempt to cause insubordination"? Would a public speech denouncing the draft be deemed a deliberate obstruction of "the recruiting or enlistment service"? Much would depend on the attitude and approach of the Wilson Justice Department. The administration was clearly disappointed with the legislation. Not only had Wilson's personal appeal to Congress been rebuffed, but a year later Attorney General Thomas Gregory publicly expressed the administration's frustration with the act. Gregory complained that when war broke out the administration had "secured the passage of the Espionage Act, but most of the teeth which we tried to put in it were taken out."[29]

In light of the president's caustic statements about disloyalty, and the attorney general's evident disappointment with the legislation, there was little reason to expect much prosecutorial restraint. Any doubt on this score was erased when Attorney General Gregory, referring to war dissenters, declared in November 1917, "May God have mercy on them, for they need expect none from an outraged people and an avenging government."[30]

BECAUSE THERE HAD BEEN NO direct attack on the United States, and no direct threat to America's national security, the Wilson administration needed to *create* an "outraged public." To build a sense of patriotic fervor, Wilson established the Committee on Public Information (CPI), under the direction of George Creel, a journalist and public relations expert. Creel's task was to generate enthusiasm for the war. Under his direction, the CPI produced a flood of pamphlets, news releases, speeches, newspaper editorials, political cartoons, and even motion pictures. His efforts concentrated on two main themes: feeding hatred of the enemy and promoting a suspicion of anyone who might be "disloyal." As the CPI whipped the nation into a frenzy of patriotism, many communities went so far as to ban German-language teaching and burn German-language books.

In the first month of the war, Attorney General Gregory urged "loyal" Americans to act as voluntary detectives and to report their suspicions directly to the Department of Justice. The results were staggering. Each day, thousands of accusations of disloyalty flooded into the department. Adding to the furor, the CPI encouraged citizens to form voluntary associations dedicated to informing the authorities of possible disloyalty. The largest of these citizen groups, the American Protective League, quickly enlisted more than 200,000 members. APLers ferreted out disloyalty wherever they could find it. They reported thousands of individuals to the authorities on the basis of hearsay, gossip, and slander.

The activities of these organizations went well beyond reporting alleged disloyalty. With implicit immunity, they engaged in wiretaps, breaking and entering, bugging offices, and examining bank accounts and medical records. Vigilantes ransacked the homes of German-Americans. In Oklahoma, a former minister who opposed the sale of Liberty bonds was tarred and feathered. In Texas, six farmers were horsewhipped because they declined to contribute to the Red Cross. In Illinois, an angry mob wrapped an individual suspected of disloyalty in an American flag and then murdered him on a public street. Wilson, Gregory, and Creel helped create not only an "outraged public" but a fearful and intolerant nation. It was in this atmosphere of accusation and suspicion that federal judges were called upon to interpret and apply the Espionage Act of 1917.

FACED WITH AN AGGRESSIVE Justice Department and an increasingly outraged public, how would judges construe the Espionage Act? The federal judiciary was a product of its times. The predominant view during this era was that civil liberties were intended for respectable, law-abiding citizens. This did not bode well for those whose views could readily be labeled "disloyal," "radical," or "seditious." Moreover, there was as yet no deeply rooted commitment to civil liberties within the legal profession, and no well-developed understanding of the freedom of speech. Before the Espionage Act, there was scant judicial precedent on the meaning of the First Amendment. Most judges continued to assume that the First Amendment implicitly incorporated the English common law and that the government could punish speech whenever it might have harmful effects, without regard to its value to public discourse.

This approach to the First Amendment was roundly criticized in the scholarly commentary. Drawing on the controversy over the Sedition Act of 1798, prominent late nineteenth- and early twentieth-century scholars disputed the assumption that the Constitution's framers intended to import the English common law of free speech. Professor Henry Schofield of Northwestern University, for example, argued that a central goal of the American Revolution "was to get rid of the English common law on liberty of speech."[31] Like most other scholars of his generation, Schofield argued that speech about matters of public concern should generally be immune from regulation.

It was an open question whether federal judges would embrace this understanding of the Constitution. As it turned out, without any clear judicial precedents to guide them, few federal judges had either the inclination or the fortitude to withstand the mounting pressure for suppression. The First Amendment was swept away in the tide of patriotic fervor.

A few courageous judges did take a clear stand in favor of free speech, however, and we should acknowledge their contributions. Not surprisingly, each of these judges had a strong streak of independence. Federal District Judge George Bourquin of Montana presided over the prosecution of Ves Hall, who was alleged to have said that "Germany would whip the United States" and that "the

United States was only fighting for Wall Street millionaires." The government charged Hall with violating the Espionage Act. Judge Bourquin directed a verdict of acquittal. Noting that Hall had made these comments in a village of some sixty people, sixty miles from the nearest railway, Bourquin concluded that any claim that Hall had intended his remarks to interfere "with the operation or success of the military" must be dismissed as "absurd."[32] He held that mere criticism of the war, or even expressions of disloyalty, were not prohibited by the act.

Judge Charles Fremont Amidon was a man of impressive learning, intellect, and dignity. In a series of decisions in 1917 and 1918, he too argued for a narrow construction of the act. In one case, a farmer, E. H. Schutte, allegedly stated that the war "is a rich man's war and it is all a damned graft and a swindle." The United States charged him with violating the Espionage Act. Judge Amidon dismissed the indictment because there was no evidence that Schutte's comments had been made to an audience containing men who were in the armed forces or eligible for the draft.[33]

The most important decision in which a federal judge held fast against a broad construction of the Espionage Act was *Masses Publishing Co. v. Patten*.[34] The *Masses* was a monthly "revolutionary" journal that regularly featured a remarkable collection of writers, poets, playwrights, and philosophers, including Max Eastman, John Reed, Vachel Lindsay, Emma Goldman, Carl Sandburg, Bertrand Russell, Louis Untermeyer, and Sherwood Anderson. Iconoclastic, impertinent, and confrontational, it was filled with sparkling social satire, intellectual commentary, and political criticism.

In the summer of 1917, Postmaster General Albert Burleson ordered the August issue of the *Masses* excluded from the mail, exercising his authority under the Espionage Act. The *Masses* sought an injunction to prohibit the local postmaster from refusing to accept the issue for mailing. The postmaster argued that four cartoons and four items of text violated the act, thus justifying the order of exclusion. Illustrative of the contents was a poem by Josephine Bell that praised the courage of Emma Goldman and Alexander Berkman, who were then in jail for opposing the draft. Judge Learned Hand granted the injunction and prohibited the postmaster from excluding the *Masses* from the mail.

From the moment he was assigned the case, Hand fully appreciated its significance for him personally. Hand knew he was under consideration for promotion to the court of appeals, a promotion he richly deserved and much desired. He wrote his wife that if the case were not quickly settled, his decision would go against the government, and then "whoop-la your little man is in the mud." He added that "there are times when the old bunk about an independent and fearless judiciary means a good deal."[35]

In his opinion, Judge Hand conceded the postmaster's claim that "to arouse discontent and disaffection among the people with the prosecution of the war and with the draft tends to promote a mutinous and insubordinate temper among the troops." But, he argued, to read the word "cause" in the statute so broadly would allow "the suppression of all . . . criticism, and of all opinion except what encouraged and supported the existing policies." Hand reasoned that such an interpretation of the act "would contradict the normal assumption of democratic government" and would be "contrary to the use and wont of our people." He therefore held that the act should not be construed so broadly.[36]

But what, then, did the act prohibit? Hand observed that Anglo-American law had always held that "one may not counsel or advise others to violate the law." Moreover, words "which have no purport but to counsel the violation of law cannot . . . be a part of that public opinion which is the final source of government in a democratic state." Hand thus concluded that if one stops short of expressly urging others to violate the law, "one should not be held to have attempted to cause its violation." This principle, he emphasized, "is not a scholastic subterfuge, but a hard-bought acquisition in the fight for freedom." Applying this approach to the facts of *Masses*, Hand held that neither the cartoons nor the text crossed the line of *express advocacy* of unlawful conduct and therefore did not violate the act.[37]

As Hand had predicted, his opinion in *Masses*, one of the most brilliant ever written on the subject of free speech, was not greeted warmly. It was promptly reversed by the court of appeals, and Hand was passed over for promotion.[38] Several days later, seven of the *Masses*'s editors and staff were indicted for conspiracy to violate the Espionage Act. By the end of the year, the *Masses* had ceased publication.

FEW OTHER JUDGES FOLLOWED the lead of Bourquin, Amidon, and Hand. Most were determined to impose severe sentences on those charged with disloyalty, and no details of legislative interpretation or appeals to the First Amendment could stand in their way. These judges were operating in a feverish atmosphere, not conducive to careful judicial reflection. During the war, the United States prosecuted more than *2,000* dissenters for allegedly disloyal, seditious, or incendiary speech.

The prevailing approach in the federal courts is well illustrated by *Shaffer v. United States*.[39] Frank Shaffer was charged with mailing copies of a book, *The Finished Mystery*, which argued that the "war itself is wrong" and that "its prosecution will be a crime."[40] Shaffer was convicted under the act, and the court of appeals affirmed his conviction, with the following reasoning:

> It is true that disapproval of the war and the advocacy of peace are not crimes under the Espionage Act; but the question here . . . is whether the natural and probable tendency and effect of the words [may] produce the result condemned by the statute. . . .
>
> Printed matter may tend to obstruct the . . . service even if it contains no mention of recruiting or enlistments. . . . The service may be obstructed by attacking the justice of the cause for

which the war is waged, and by undermining the spirit of loyalty which inspires men to enlist or to register for conscription
in the service of their country. . . .

It is argued that the evidence fails to show that [Shaffer
intended this result]. But . . . he must be presumed to have
intended the natural and probable consequences of what he
knowingly did.[41]


This "bad tendency" approach was embraced by almost every federal court that applied the Espionage Act during World War I. As
Gilbert Roe had predicted in his testimony to the House Judiciary
Committee, judges and juries were overwhelmed by wartime hysteria. Consider the following:

• Rose Pastor Stokes was convicted for saying, "I am for the people
and the government is for the profiteers," during an antiwar talk to
the Women's Dining Club of Kansas City. Although there were no
soldiers—indeed, no men—in her intended audience, the government successfully argued that she had violated the act because "our
armies . . . can operate and succeed only so far as they are supported
and maintained by the folks at home," and Stokes's statement had
the tendency to "chill enthusiasm, extinguish confidence, and retard
cooperation" of mothers, sisters, and sweethearts. She was sentenced to ten years in prison.[42]

• The Reverend Clarence H. Waldron was convicted for distributing a pamphlet stating that "if Christians [are] forbidden to fight to
preserve the Person of their Lord and Master, they may not fight to
preserve themselves, or any city they should happen to dwell in." The
government charged that in distributing this pamphlet Waldron had
obstructed the recruiting service. He was sentenced to fifteen years in
prison.

• Robert Goldstein was convicted for producing and exhibiting a
motion picture about the American Revolution. *The Spirit of '76*
depicted Paul Revere's ride, the signing of the Declaration of Independence, and Washington at Valley Forge. But it also included a

scene accurately portraying the Wyoming Valley Massacre, in which British soldiers bayoneted women and children. The government charged that this could promote insubordination because it negatively portrayed America's ally in the war against Germany. Goldstein was sentenced to ten years in prison.[43]

None of these defendants had *expressly advocated* insubordination, refusal of service, or any other unlawful conduct. But by questioning the morality or conduct of the war, each had increased the possibility that some listener, reader, or viewer might engage in unlawful conduct, or encourage someone else to do so. As these cases illustrate, under the "bad tendency" interpretation of the Espionage Act, it became impossible to question the war or the draft without running the risk of being accused of unlawfully obstructing the war effort.

Against this background, and especially in light of the severity of the sentences meted out, no sensible person dared criticize the Wilson administration's policies. As Professor Zechariah Chafee observed at the time, under this construction of the Espionage Act "all genuine discussion" of the justice and wisdom of continuing the war became "perilous."[44]

Even with the "bad tendency" test well entrenched and the prosecutions of dissenters mounting daily, the Department of Justice sought in 1918 to amend the Espionage Act to close what it described as "loopholes" in the original legislation. Pointing to the recent lynching of a German-American suspected by neighbors of disloyalty, Attorney General Gregory argued that such incidents occurred because otherwise law-abiding citizens believed existing laws inadequate to prevent disloyalty and therefore felt justified in taking the law into their own hands. He insisted that Congress make the Espionage Act "more drastic," warning that unless citizens were satisfied that disloyal individuals would not be allowed to roam free, and "unless the hysteria, which results in the lynching of men, is checked," the nation would fall into "a condition of lawlessness."[45] What seems most remarkable about this argument is that instead of seeking federal authority to *protect* dissenters from mob violence, Gregory sought to expand the prohibition of dissent.*

As a result of this prodding, Congress enacted the Sedition Act of 1918, which forbade any person, "when the United States is in war," to utter or write any "abusive language about the form of government of the United States, or the Constitution of the United States, or the military or naval forces of the United States, or the flag of the United States, or the uniform of the Army or Navy of the United States."[46]

The analogy to the Sedition Act of 1798 did not pass unnoticed. Senator James Reed asked his colleagues to note how closely the bill paralleled the "old" Sedition Act, adding pointedly that the proposed statute was even worse, for "a conviction under the old sedition law" required the government to prove falsity and malice, whereas the new act "omits both of those important qualifying terms."[47] Despite these objections, the Sedition Act of 1918 was approved by Congress and signed into law by President Wilson. With the passage of this law, the Wilson administration had put in place the perfect instrument to suppress dissent.

WHAT WOULD THE SUPREME COURT say about the constitutionality of the Espionage Act of 1917 and the Sedition Act of 1918? At this time, the Court was in firmly conservative hands. These justices were not likely to take a bold stand in favor of those who challenged the established order.

*Schenck v. United States*[48] was the Supreme Court's first significant

---

*This logic took the idea of the "heckler's veto" to a new extreme. In the "heckler's veto" situation, the government cannot constitutionally silence the speaker. But if other citizens threaten violence because *they* do not like what the speaker is saying, the government can claim that by punishing the speaker it is merely preserving order. If the government is allowed to do this, it effectively transfers the power of censorship to the mob. The net result is the suppression of constitutionally protected speech. Moreover, the more the government acts in this manner, the more it encourages the speaker's opponents to use or threaten to use violence in order to silence unpopular expression. The proper response of the government is not to cater to the "heckler's veto," but to protect the speaker.

decision interpreting the First Amendment. The defendants in *Schenck* were charged with attempting to obstruct the recruiting and enlistment service by circulating a pamphlet to men who had been called and accepted for military service. The pamphlet argued that the draft was unconstitutional, described a conscript as "little better than a convict," and intimated that conscription was a "monstrous wrong" designed to further the interests of Wall Street. It encouraged readers to join the Socialist Party, write their congressmen to protest conscription, and "petition for the repeal" of the Conscription Act. The defendants were convicted at trial because the "natural and probable tendency" of the pamphlet was to dampen the willingness of men to serve in the armed forces. It was, all in all, an unexceptional case under the Espionage Act.

Justice Oliver Wendell Holmes wrote the opinion for a unanimous Supreme Court, upholding the conviction. In considering the First Amendment, Holmes penned the following passage, one of the most famous in the annals of American legal history:

> We admit that in many places and in ordinary times the defendants, in saying all that was said in the circular, would have been within their constitutional rights. But the character of every act depends upon the circumstances in which it is done. The most stringent protection of free speech would not protect a man in falsely shouting fire in a theater, and causing a panic. . . .
>
> The question in every case is whether the words used are used in such circumstances and are of such a nature as to create a clear and present danger that they will bring about the substantive evils that Congress has a right to prevent. . . .[49]

Note that Holmes invoked the "false cry of fire" for two purposes. First, he used it to refute the "absolutist" interpretation of the First Amendment. The phrase "Congress shall make no law . . . abridging the freedom of speech, or of the press" might literally be taken to prohibit *any* law limiting free speech. But such an interpretation would mean that even the false cry of fire would be constitutionally protected. Because Holmes sensibly regarded that result as absurd, it follows that the First Amendment cannot be taken literally. Its meaning must turn on the interpretation of the phrase "the freedom of speech, or of the press," for it is *that* freedom that may not be "abridged."

Second, Holmes used the false cry of fire to define the circumstances in which speech is *not* protected by the First Amendment. That is, he derived his "clear and present danger" test from his hypothetical. Why can a false cry of fire be punished? Because it creates a clear and present danger of harm. Hence, that is the test for restricting speech under the First Amendment.[*]

At first blush, the clear-and-present-danger standard seems much more protective of speech than the "bad tendency" test. Whereas the latter requires only a remote connection between the speech and the harm, Holmes's test (as illustrated by the false cry of fire) implies that speech can constitutionally be restricted only if the connection is *likely* and *immediate*.

But if the Court had actually applied a clear-and-present-danger standard in *Schenck*, shouldn't it have *reversed* the conviction? Although the circulation of the pamphlet satisfied the bad tendency test, surely it did not pose a clear and present danger analogous to causing a panic in the theater. So why did the Court *affirm* Schenck's conviction? At the very least, shouldn't the Court have ordered a new trial at which the jury could apply the Holmes standard?

The most plausible explanation is that the Court did not intend the phrase "clear and present danger" to reflect a change in the law. Any doubt on this score was erased only a week later, when the Court

---

[*] Suppose the "cry of fire" were *true*. Would it still be punishable? If not, does that suggest a possible error in Holmes's reasoning?

handed down its decisions in *Frohwerk v. United States*[50] and *Debs v. United States*,[51] which unanimously upheld convictions under the Espionage Act without even mentioning clear and present danger. In both opinions, also written by Justice Holmes, the Court clearly approved the bad tendency test.* Thus, in its first three decisions on the meaning of the First Amendment, the Supreme Court unanimously embraced a very narrow view of "the freedom of speech, or of the press."

In the fall of 1919, six months after *Schenck*, *Frohwerk*, and *Debs*, the Court handed down its decision in *Abrams v. United States*.[52] The defendants, a group of young Russian-Jewish émigrés, distributed several thousand copies of each of two leaflets, one in English, the other in Yiddish, on the Lower East Side of New York. The leaflets called for a general strike to protest the sending of American troops into Russia. After a highly contentious trial that called to mind some of the prosecutions under the Sedition Act of 1798, the defendants were convicted of violating the Sedition Act of 1918. They were sentenced to terms ranging up to twenty years in prison. The Supreme Court affirmed the convictions, summarily rejecting the defendants' First Amendment argument as having already been "negatived" in *Schenck*, *Frohwerk*, and *Debs*.

Surprisingly, Justice Holmes, joined by Justice Louis D. Brandeis, dissented. Holmes noted that the power of government to restrict speech "is greater in time of war than in time of peace because war opens dangers that do not exist at other times." But, he insisted, "the principle . . . is always the same." It is "only the present danger of immediate evil . . . that warrants Congress in setting a limit to the expression of opinion."[53]

Turning to the case at hand, Holmes declared that "nobody can suppose" that the distribution of this leaflet presented "any immedi-

---

*The *Debs* case, by the way, involved Eugene V. Debs, the national leader of the Socialist Party, who had given a speech questioning the morality of the draft. He was sentenced to ten years in prison. In 1920, while in prison for this offense, Debs received a million votes for president.

ate danger that its opinions would hinder the success of the government arms."[54] Indeed, in Holmes's view, the defendants had as much right to publish their leaflets "as the Government has to publish the Constitution of the United States."[55] In reaching this conclusion, Holmes offered one of the most eloquent statements ever made about the freedom of speech:

> Persecution for the expression of opinions seems to me perfectly logical. If you have no doubt of your premises or your power and want a certain result with all your heart you naturally express your wishes in law and sweep away all opposition. . . . But when men have realized that time has upset many fighting faiths, they may come to believe even more than they believe the very foundations of their own conduct that the ultimate good desired is better reached by free trade in ideas—that the best test of truth is the power of the thought to get itself accepted in the competition of the market, and that truth is the only ground upon which their wishes safely can be carried out. That at any rate is the theory of our Constitution. It is an experiment, as all life is an experiment. . . . While that experiment is part of our system I think that we should be eternally vigilant against attempts to check the expression of opinions that we loathe and believe to be fraught with death, unless they so imminently threaten immediate interference with the lawful and pressing purposes of the law that an immediate check is required to save the country.[56]

The explanation for Holmes's dramatic transformation over the summer of 1919 remains a delicious mystery. It seems clear, though, that his extensive conversations and correspondence that summer with Judge Learned Hand, the Harvard law professor Zechariah Chafee, and the political scientist Harold Laski sparked the change in his thinking. For the first time in American history, a justice of the

Supreme Court passionately advocated meaningful protection of free speech, even in wartime.*

But Holmes and Brandeis still represented a minority of two. In a series of subsequent decisions involving prosecutions of individuals who dissented during World War I, the Court continued to uphold convictions under the Espionage and Sedition Acts, and Holmes and Brandeis continued to dissent. These decisions left no doubt of the Supreme Court's understanding of the First Amendment at this time in our history: While the nation is at war, "serious, abrasive criticism" was "beyond constitutional protection." As the First Amendment scholar Harry Kalven sadly observed, these decisions were "dismal evidence of the degree to which the mood of society" can "penetrate judicial chambers."[57]

AFTER THE WAR, HOWEVER, THE American people began to reflect on what they had done. Attorney General Gregory recommended the release of most prisoners still in jail for Espionage Act or Sedition Act convictions. He explained that in many cases injustices had been done because of the "intense patriotism" of the judges and jurors.[58]

---

*The defendants in Abrams were a fascinating group. Mollie Steimer, for example, arrived at Ellis Island in 1913 with her parents and her five brothers and sisters, part of the flood of immigrants fleeing poverty and anti-Semitism in czarist Russia. Two days after her arrival, the fifteen-year-old went to work in a grimy garment factory amid the crowded tenements of New York's Lower East Side. Faced with continuing hardship and bleak prospects for the future, she began to explore radical literature and soon became a committed anarchist.

At the time of her trial, she was twenty years old, but looked much younger. At four feet nine inches and less than ninety pounds, she was tiny, but she was tough as nails. After her conviction, she was sentenced to fifteen years in prison. In 1922, she was ordered deported to the Soviet Union. When she was informed of this action, she refused to leave the federal penitentiary, because there was a threatened railroad strike and she would not ride on a train run by strikebreakers. After the strike was resolved, she was shipped back to Russia.

Once there, she immediately began protesting the injustices of Soviet society. In 1923, the Soviets deported Mollie Steimer to Germany. Few other people have the distinction of having been deported by both the United States and the Soviet Union. In 1933, when Hitler came to power, Steimer fled to Paris. Her Jewish and anarchist identities caught up with her, however, and after the Nazis occupied France, she escaped to Mexico. Through her entire life, she remained a dedicated anarchist. Mollie Steimer died in Cuernavaca in 1980 at the age of eighty-two.

In 1920, Congress repealed the Sedition Act of 1918 (the Espionage Act of 1917 remains on the books). In 1923, President Coolidge ordered the release of all the remaining prisoners. A decade later, President Roosevelt granted amnesty to all persons convicted under the Espionage and Sedition Acts and restored their full political and civil rights. In later years, the Supreme Court effectively overruled *Schenck*, *Frohwerk*, *Debs*, *Abrams*, and the other World War I–era decisions, implicitly acknowledging that these convictions had all violated the First Amendment.

The government's repression of dissent during World War I had a significant impact on American society.* It was in reaction to these abuses that the modern civil liberties movement came into being. With the benefit of hindsight, many supporters of the Wilson administration were shocked by what they had done in the name of patriotism and national security. Before the war, the philosopher-educator John Dewey, one of the leading intellectuals of his day, argued that the government's suppression of dissent was justified on grounds of pragmatism. After the war, he wrote that "the increase of intolerance of discussion to the point of religious bigotry" had led the nation to condemn as seditious "every opinion and belief which irritates the majority of loyal citizens."[59] Dewey admitted that he had underestimated the determination of the American people to "grovel in the sacrifice of their liberties" in order to prove their devotion to the cause,[60] and warned that those who are dedicated to preserving civil liberties in wartime must steel themselves to be attacked as "enemies of the nation."[61] In 1920, Dewey helped found the American Civil Liberties Union.

---

*The suppression of free speech during World War I was compounded by the Red Scare of 1919–20, during which thousands of noncitizens were rounded up in dragnet arrests and summarily deported because of their suspected radical beliefs. It was a period of rampant xenophobia, intolerance, and public hysteria.

CHAPTER IV

# World War II
## "A Jap's a Jap"

❧❧

A S illustrated by the Alien Friends Act of 1798, war fever often translates into xenophobia. To some extent, this is understandable. In a war, citizens of an enemy nation who reside in the United States will often have divided loyalties. It is reasonable to suppose that enemy aliens pose greater risks of espionage, sabotage, and subversion than either American citizens or other noncitizen residents. As the Supreme Court observed in 1950, the "alien enemy is bound by an allegiance which commits him to . . . the cause of our enemy; hence the United States . . . regards him as part of the enemy resources" and may therefore take appropriate "measures to disable him from commission of hostile acts."[1]

Even noncitizens who are not enemy aliens may pose special risks because they do not have the same allegiance to the nation as American citizens. It is therefore predictable that a nation at war will keep tabs on both "alien enemies" and "alien friends." But how a nation addresses these risks speaks volumes about its values, its sense of fairness, and its willingness to judge individuals as individuals.

IN ANTICIPATION OF OUR POSSIBLE ENTRY into World War II, the Alien Registration Act of 1940 (known as the Smith Act) required all resident aliens to register with the Immigration and Naturalization Service (INS).[2] This was the first time the United States had ever made such an "inventory" of noncitizens. Of the almost 5 million aliens who registered, approximately 600,000 were Italian nationals, 260,000 were German nationals, and 40,000 were Japanese nationals. Immediately after the attack on Pearl Harbor, the government classified all 900,000 of these individuals as "enemy aliens" under the Alien Enemies Act of 1798, which authorized the government to apprehend, detain, and deport enemy nationals.

When Attorney General Francis Biddle asked President Roosevelt to sign the proclamations necessary to authorize the detention of enemy aliens, Roosevelt suggested that it might be wise to intern all German nationals. He explained that he wasn't much concerned about the Italians, because "[t]hey are a lot of opera singers," but the Germans "are different, they may be dangerous." Having learned from the excesses of World War I, however, Biddle was determined not to overreact. He was convinced that the right approach was to consider enemy aliens as individuals. But how to decide which enemy aliens to detain?

In the years leading up to America's entry into World War II, the FBI had prepared a custodial detention list of "potentially danger-ous" German, Italian, and Japanese citizens in the United States. On the night of December 7, 1941, the FBI took the most dangerous of these individuals into custody. Over the next several months, the FBI detained 9,121 enemy aliens in this manner. Approximately 5,100 (57 percent) were Japanese nationals, 3,250 (36 percent) were Ger-man nationals, and 650 (7 percent) were Italian nationals. Accord-ing to Biddle, each of these detentions "was made on the basis of information concerning the specific alien taken into custody." Biddle authorized "no dragnet techniques."[3] In this program, the govern-ment detained approximately 1 of every 923 Italian nationals, 1 of every 80 German nationals, and 1 of every 8 Japanese nationals.

Although the Alien Enemies Act does not require a hearing before an enemy alien is detained, Biddle insisted that each individual taken into custody have a hearing. More than a hundred Enemy Alien

Hearing Boards were established for this purpose. As a result of these hearings, by June 30, 1943, more than half of these detainees had been released. By June 1944, the number of enemy aliens interned in this program had dwindled to 2,525.

After Pearl Harbor, all enemy aliens who had not been taken into custody—approximately 890,000—were subjected by presidential proclamation to restrictions on their freedom of movement and forbidden to possess such items as radios, cameras, and weapons. In October 1942, Biddle lifted these restrictions for all 600,000 Italian nationals (representing two-thirds of the enemy aliens in the United States), explaining that this was "an act of justice" and "an important weapon" in laying the foundation for military operations in Italy.[4]

German nationals did not fare quite as well, but on the whole they were treated well. The vast majority of German nationals lived relatively quiet lives without serious inconvenience. In part, this was because German-Americans made up almost 25 percent of the population and therefore constituted an important voting bloc that wielded significant economic power. Any government policy that subjected German nationals to dragnet roundups or serious deprivations would have alienated an influential element in American society.

The United States was not so sympathetic to Japanese aliens or even Japanese-Americans. Japan's attack on Pearl Harbor killed more than 2,000 people and destroyed much of the Pacific fleet. Two months later, on February 19, 1942, President Roosevelt signed Executive Order No. 9066, which authorized the Army to "designate . . . military areas" from which "any or all persons may be excluded." Although the words "Japanese" or "Japanese-American" never appeared in the order, it was understood to apply only to persons of Japanese ancestry.[5]

Over the next eight months, almost 120,000 persons of Japanese descent were ordered to leave their homes in California, Washington, Oregon, and Arizona. Two-thirds of these individuals were *American citizens*, representing almost 90 percent of all Japanese-Americans.

No charges were brought against these individuals. There were no hearings. They did not know where they were going, how long they would be detained, what conditions they would face, or what fate would await them. They were ordered to bring only what they could carry. Many families lost everything.

On the orders of military police, these men, women, and children were assigned to temporary "detention camps," which had been set up in converted racetracks and fairgrounds. Many families lived in crowded horse stalls, often in unsanitary conditions. Barbed-wire fences and armed guard towers surrounded the compounds. From there, the internees were transported to one of ten permanent internment camps, which were located in isolated areas in wind-swept deserts or vast swamplands. They were confined in over-crowded rooms with no furniture other than cots. Although the internees had been led to believe that these would be "resettlement communities" rather than detention camps, they once again found themselves surrounded by barbed wire and military police. There they remained for three years.

WHY DID THIS HAPPEN? CERTAINLY, the days following Pearl Harbor were dark days for the American spirit. Fear of possible Japanese sabotage and espionage was rampant, and an outraged public felt an understandable desire to lash out at those who had attacked the nation. But the internment was also an extension of more than a century of racial prejudice against the "yellow peril." Laws passed in the early 1900s denied immigrants from Japan the right to become naturalized American citizens, to own land, and to marry outside their race. In 1924, immigration from Japan was halted altogether.

President Roosevelt, who was not exempt from the pervasive American prejudice against "Orientals," was concerned long before 1941 about a possible pro-Japanese fifth column in the United States. As early as 1936, he initiated an investigation of potential disloyalty among Japanese-Americans. By December 1941, the FBI had compiled a list of some 2,000 individuals of Japanese ancestry whom it deemed "suspect." This list included "nearly the entire leadership of first-generation West Coast Japanese-Americans."[6] Roosevelt's willingness to consider such measures against Japanese-Americans was not matched by any similar effort to monitor Americans of German or Italian ancestry.

In the immediate aftermath of Pearl Harbor, there was no clamor for the mass internment of Japanese aliens or Japanese-Americans. To the contrary, Eleanor Roosevelt announced that "no law-abiding aliens of any nationality would be discriminated against by the government," and Judge Jerome Frank, a distinguished federal judge and close friend of the president, observed that "if ever any Americans go to a concentration camp, American democracy will go with them."[7] A few days later, Attorney General Biddle assured the nation that there would be "no indiscriminate, large-scale raids."[8] On December 10, FBI Director J. Edgar Hoover reported that almost all the persons the FBI intended to arrest had been taken into custody.

In the weeks that followed, however, a demand for the removal of all persons of Japanese ancestry reached a crescendo along the West Coast. The motivations for this delayed outburst of anxiety were many and complex. Certainly, it was fed by fears of a Japanese invasion. Conspiracy theories abounded, and neither government nor military officials effectively allayed these concerns. Mayor Fletcher Bowron of Los Angeles and other local officials eagerly passed on to the public as true "even the wildest rumor of Oriental treachery." By mid-January, California was awash in unfounded rumors of sabotage and espionage.[9]

General John DeWitt, the top Army commander on the West Coast, was determined not to be caught up short like his counterpart in Hawaii. Several days after Pearl Harbor, he reported as fact rumors that a squadron of enemy airplanes had passed over California, that there was a planned uprising of 20,000 Japanese-Americans in San Francisco, and that "Japanese Americans were aiding submarines by signaling them from the shore."[10] The FBI and other government agencies debunked all these rumors as false.

On January 2, the Joint Immigration Committee of the California legislature issued a manifesto charging that even ethnic Japanese born in the United States were "unassimilable," that American citizens of Japanese descent could "be called to bear arms for their Emperor," and that Japanese-language schools were teaching students that "every Japanese, wherever born, or residing," owed primary allegiance to "his Emperor and Japan."[11]

Two days later, the newspaper columnist Damon Runyon erroneously reported that a radio transmitter had been discovered in a rooming house that catered to Japanese residents. Who could doubt, he asked, the "continued existence of enemy agents" among the Japanese population? On January 14, California Congressman Leland Ford insisted that the United States place "all Japanese, whether citizens or not," in "inland concentration camps." The American Legion demanded the internment of all 93,000 individuals of Japanese extraction then living in California.[12]

Such demands were further ignited by the January 25 report of the Commission on Pearl Harbor, which was chaired by Supreme Court Justice Owen Roberts. The report, which was hastily researched and written, erroneously asserted that persons of Japanese ancestry in Hawaii had facilitated Japan's attack on the United States. A few days later, Henry McLemore wrote a column in the *San Francisco Examiner* calling for "the immediate removal of every Japanese on the West Coast." He added, "Personally, I hate the Japanese. And that goes for all of them."[13]

On February 4, California Governor Culbert Olson declared in a radio address that it was "much easier" to determine the loyalty of Italian and German aliens than of Japanese aliens and Japanese-Americans. "All Japanese people," he added, "will recognize this fact."[14] California's attorney general, Earl Warren, argued that whereas it was relatively easy to find out which German- or Italian-Americans were loyal, it was simply too difficult to determine which Americans of Japanese ancestry were loyal and which were not. Warren later opined that "there is more potential danger among the group of Japanese who are born in this country than from the alien Japanese who were born in Japan."[15]

General DeWitt initially resisted demands for "wholesale internment," insisting that "we can weed the disloyal out of the loyal and lock them up, if necessary." In early January, he condemned the idea of mass internment as "damned nonsense." But as political pressure mounted, DeWitt changed his tune. As California's governor, the mayor of Los Angeles, and most members of the West Coast congressional delegations insisted that all persons of Japanese ancestry be removed from the West Coast, DeWitt came to the rather startling view that "[t]he very fact that no sabotage has taken place to date is a disturbing and confirming indication" that the Japanese have carefully orchestrated their subversion so that when the sabotage comes it will be massive.[16]

Crudely racist sentiments permeated the debate over the "Japanese problem." At a meeting in January, General DeWitt stated, "The Japanese race is an enemy race and while many second and third generation Japanese born on United States soil, possessed of United States citizenship, have become 'Americanized,' the racial strains are undiluted." He later emphasized that "[i]t makes no difference whether he is an American citizen, he is still a Japanese." This was not true, however, of Germans and Italians. To the contrary, "[y]ou needn't worry about the Italians" and "the same for the Germans." "But we must worry about the Japanese all the time until he is wiped off the map." On another occasion, DeWitt proclaimed, "[A] Jap's a Jap."[17]

Similar sentiments, and worse, were expressed throughout the West Coast. The following statement by the manager of the Salinas Vegetable Grower-Shipper Association, a group that would gain financially from the roundup of Japanese-Americans, captures the spirit of the moment:

We're charged with wanting to get rid of the Japs for selfish reasons. . . . We do. It's a question of whether the white man lives on the Pacific Coast or the brown men. They came into this valley to work, and they stayed to take over. . . . If all the Japs were removed tomorrow, we'd never miss them in two weeks, because the white farmers can take over and produce everything the Jap grows. And we don't want them back when the war ends, either.[18]

THROUGHOUT THIS PERIOD, ATTORNEY General Biddle strongly opposed internment as "ill-advised, unnecessary, and unnecessarily cruel." In late January, the California congressional delegation attempted to pressure Biddle to support internment. Biddle replied that "unless the writ of habeas corpus were suspended" he knew of no way in which "Japanese born in this country could be interned." On February 1, Biddle convened a meeting in his office with representatives of the War Department to discuss the question. He made clear that he would have "nothing to do with any interference with citizens," nor would he "recommend the suspension of the writ of habeas corpus."[19]

In the first two weeks of February, Biddle continued to argue the point. On February 7, over lunch with the president, he told Roosevelt that "mass evacuation" was inadvisable because the army had offered "no reasons" that would justify it as a military measure.[20] Two days later, he wrote Secretary of War Henry Stimson that the Department of Justice would not "under any circumstances" participate in the evacuation of American citizens on the basis of race. On February 12, he again wrote Stimson that although "the Army could legally evacuate all persons in a specified territory if such action was deemed essential from a military point of view," it could not single out American citizens of Japanese origin.[21]

Biddle informed Stimson that J. Edgar Hoover had concluded that the demand for mass evacuation was based on "public hysteria" and that the FBI had already taken into custody all suspected Japanese agents. By early February, Hoover, the Office of Naval Intelligence, and military intelligence "all agreed that they had destroyed the Japanese espionage organization," and Hoover accused DeWitt of "getting a bit hysterical."[22]

Stimson himself had grave doubts about the constitutionality of a plan based on the "racial characteristics" of a particular minority group. He confided to his diary the absence of any persuasive "military necessity" for evacuation and his belief that the evacuation of all Japanese-Americans from the West Coast would "make a tremendous hole in our constitutional system."[23]

The public clamor on the West Coast continued to build, however. The American Legion, the Native Sons and Daughters of the Golden West, the Western Growers Protective Association, the California Farm Bureau Federation, the Chamber of Commerce of Los Angeles, and all the West Coast newspapers cried out for the prompt removal of Japanese aliens and citizens alike. American "patriots" began to commit ugly acts of vigilantism and vandalism against Japanese-Americans and their property.

In mid-February, national columnists like Walter Lippmann and Westbrook Pegler demanded severe measures to deal with the ethnic Japanese. The attorney general of Idaho announced that all Japanese and Japanese-Americans should "be put in concentration camps, for the remainder of the war," adding pointedly, "We want to keep this a white man's country." The attorney general of Washington chimed in that he favored the removal of all "citizens of Japanese extraction."[24]

On February 14, General DeWitt officially recommended that all persons of Japanese extraction be removed from "sensitive areas."[25] In a last-ditch effort to stave off mass internment, Biddle wrote the president on February 17. His letter blasted Lippmann and Pegler as "Armchair Strategists and Junior G-Men" whose columns came "close to shouting FIRE! in the theater."[26] Shortly thereafter, Biddle spoke with Roosevelt by phone. At the end of that conversation, a dejected Biddle agreed that he would no longer resist the mass incarceration of Japanese-Americans. According to Biddle, his Justice Department lawyers were "devastated."[27]

On February 19, President Roosevelt signed Executive Order No. 9066. The matter was never discussed in the cabinet, "except in a desultory fashion,"[28] and the president did not consult General

George Marshall or his primary military advisers, the Joint Chiefs of Staff.[29] The public rationale for the decision, laid out in General DeWitt's final report on the evacuation of the Japanese from the West Coast, was that time was of the essence and that the government had no reasonable way to distinguish loyal from disloyal persons of Japanese descent.

This report has rightly been condemned as a travesty. It relies upon unsubstantiated and even fabricated assertions; the government had already postponed action until more than two months after Pearl Harbor and did not actually initiate the process of internment for several months after February 19; the FBI had already taken into custody those individuals it suspected of potential subversion; two weeks before Roosevelt signed the executive order, General Mark Clark and Admiral Harold Stark testified before a House committee that the danger of a Japanese attack on the West Coast was "effectively nil"; and "[n]o proven instance of espionage after Pearl Harbor among the Japanese population in either Hawaii or the continental United States has ever been disclosed."[30] Moreover, the military did not intern the ethnic Japanese in Hawaii even though Hawaii had by far the greatest concentration of individuals of Japanese descent and even though it had been the site of the Japanese attack. The argument of military necessity was simply not credible.

WHY, THEN, DID THE PRESIDENT sign the executive order? Robert Jackson, who had served as Roosevelt's attorney general before being appointed to the Supreme Court, once observed that Roosevelt was a "strong skeptic of legal reasoning" and, despite his reputation, was not a "strong champion of . . . civil rights." He "had a tendency to think in terms of right and wrong, instead of terms of legal and illegal. Because he thought that his motives were always good for the things that he wanted to do, he found difficulty in thinking that there could be legal limitations on them."[31] Jackson's successor as attorney general, Francis Biddle, speculated about why Roosevelt signed Executive Order No. 9066:

I do not think he was much concerned with the gravity or implications of this step. He was never theoretical about things. What
must be done to defend the country must be done. The decision
was for his Secretary of War, not for the Attorney General, not
even for J. Edgar Hoover, whose judgment as to the appropriate-
ness of defense measures he greatly respected. The military
might be wrong. But they were fighting the war. Public opinion
was on their side, so that there was no question of any substantial opposition. . . . Nor do I think that the constitutional difficulty plagued him—the Constitution has never greatly bothered
any wartime President. That was a question of law, which ultimately the Supreme Court must decide. And meanwhile—
probably a long meanwhile—we must get on with the war.[32]

Undoubtedly, public opinion played a key role in the thinking of
both the military and the president. Even Secretary of War Stimson
thought internment a "tragedy," and it seems certain that the War
Department yielded to political pressure. Indeed, there was almost no
public protest of Roosevelt's decision. Only two West Coast public
officials opposed internment—Senator Sheridan Downey of California and Mayor Harry P. Cain of Tacoma, Washington, and even most
civil liberties groups kept relatively quiet, presumably in the interest
of national unity.

Although Roosevelt explained the order in terms of military
necessity, there is little doubt that domestic politics played a role in
his thinking, particularly since 1942 was an election year and Roosevelt was hardly immune to politics. Because of the attack on Pearl
Harbor, public opinion strongly urged the president to focus American military force on the Pacific. Roosevelt preferred a Europe-first
policy. The incarceration of almost 120,000 individuals of Japanese
ancestry was, in part, a way to pacify the "Asia-Firsters." As the legal
historian Peter Irons has observed, the internment decision "illustrates the dominance of politics over law in a setting of wartime concerns and divisions among beleaguered government officials."[33]

* * *

IN HIS SPECULATION ABOUT Roosevelt's thinking, Biddle noted that "ultimately the Supreme Court must decide." And so it did, in a series of three decisions, each addressing the constitutionality of a different aspect of the military orders: the nighttime curfew for Japanese-Americans, the exclusion of Japanese-Americans from certain areas of the West Coast, and the internment of Japanese-Americans in detention camps.

In June 1943, the Court handed down its decision in *Hirabayashi v. United States*.[34] Chief Justice Harlan Fiske Stone wrote the opinion of the Court. Although Stone observed privately that he was shocked that "U.S. citizens were subjected to this treatment,"[35] he nonetheless upheld the constitutionality of the curfew:[*]

> The war power of the national government is "the power to wage war successfully." . . . We cannot say that the war-making branches of the Government did not have ground for believing that in a critical hour such persons . . . constituted a menace to the national defense and safety, which demanded that prompt and adequate measures be taken to guard against it. . . . Distinctions between citizens solely because of their ancestry are by their very nature odious to a free people. . . . [But] it by no means follows that, in dealing with the perils of war, Congress and the Executive are wholly precluded from taking into account those facts and circumstances which are relevant to measures for our

[*] Gordon Hirabayashi was born in 1918 in Auburn, Washington. His father ran a roadside fruit market. His parents were pacifists. He attended the University of Washington, where he assumed a leadership role in the YMCA and the Japanese Students Club. As a YMCA officer, he attended in the summer of 1940 the "President's School," held jointly at Columbia University and the Union Theological Seminary in New York City, where he participated in passionate debates about pacifism and social activism. After President Roosevelt signed Executive Order No. 9066, Hirabayashi, with the help of a local legislator and the ACLU, decided to challenge the constitutionality of General DeWitt's curfew order by turning himself in to the FBI. He was prosecuted and convicted of violating a federal statute that makes it a crime for any person knowingly to disregard restrictions in a military area.

national defense . . . and which may in fact place citizens of one ancestry in a different category from others. . . .[36]

The following year, in *Korematsu v. United States*,[37] the Court upheld the exclusion order in a 6-to-3 decision. Justice Hugo Black delivered the opinion for the majority:*

> We cannot reject as unfounded the judgment of the military authorities . . . that there were disloyal members of [the Japanese-American] population, whose number and strength could not be precisely and quickly ascertained. . . . [W]e are not unmindful of the hardships imposed . . . upon a large group of American citizens. But hardships are part of war, and war is an aggregation of hardships. All citizens alike, both in and out of uniform, feel the impact of war in greater or lesser measure. . . .
>
> To cast this case into outlines of racial prejudice . . . confuses the issue. Korematsu was not excluded from the [West Coast] because of hostility to . . . his race . . . [but] because the . . . military authorities . . . decided that the . . . urgency of the situation demanded that all citizens of Japanese ancestry be segregated from the [area]. . . . We cannot—by availing ourselves of the calm perspective of hindsight—now say that at that time these actions were unjustified.[38]

*Fred Korematsu was born in 1919 in Oakland, California. After graduating from high school, he worked as a shipyard welder. In June 1941, he sought to enlist in the U.S. Navy but was turned down because of gastric ulcers. On May 30, 1942, the police in San Leandro, California, stopped and questioned Korematsu, who was walking down the street with his girlfriend. He explained that the rest of his family had been sent to the Tanforan assembly center, located in a converted racetrack, but that he had not reported. He maintained that General DeWitt's Exclusion Order was unlawful. Korematsu was arrested, prosecuted, and convicted of violating the order directing that all persons of Japanese ancestry must be excluded from the area under the supervision of the Western Command of the U.S. Army. For the rest of his life, Korematsu continued to challenge the legality of the Japanese internment. In 1998, President Clinton honored him with the Presidential Medal of Freedom, the highest honor the United States can bestow upon a civilian. Fred Korematsu died in 2005.

The three dissenting Justices were Owen Roberts, who had issued the report on Pearl Harbor, Frank Murphy, and Robert Jackson. Justice Roberts argued that it was patently unconstitutional for the government to insist that an individual submit "to imprisonment in a concentration camp" for no reason other than "his ancestry, without evidence or inquiry concerning his loyalty and good disposition towards the United States."[39] Justice Jackson's dissenting opinion took a somewhat different turn. Jackson argued, "My duties as a justice as I see them do not require me to make a military judgment as to whether General DeWitt's evacuation and detention program was a reasonable military necessity." But although the courts should not "interfere with the Army in carrying out its task," they also may not "be asked to execute a military expedient that has no place in law under the Constitution." Jackson concluded, "I would . . . discharge the prisoner."[40]

Justice Murphy wrote an angry dissent:

No adequate reason is given for the failure to treat these Japanese-Americans on an individual basis by holding investigations and hearings to separate the loyal from the disloyal, as was done in the case of persons of German and Italian ancestry. . . . It is asserted merely that the loyalties of this group "were unknown and time was of the essence." Yet nearly four months elapsed after Pearl Harbor before the first exclusion order was issued; nearly eight months went by until the last order was issued; and the last of these "subversive" persons was not actually removed until almost eleven months had elapsed. Leisure and deliberation seem to have been more of the essence than speed. . . . Moreover, there was no adequate proof that the Federal Bureau of Investigation and the military and naval intelligence services did not have the espionage and sabotage situation well in hand during this long period. . . . I dissent, therefore, from this legalization of racism.[41]

The third case in the trilogy, *Ex parte Endo*,[42] decided on the same day as *Korematsu*, involved a petition for a writ of habeas corpus filed on behalf of Mitsuye Endo, who alleged that she was a loyal citizen who had been unlawfully interned. The government conceded that Endo was a loyal American.* The Court held that Endo "should be given her liberty." The Court explained that Executive Order No. 9066 had to be construed as "sensitive to and respectful of the liberties of the citizen." Because "[a] citizen who is concededly loyal presents no problem of espionage or sabotage," and because Executive Order No. 9066 had been designed to prevent such activities, the order could not be interpreted as authorizing the detention of a citizen whom the government *conceded* to be loyal. "Loyalty," the Court emphasized, "is a matter of the heart and mind, not of race, creed, or color." The Court therefore concluded that Endo was "entitled to an unconditional release."[43]

The Court issued this decision on December 18, 1944—one day *after* the Roosevelt administration had announced that it would release the internees. The timing was no accident. There is good reason to believe that the Court intentionally delayed its decision in *Endo* to allow the president rather than the Court to end the internment.

There had been a lengthy struggle within the Roosevelt administration about when to end the internment. In December 1943, Biddle and Secretary of the Interior Harold Ickes strenuously argued for the immediate release of all loyal Japanese-Americans. In May 1944, Secretary of War Stimson made clear to Roosevelt that the internment could be ended "without danger to defense considerations." Nonetheless, the president chose to postpone the decision, explaining

---

*Mitsuye Endo was a twenty-two-year-old clerical worker in the California Department of Motor Vehicles. She did not read or speak Japanese and had never visited Japan. Her brother was serving in the U.S. Army. Endo's petition alleged that she was a loyal citizen who had been unlawfully interned in a relocation center under armed guard. During the course of her litigation, the government offered to release her from the detention camp if she agreed to drop the suit and resettle in the East. Endo refused to drop the case, and she therefore remained in the camp for two additional years, until the Supreme Court finally ordered her release.

that "the whole problem, for the sake of internal quiet, should be handled gradually." In plain truth, Roosevelt did not want to release the internees until after the 1944 presidential election, because such a decision might upset voters on the West Coast. The president's "desire for partisan advantage in the 1944 elections provides the only explanation for the delay in ending internment."[44]

IN THE YEARS IMMEDIATELY AFTER World War II, attitudes about the Japanese internment began to shift. In the Evacuation Claims Act of 1948,[45] Congress authorized compensation for specific property losses suffered by the internees. Several factors spurred the enactment of this legislation, including a growing sense of guilt, gratitude to the Nisei fighting units that had served the nation during the war, and international condemnation of the internment. The process for obtaining compensation was agonizingly slow, however. By 1958, only 26,000 internees had received any compensation, at an average of $1,400 per internee. As one critic acidly observed, the goal of the program was not to offer reparations for the moral, constitutional, reputational, and economic wrongs done to Japanese-Americans but to compensate them for lost "pots and pans."[46]

Many participants in the Japanese internment have reflected on the roles they played. Some knew at the time that internment was unconstitutional and immoral. In April 1942, Milton Eisenhower, the national director of the War Relocation Authority, which was responsible for running the detention camps, lamented that "when this war is over . . . we, as Americans, are going to regret the . . . injustices" we have done.[47] Two months later, he resigned his position.

Francis Biddle, who had vigorously and consistently opposed internment, continued to deplore the government's action. In 1962, he wrote that internment had "subjected Americans to the shame of being classed as enemies of their native country without any evidence indicating disloyalty." Unlike citizens of German and Italian descent, Japanese-Americans had been treated as "untouchables, a group who could not be trusted and had to be shut up only *because* they were of Japanese descent." Biddle concluded that this episode showed "the power of suggestion which a mystic cliché like 'military necessity' can exercise on human beings." Because of a lack of "courage and faith" in American values, the nation had missed a unique opportunity to "assert the human decencies for which we were fighting."[48]

Justice Wiley Rutledge, who voted with the majority in *Hirabayashi*, *Korematsu*, and *Endo*, once told Chief Justice Stone that he had suffered "more anguish" over *Hirabayashi* than over any other case he had decided as a justice. Rutledge's biographer later observed that the Japanese internment cases "pushed Wiley Rutledge along the path to his premature grave."[49]

Justice Hugo Black, on the other hand, the author of *Korematsu*, did not find these cases difficult. Years later, he volunteered that he would have done "precisely the same thing" again. Justifying his position, Black noted, "We had a situation where we were at war. People were rightly fearful of the Japanese in Los Angeles, many loyal to the United States, many undoubtedly not." Black added that this was especially problematic because "they all look alike to a person not a Jap."[50]

Justice William O. Douglas, who also joined the majority in these cases, vacillated between regretting his vote to uphold the Japanese exclusion and defending, or at least explaining, the Court's action. In 1980, Douglas confessed, "I have always regretted that I bowed to my elders" in these cases, noting that these decisions were "ever on my conscience." On the other hand, Douglas explained that the Court "is not isolated from life. Its members are very much a part of the community and know the fears, anxieties, craving and wishes of their neighbors." Although this "does not mean that community attitudes are necessarily translated" into Supreme Court decisions, it does mean that "the state of public opinion will often make the Court cautious when it should be bold."[51]

In 1962, Chief Justice Earl Warren, who played a pivotal role as California's attorney general, reflected on *Korematsu*. Warren observed that war is "a pathological condition" for the nation, and that in such a condition "[m]ilitary judgments sometimes breed action that, in more stable times, would be regarded as abhorrent." This places judges in a dilemma because the Court may conclude that it is not in a very good position "to reject descriptions by the Executive of the degree of military necessity." Moreover, judges cannot easily detach themselves from the pathological condition of warfare, although with "hindsight, from the vantage point of more tranquil times, they might conclude that some actions advanced in the name of national survival" had in fact violated the Constitution.[52] In his 1974 memoir, Warren conceded that Japanese internment was "not in keeping with our American concept of freedom and the rights of citizens,"[53] and in later years he admitted privately that he regretted his own actions in the matter.[54]

Years before he was appointed to the Supreme Court, Tom Clark had served as an assistant attorney general under Francis Biddle. In that capacity, Clark had acted as Biddle's liaison with General DeWitt's legal staff. Clark assigned lawyers to assist the local U.S. attorneys in criminal prosecutions for violation of the military orders.[55] Upon retiring from the Supreme Court in 1966, Clark stated, "I have made a lot of mistakes in my life. . . . One is my part in the evacuation of the Japanese from California. . . . [A]s I look back on it—although at the time I argued the case—I am amazed that the Supreme Court ever approved it."[56]

THE COURT'S DECISIONS IN *Hirabayashi* and *Korematsu* were immediately condemned in both the public and professional literature. In 1945, Eugene Rostow, then dean of the Yale Law School, termed the decision a "disaster." He chastised the Court for dealing with the facts as "Kiplingesque folklore" and for upholding a military policy that clearly had been based not on military necessity but on "ignorant race prejudice."[57] There is little doubt that even at the time of the decision the justices knew, or should have known, that the government's justifications for the internment were without merit, but they chose to ignore the facts. Over the years, *Hirabayashi* and *Korematsu* have become constitutional pariahs. The Supreme Court has never cited either decision with approval of its result.

The immorality and unconstitutionality of the internment have continued to reverberate. As part of the celebration of the Bicentennial of the Constitution in 1976, President Gerald Ford issued Presidential Proclamation No. 4417, in which he acknowledged that we must recognize "our national mistakes as well as our national achievements." "February 19th," he noted, "is the anniversary of a sad day in American history," for it was "on that date in 1942 . . . that Executive Order 9066 was issued." Ford observed that "[w]e now know what we should have known then"—that the evacuation and internment of loyal Japanese American citizens was "wrong."[58]

Four years later, Congress established the Commission on Wartime Relocation and Internment of Civilians to review the implementation of Executive Order No. 9066. The commission comprised former members of Congress, the Supreme Court, and the cabinet, as well as distinguished private citizens. It heard testimony from more than seven hundred witnesses, including key government personnel who were involved in the issuance and implementation of Executive Order No. 9066. It reviewed hundreds of documents that had previously been unavailable. In 1983, the commission unanimously concluded that the factors that had shaped the internment decision "were race prejudice, war hysteria and a failure of political leadership," *not* military necessity. It recommended that "Congress pass a joint resolution, to be signed by the President, which recognizes that a grave injustice was done and offers the apologies of the nation for the acts of exclusion, removal and detention."[59]

That same year, Fred Korematsu and Gordon Hirabayashi filed petitions for writs of error *coram nobis* to have their convictions set aside for "manifest injustice."* The following year, Judge Marilyn

---

* A petition for a writ of *coram nobis* asks a court to set aside a previously entered judgment on the ground that the defendant had failed to establish a valid defense in the original proceeding because of fraud, duress, or excusable neglect.

Patel granted Korematsu's petition.[60] Patel found that in its presentation of evidence to the federal courts in the course of Korematsu's prosecution and appeal, including in the Supreme Court, the government had *knowingly and intentionally* failed to disclose critical information that directly contradicted key statements in General DeWitt's final report, on which the government had asked the courts to rely.

Judge Patel observed that the Supreme Court's decision in *Korematsu* "stands as a constant caution that in times of war or declared military necessity our institutions must be vigilant in protecting constitutional guarantees." It stands "as a caution that in times of distress the shield of military necessity and national security must not be used to protect governmental actions from close scrutiny and accountability." And it stands "as a caution that in times of international hostility" the judiciary "must be prepared to exercise [its] authority to protect all citizens from the petty fears and prejudices that are so easily aroused."[61]

In 1987, a federal court of appeals granted Gordon Hirabayashi's petition for a writ of *coram nobis* and vacated his conviction. In an opinion by Judge Mary Schroeder, the court found serious deceit in the United States's presentation of its case to the Supreme Court.[62] Judge Schroeder found that the original version of DeWitt's final report, which was designed to justify the military orders, did not "purport to rest on any military exigency, but instead declared that because of traits peculiar to citizens of Japanese ancestry it would be impossible to separate the loyal from the disloyal." When officials of the War Department received DeWitt's report in early 1942, they ordered him to excise the racist overtones and to add statements of military necessity. Copies of the original report were burned. When officials of the Justice Department were preparing to argue the *Hirabayashi* case in the Supreme Court, they sought all materials relevant to General DeWitt's decision making. The War Department did not disclose to the Justice Department the original version of the report.

Judge Schroeder found that, given the importance the justices attached to the government's claims of military necessity, "the reasoning of the Supreme Court would probably have been profoundly and materially affected" had it been advised "of the suppression of evidence" that would have "established the . . . real reason for the exclusion order."[63]

In the last year of his presidency, Ronald Reagan signed the Civil Liberties Act of 1988,[64] which officially declared the Japanese internment a "grave injustice" that was "carried out without adequate security reasons" and without any documented acts of "espionage or sabotage." The act declared that the program of exclusion and internment had been "motivated largely by racial prejudice" and "wartime hysteria," and offered an official presidential apology and reparations to each of the Japanese-American internees who had suffered discrimination, deprivation of liberty, loss of property, and personal humiliation at the hands of the U.S. government.

The World War I and World War II episodes involved quite different issues. In World War I, the primary civil liberties issue was freedom of speech. In World War II, it was freedom from racial discrimination and unlawful detention. But both episodes carry the same fundamental lesson for the future. In periods of war fever, we are likely to lose our sense of perspective and needlessly sacrifice fundamental liberties—particularly the fundamental liberties of those we already fear and despise. In both of these episodes, the president, the Congress, and the Supreme Court all failed in their responsibility to preserve and protect the Constitution, and the public sat by silently or, worse, cheered them on.

## CHAPTER V

# The Cold War
# "The Scaremongers"

❧❧

IN August 1945, World War II drew to a close. For the first time in over a decade the world was at peace. The United States had the strongest economy and the most powerful military in the world. The prospect for civil liberties seemed bright, and Americans expected to be able to enjoy the hard-won fruits of national sacrifice. But optimism faded quickly. The new year brought severe economic dislocations as shortages and strikes racked the nation, and the collapse of the Soviet-American wartime alliance soured the national mood. Franklin Roosevelt had promised an era of U.S.-Soviet collaboration, but by early 1946, President Truman was bitterly assailing the Soviets for blocking free elections in Eastern Europe.

At the same time, two spy scares stunned the nation. The public learned that secret documents about China had been leaked to a leftist journal, and Canada charged that twenty-two individuals had conspired to steal information about the atom bomb for the Soviet Union. In July 1946, a House subcommittee recommended a new federal loyalty program to protect the United States against those whose primary loyalty was to "governments other than our own."[1]

As the 1946 midterm elections approached, President Truman came under increasing attack from an anti–New Deal coalition of Republicans and Southern Democrats who excited fears of Communist subversion. In California, Richard Nixon, just thirty-three years old, charged that his congressional opponent voted the "Moscow" line. In Nebraska, Senator Hugh Butler declared that "if the New Deal is still in control of Congress after the election, it will owe that control to the Communist party."[2] B. Carroll Reece, chairman of the Republican National Committee, proclaimed that the "choice which confronts Americans" is between Republicanism and Communism.[3] The Republicans won a major victory, picking up fifty-four seats in the House and eleven in the Senate, taking control of both chambers. Fear had proved a potent political weapon. As the Democrats scrambled to respond, Truman's labor secretary demanded that the Communist Party should be outlawed. "Why," he asked, "should they be able to elect people to public office?"[4]

The new Republican-controlled Congress promptly declared its intention to play the Red card. The House Un-American Activities Committee (HUAC) announced an aggressive program to expose Communists and Communist sympathizers. J. Parnell Thomas, the rabid new chairman of HUAC, pledged that his committee would "ferret out" those who sought to subvert the American way of life.[5]

Truman was caught in a vise. Conservatives accused him of being soft on Communism, while progressives in his own party attacked him for being too rigid in dealing with the Soviets. In response, the president launched a bold two-pronged program to protect his flanks. On March 12, 1947, he announced what became known as the Truman Doctrine, pledging that the United States would commit all of its might to confront the Soviets whenever and wherever they encroached "upon the interests of a peaceful and stable world."[6] Noting the enormity of this commitment, Michigan Senator Arthur Vandenburg advised Truman that if he wanted the American people's support he would have to "scare the hell" out of them.[7] Truman agreed. With this stroke, Truman effectively defined the progressives as "soft on Communism."

Nine days later, Truman announced the second prong of his strategy. In order to defang the conservatives, he established by executive order a loyalty program for all federal employees.[8] Under this program, the first of its kind in American history, *every* present and prospective federal employee—more than 4 million people—would be subjected to a loyalty investigation. The executive order provided that no individual could work for the federal government if "reasonable grounds exist" for believing that he might be "disloyal."[9] Among the activities that could be deemed "disloyal" was "[m]embership in, affiliation with or sympathetic association with any organization . . . designated by the Attorney General as Communist, or subversive."[10]

WHO WERE THE "REDS" about whom everyone was so excited? The Communist Party of the United States of America, or CPUSA, which was founded in 1919, never attained any appreciable size. At the peak of its membership, in 1940, it had barely 100,000 dues-paying members. From an electoral standpoint, the party was effectively irrelevant. Whereas Eugene Debs had received almost a million votes in both 1912 and 1920 as the Socialist Party candidate for president, Communist Party candidates never garnered even 10 percent of that number, and no member of the Communist Party was ever elected to Congress.

Who joined the Communist Party or became so-called "fellow travelers"? The vast majority of American Reds were drawn to Communism in the 1930s, not to serve the Soviet Union, but because Communism seemed a viable hope in the struggle for justice at home and against fascism abroad. Most of those who turned to Communism did so as a consequence of the Depression, which brought with it a profound sense of despair and dislocation. With a third of all Americans unemployed, the Depression triggered a severe loss of confidence in America's business and political leaders, a widespread demand for economic and social reform, and a desperate search for answers.

After 1929, people listened more attentively to pleas for a planned, classless society. On urban breadlines and devastated farms, Americans increasingly questioned the harsh consequences of unrestrained capitalism. Moreover, with President Roosevelt's recognition of the Soviet Union in 1933, Americans were more open than ever to learning about Communism. The CPUSA advocated public housing to replace slums, and public works to provide jobs; it championed racial equality and the rights of labor; it opposed fascism abroad and repressive social and economic structures at home. As such progressive voices as the *New Republic* and the *Nation* acknowledged, New Deal liberalism and Communism shared some of the same ideals.

In an era of intense social turbulence and political energy, hundreds of clubs, associations, committees, and alliances sprang into being to fight for economic, social, political, racial, and international justice. The overlap between these groups and the CPUSA in the causes they supported, their memberships, and their cooperation in sponsoring rallies and other events was often extensive. Most members of these groups were not Communists, or even Communist "sympathizers," but they and the Communists shared many of the same goals. Hundreds of thousands—perhaps millions—of Americans joined such organizations in the 1930s, not because they wanted to overthrow the government, but because they wanted to help in good causes as a civic duty.

After the United States entered World War II as an ally of the Soviet Union, Americans viewed both Russia and the CPUSA more favorably than at any time since the Russian Revolution. President Roosevelt confidently assured Americans that "we are going to get along very well with . . . the Russian people—very well indeed."[11] With the end of World War II, and as the international situation deteriorated, most Americans who still had ties to the Communist Party or to organizations or causes connected to the Communist Party quickly severed them. But, by then, it was too late. The most infamous question of the next two decades—"Are you now or *have you ever been . . . ?*"—encompassed the past.

AS ALREADY NOTED, THE TRUMAN LOYALTY program defined as "disloyal" any sympathetic association with any organization "designated by the Attorney General as Communist, or subversive."[12] The attorney general's list initially encompassed 78 organizations but quickly swelled to more than 250, including, for example, the International Workers Order, a fraternal benefit society that specialized in low-cost insurance, and the Joint Anti-Fascist Refugee Committee, which provided relief for refugees of the Spanish Civil War. Inclusion of an organization on the attorney general's list was tantamount to public branding. Contributions dried up, membership dwindled, meeting places disappeared. The greatest impact of the list, however, was on the freedom of American citizens. Because the criteria for listing were vague and undisclosed, because organizations had no right to contest their listing, and because new groups were constantly being added to the list, individuals had to be wary of joining *any* organization. The only "safe" course was to join nothing.

How did the loyalty program work? Every federal employee and every applicant for federal employment was subjected to a preliminary investigation. If that investigation uncovered any "derogatory" information, the FBI would conduct a "full field investigation"—a thorough probe of the individual's relationships, sympathies, associations, beliefs, writings, and intentions. FBI agents would interview the individual's current and former friends, neighbors, teachers, coworkers, employers, and employees in an effort to learn what they thought of his loyalty, what organizations he had joined, what journals and books he had read, and what sentiments he had expressed.

All this information was then compiled in an FBI dossier and turned over to a loyalty board, which convened a formal hearing if there were "reasonable grounds" to doubt the individual's loyalty. Although the "suspect" could appear before the loyalty board, consult with counsel, and present witnesses in his "defense," he had no right to confront the witnesses against him—or even to learn their identity. These hearings took on the character of a "medieval inquisition."[13] The impact of the program was devastating. Merely to be suspected and called to defend oneself in a loyalty investigation was terrifying and ruinous to reputation, regardless of outcome.

This program harmed not only those hauled before a loyalty board, but the very system of American freedom. Because of the elusiveness of the concept of "disloyalty," no federal employee or prospective federal employee could ever consider herself exempt from the perils of investigation. Was it disloyal to advocate disarmament, to argue that the Communist Party should be legal, to subscribe to the Communist Party newspaper, to read books by "Communist" authors? Any slip of the tongue, any unguarded statement, any criticism of government policy, could lead to one's undoing. The anonymity of informers left every individual open to fools, schemers, paid informers, scandalmongers, and personal enemies. The only sane approach was to keep one's head down, and never look up. As one government employee tellingly remarked, "If Communists like apple pie and I do, I see no reason why I should stop eating it. But I would."[14]

IN EARLY 1949, CHINA FELL to the Communists. Overnight, almost a quarter of the world's population was "lost" to the Reds. Americans were stunned and frightened. Then, only a month later, the Soviet Union detonated its first atom bomb. Americans were thrown into a panic. Some communities issued dog tags to children so their bodies could be identified after a nuclear attack. Americans began to build bomb shelters and to discuss the need for mass graves in the event of nuclear war. Editorials advocated a preemptive war against the Soviet Union "before it is too late." Everywhere were the questions: How had we lost China? How had Russia gotten the bomb? Self-proclaimed patriots immediately linked these questions to their charges of Communist infiltration. Only perfidy, they argued, could have caused such disasters.

In 1950, Klaus Fuchs, a British physicist, confessed to passing U.S. atomic secrets to the Soviets. Fuchs's confession led to the arrest of several alleged conspirators, including Julius and Ethel Rosenberg. Americans increasingly came to believe that the greatest threat to the national security was the betrayal of America by Americans.

Republican Senator Homer Capehart of Indiana fumed, "How much more are we going to have to take? . . . In the name of heaven, is this the best America can do?"[15]

It was at this moment that Senator Joseph McCarthy burst upon the scene. After graduating from Marquette University Law School, McCarthy struggled for several years as a small-town lawyer in Wisconsin. Then, in 1939, he ran successfully for a state circuit judgeship. At thirty years of age, he was the youngest judge ever elected in the county. His campaign tactics were described at the time as bare-knuckled, ferocious, dishonest, and devastatingly effective.

After Pearl Harbor, McCarthy enlisted in the Marines and was sent to the South Pacific. Planning a run for the Senate, he issued his own press releases and labeled himself "Tail Gunner Joe"—though he was not a tail gunner. After fracturing his foot during a prank, he falsified a military citation, claiming he had been injured in combat. In 1946, he campaigned for the Senate, first playing the "Red card" when he charged his opponent with paving the way for the Russians in Eastern Europe. As the election neared, he promised to remove the "Communists from the public payroll" and accused President Truman of attempting to "Sovietize our farms." He won handily.[16]

At the age of thirty-eight, Joe McCarthy arrived in the Senate with an impressive head of steam. But he soon floundered. He was perceived as an "uncouth outsider" devoid of personal charm or legislative ability. He earned the degrading nickname the "Pepsi-Cola Kid," because of his work for the soft-drink lobby. He "needed a new direction."[17] He returned to the Communist issue.

And so it was that on February 9, 1950, this little-known first-term senator from Wisconsin exploded into the national headlines. McCarthy was scheduled to deliver a routine Lincoln Day address at a dinner sponsored by a Republican women's club in Wheeling, West Virginia. His speech incorporated the usual bombast about traitors in the federal government. But McCarthy then departed from his script and asserted that he was privy to inside information: "And ladies and gentlemen," he said, "while I cannot take the time to name all the men in the State Department who have been named as active members of the Communist Party and members of a spy ring, I have here in my hand a list of 205—a list of names that were made known to the secretary of state as being members of the Communist Party and who nevertheless are still working on and shaping policy in the State Department."[18]

This was a complete fabrication. McCarthy had no such list. The State Department immediately issued a furious denial. Over the next few days, the story picked up steam, and McCarthy found himself at the center of a storm. When called on his lie, he bluffed. On February 10, he offered to show his "list" to a reporter, but then "discovered" he had left it in another suit. President Truman declared there was not a word of truth in McCarthy's charges. With a breathtaking audacity that was to become his hallmark, McCarthy scornfully replied that the president "should refresh his memory."[19]

Senate Democrats demanded that McCarthy prove his accusations. After lengthy machinations, McCarthy agreed to give a Senate committee "detailed information" about Communists in the State Department. Senator Millard Tydings of Maryland, a conservative Democrat, was appointed to chair the committee. As the Tydings Committee worked on its report, McCarthy lashed out, decrying those "egg-sucking liberals" whose "pitiful squealing . . . would hold sacrosanct those Communists and queers" who had sold China into "atheistic slavery."[20] He warned that "the time has come to pinpoint . . . the most dangerous Communists, and if lumberjack tactics are the only kind they understand, then we shall use those tactics."[21]

On July 14, 1950, the Tydings Committee issued its report. It concluded that McCarthy's accusations represented "perhaps the most nefarious campaign of half-truths and untruth in the history of this Republic."[22] McCarthy immediately labeled the report "a clear signal" to the traitors in our government that they need not fear "exposure from this Administration."[23]

Although McCarthy's charges had been proved both spurious and highly damaging to innocent individuals, most Republicans rallied to his cause. Bolstered by opinion polls showing growing support for his crusade, mainstream Republicans, out of the White House for sixteen years, saw McCarthy as their ticket to political power.* He was suddenly the most sought-after speaker in the nation. In addresses across America, McCarthy charged that there was a "plot" at the highest levels of government "to reduce security . . . to a nullity."[24] Audiences were swept away by his certitude and patriotism.

AND THEN IT ALL GOT WORSE. On June 25, 1950, North Korean artillery opened fire on South Korea. Five days later, with UN approval, Truman authorized General Douglas MacArthur to defend South Korea. Within a year, 300,000 Communist Chinese troops entered the war, and American soldiers were bogged down in a miserable conflict in which more than 30,000 lost their lives. Coming hard on the heels of the loyalty program, the fall of China, and McCarthy's accusations, the Korean War unleashed a frenzy of anti-Red hysteria. State and local governments frantically enacted their own loyalty programs, established their own investigating committees, and removed thousands of "Communistic" books from schools and public libraries.

In a similar frenzy, Congress hastily enacted the McCarran Internal Security Act of 1950, which required all Communist and other subversive organizations to disclose the names of their members.[25] The act prohibited any person who was a member of such an organization from working in any capacity for the government or for any private employer engaged in defense work.[26] Harry Truman vetoed the legislation, explaining that "instead of striking blows at Communism," the act would "strike blows at our own liberties."[27] Truman's

---

*Not all Republicans supported McCarthy. On the same day that the Tydings Committee released its report, the freshman Republican Senator Margaret Chase Smith of Maine read on the Senate floor a "Declaration of Conscience," which she and six other Republicans had signed. It was a direct attack on McCarthy and the right wing of the Republican Party: "[C]ertain elements of the Republican Party have materially added to this confusion in the hopes of riding the Republican Party to victory through the selfish exploitation of fear, bigotry, ignorance and intolerance."

veto was courageous, but by 1950 his credibility on these issues had been destroyed by his own anti-Communism. A rising tide of fear swamped Truman's plea for moderation, and his veto was swiftly overridden.

As the 1950 elections approached, Joe McCarthy appeared on the covers of both *Time* and *Newsweek*. He raced across the country campaigning for his favored candidates and against those he opposed. He attacked Democrats as "parlor pinks and parlor punks." He pilloried Senator Millard Tydings with a particular vengeance, accusing him of "protecting Communists."[28] McCarthy's staff worked hand-in-glove with Tydings's opponent in an effort to bring him to his knees. They even helped orchestrate the circulation of a doctored photograph that purported to show Tydings huddling in secret conversation with leaders of the Communist Party.

Red-baiting reached unprecedented levels. John Foster Dulles, challenging Herbert Lehman for the U.S. Senate in New York, said of Lehman, "I know he is no Communist, but I know also that the Communists are in his corner." In California, Congressman Richard Nixon secured election to the Senate by circulating a pink sheet accusing his Democratic opponent, Helen Gahagan Douglas, of voting the Communist line. And in Florida, Congressman George Smathers defeated Claude Pepper by attacking him as "Red Pepper."[29]

The Democrats attempted desperately to fend off these assaults. Truman argued that those who claimed that the nation was in peril from domestic subversion had "lost all proportion, all sense of restraint, all sense of patriotic decency."[30] But to no avail. The Republicans scored major gains in both the House and Senate and, most satisfying of all to Joseph McCarthy, his nemesis—Millard Tydings—was driven from office.

Mainstream Republicans drew even closer to McCarthy. They invited him to deliver a major address at the 1952 Republican National Convention. He roused the audience, thundering: "I say one Communist in a defense plant is one Communist too many. One Communist on the faculty of one university is one Communist too many.

. . . And even if there were only one Communist in the State Department, that would still be one Communist too many."[31] The 1952 Republican platform formally charged the Democrats with shielding "traitors," and the party's nominee for President, General Dwight D. Eisenhower, selected as his running mate Richard Nixon, one of the nation's most infamous Red-baiters. The Republicans swept the '52 elections, winning not only the House and Senate, but the White House as well.

Joe McCarthy, reelected to the Senate, was now seen as invincible, and as the most feared man in America. Democrats were thoroughly intimidated. Even Lyndon Johnson, leader of the Senate Democrats, was wary of McCarthy, cautioning his colleagues, "You don't get in a pissin' contest with a polecat."[32] The extent to which McCarthy had intimidated the Senate had been made strikingly evident earlier that session. During a speech on the floor, McCarthy piled hundreds of documents in front of him, supposedly substantiating charges of Communist infiltration. He defiantly dared any senator to inspect them. Senator Herbert Lehman, a distinguished public servant who had been accused by Dulles of "having Communists in his corner," walked to McCarthy's desk and held out his hand for the documents. There was silence. Then, "McCarthy giggled his strange, rather terrifying little giggle." As Lehman looked around the chamber for support, "not a man rose." His fellow senators lowered their eyes or looked away. McCarthy snarled under his breath, "Go back to your seat, old man."[33]

WITH THE SENATE NOW FIRMLY in Republican hands, McCarthy became chair of the Permanent Subcommittee on Investigations. He immediately declared his intention to investigate Communist infiltration of the federal government and of the nation's colleges and universities. He ruthlessly pursued his targets in a marble caucus room that, in the words of one witness, "stank with the odor of fear."[34]

In February 1953, McCarthy launched an investigation of Voice of America (VOA), an agency established during World War II to promote a positive view of the United States around the world. McCarthy charged that the VOA was riddled with Communists and fellow travelers. In televised hearings, he asserted that VOA libraries contained books by "known Communists." When his staff examined VOA catalogues, they rooted out more than 30,000 volumes written by such "Communist" and "un-American" authors as Lillian Hellman, Jean-Paul Sartre, Dashiell Hammett, Theodore White, Arthur Schlesinger, Jr., John Dewey, W. H. Auden, Edna Ferber, and Stephen Vincent Benét.

The Eisenhower State Department, which oversaw the VOA, immediately banned all books, music, and paintings by "Communists, fellow-travelers, et cetera" from all VOA programs.[35] Terrified VOA librarians hurriedly discarded and even burned books that had been placed on what appeared to be an official blacklist. McCarthy badgered and humiliated VOA personnel. Some resigned in protest; others were fired for refusing to cooperate. During the investigation, one VOA employee committed suicide, writing to his wife, "[O]nce the dogs are on you, everything you have done since the beginning of time is suspect."[36] The hearings uncovered no evidence of unlawful conduct. As Americans were whipped into a frenzy over possible Communist espionage, sabotage, and subversion, they increasingly came to suspect each other of disloyalty. "Is my neighbor a Communist? My daughter's teacher? The cop on the beat?" Fear bred suspicion; suspicion bred fear.

By mid-1953, both *Newsweek* and the *New York Times* were speculating that McCarthy was aiming for the White House in 1956. Fearing for the nation, former President Truman made a nationally televised speech in which he accused the Eisenhower administration of "shameful demagoguery" and defined McCarthyism as a "horrible cancer [that] is eating at the vitals of America."[37] Even Republicans began to grow nervous. The president's brother, Milton Eisenhower, who a decade earlier had resigned his government position in protest against the Japanese internment, publicly described McCarthy as "the most dangerous menace" to the nation.[38]

* * *

IN THE MEANTIME, THE LONG SHADOW of the House Un-American Activities Committee fell across our campuses and our culture. Robert Maynard Hutchins, the president of the University of Chicago,* observed that "[t]he entire teaching profession of the U.S. is now intimidated."[39] In hearings before HUAC, a parade of prominent actors and movie producers testified that Hollywood had been infected by un-American propaganda. Red-hunters demanded, and got, the blacklisting of such writers as Dorothy Parker, Dalton Trumbo, James Thurber, and Arthur Miller. Like the Puritans in the Salem witch trials, HUAC demanded public denunciation, purgation, humiliation, and betrayal.

Government at all levels hunted down "disloyal" individuals. Forty-four states enacted legislation making it a crime to advocate "the violent overthrow of government," which served as shorthand for Communism. Connecticut made it a crime for any person to distribute "disloyal, scurrilous or abusive matter concerning the form of government of the United States." An Indiana statute declared that its purpose was to "exterminate Communism and Communists." Texas authorized a twenty-year prison sentence for members of the Communist Party. Michigan authorized life imprisonment. Tennessee authorized the death penalty.[40]

Many states excluded members of the Communist Party from the political process. Following the lead of HUAC, many states and communities established investigating committees to expose "subver-

*Hutchins was one of the "heroes" of this era. Appointed president of the University of Chicago in 1929 at the age of thirty, Hutchins was brilliant, acerbic, daring, and magnetic. He was also a fearless champion of academic freedom. When the University of Chicago was attacked for allowing professors to teach "Communist propaganda," Hutchins responded that "the answer to such charges" is "not denial, nor evasion, nor apology," but "the assertion that free inquiry is indispensable" and that "universities exist for the sake of such inquiry." Several years later, when an Illinois legislative committee demanded that the university fire a particular professor because of his political views, a group of faculty members came to Hutchins and warned that "if the trustees fire [the professor] you'll receive the resignations of twenty full professors." To which Hutchins replied, "Oh no I won't. My successor will."

sives." These committees hounded schoolteachers, labor leaders, actors, lawyers, state employees, journalists, and judges, and publicly listed thousands of individuals found to be "disloyal." As a California investigating committee noted, the goal was to "quarantine" such people as though they "were infected with smallpox."[41]

A plague of loyalty oaths spread across the nation. Forty-two states and more than 2,000 county or city governments required such oaths of public employees. Some states and municipalities went on from there. Washington required an oath of all insurance salesmen, Texas of all pharmacists, New York of all persons who sought a license to fish; all states precluded Communists and fellow travelers from becoming members of the bar. Many states and cities removed all "Communistic" books from school and public libraries.

Anyone stigmatized as possibly "disloyal" became a menace to his friends and an outcast to society. More than 11,000 people were fired from federal, state, local, or private employment for alleged disloyalty. More than a hundred were prosecuted under the federal Smith Act because of their involvement with the CPUSA. One hundred thirty-five were prosecuted for contempt of Congress because they refused to cooperate with HUAC. Fear of ideological contamination swept the nation. As Harry Truman had warned, "scaremongers" had generated such a wave of fear that their attacks on civil liberties now went "almost unchallenged."[42]

A reporter in Madison, Wisconsin, circulated a petition asking people to support the preamble to the Declaration of Independence. Ninety-nine percent refused to sign. Columnist Drew Pearson noted that this was unprecedented and diagnosed it as "a disease of fear."[43] The "Silent Generation" of the 1950s was afflicted with this disease. As the historian Henry Steele Commager observed, the political repression of this era bred a stifling "conformity" and an "unquestioning acceptance of . . . America as a finished product, perfect and complete."[44] Reflecting on these years, Norman Mailer noted that the nation was suffering "from a collective failure of nerve."[45]

* * *

THE COLD WAR GENERATED unprecedented First Amendment activity for the Supreme Court. For roughly a decade, this was the dominant issue on the Court's docket. The key decision, the one that shaped the debate, was *Dennis v. United States.*[46]

On July 28, 1948, a federal grand jury in New York indicted under the Smith Act twelve members of the national board of the Communist Party for conspiring to advocate the duty and necessity of overthrowing the government of the United States by force and violence. The defendants were convicted and sentenced to five years in prison.* Certainly, under the World War I precedents, like *Schenck, Frohwerk, Debs,* and *Abrams,* this outcome was predictable. But in the intervening three decades, the Supreme Court had moved decidedly toward the Holmes-Brandeis understanding of the First Amendment.

When the case reached the Supreme Court, Chief Justice Fred Vinson jettisoned the World War I precedents and declared that the proper test, as Holmes and Brandeis had argued, was clear and present danger. Vinson then asked what the words "clear and present danger" mean:

---

*At the trial, the government presented evidence that a central tenet of Marxism-Leninism, set forth in many pamphlets and other writings of the CPUSA, was that capitalism rests upon the oppression of those who do not own the means of production (the "proletariat"); that no entrenched faction (the "bourgeoisie") would ever voluntarily permit itself to be displaced by peaceful change; and that the transition to a more just and classless society (the "dictatorship of the proletariat") would therefore *require* the forceful overthrow of the existing government at some time in the future, when circumstances were propitious.

The defendants rejected this characterization of the CPUSA, arguing that the demands of Marxism-Leninism were contingent upon historical circumstance. Eugene Dennis, the general secretary of the party, testified that "you cannot find out what to do in 1949 [in the United States] by reading what Lenin said the Russian workers should do under quite different circumstances in 1917." William Z. Foster, the former head of the party, testified that the party sought to convert Americans to socialism not by force or violence, but by educating the masses and persuading a majority of citizens that socialism was in their best interests, contrasting czarist Russia in 1917 with democratic United States in 1949. He argued that the prosecution had taken passages from the Communist "classics" out of context. The prosecution dismissed all this as window-dressing and cover-up.

Obviously, the words cannot mean that before the Government may act, it must wait until the putsch is about to be executed, the plans have been laid and the signal is awaited. If Government is aware that a group aiming at its overthrow is attempting to indoctrinate its members and to commit them to a course whereby they will strike when the leaders feel the circumstances permit, action by the Government is required.[47]

Reasoning backward from his putsch example, Vinson argued that the phrase "clear and present danger" could not mean "clear and present danger," for that would lead to implausible results if the danger, such as a putsch, were very grave. The true meaning of "clear and present danger," he concluded, is that in each case the court "must ask whether the gravity of the 'evil,' discounted by its improbability, justifies such invasion of free speech as is necessary to avoid the danger." This was hardly what Holmes and Brandeis had in mind. Applying his newly minted version of "clear and present danger" to the circumstances in *Dennis*, Vinson predictably found that the danger was both "clear" and "present," even though it was neither. As Vinson explained, the formation by the defendants of a "highly organized conspiracy, with rigidly disciplined members subject to call when the leaders . . . felt that the time had come for action, coupled with the inflammable nature of world conditions, . . . convince us that their convictions were justified."[48]

Justices Black and Douglas dissented. Douglas conceded that there were circumstances in which the government could punish someone for teaching the techniques of sabotage or assassination. But he noted that there was no evidence that the defendants had done any such things. Moreover, he added:

Communism in the world scene is no bogeyman; but Communism as a political faction or party in this country plainly is. Communism has been so thoroughly exposed in this country that it has been crippled as a political force. Free speech has destroyed it. . . . How it can be said that there is a clear and present danger that this advocacy will succeed is, therefore, a mystery. . . . In America, [the Communists] are miserable merchants of unwanted ideas; their wares remain unsold. The fact that their ideas are abhorrent does not make them powerful.[49]

Justice Black's dissenting opinion offered a prescient observation: "Public opinion being what it now is, few will protest the conviction of these [Communists]. There is hope, however, that in calmer times, when present pressures, passions and fears subside, this or some later Court will restore the First Amendment liberties to the . . . place where they belong in a free society."[50]

Ultimately, of course, Justice Black's prediction proved correct. Over time, the Court and the nation have come to regard *Dennis* as an embarrassment, or worse. Although in the short run it legitimized a rash of repressive programs designed to stigmatize, blacklist, and punish individuals for their "subversive" beliefs or associations, in the long run it was shunted aside and effectively overruled. We must ask, though, why six of the eight justices bent over backward in *Dennis* to affirm the convictions.

As Justice Douglas observed about *Korematsu*, we see once again that judges are "not exempt from the fears and beliefs of other Americans." Indeed, it was quite natural for them to adopt the prevailing anti-Communist assumptions as a way to make sense of their times. The drumbeat of anti-Red hysteria shaped the perceptions of most Americans, including most of the justices. In the face of frenzied investigations and accusations, the Court succumbed to what Justice Black described as "present pressures, passions and fears." As the legal historian William Wiecek has noted, for the justices to have resisted "the ideological and emotional pressures of the Cold War era would have required superhuman wisdom and equanimity," qualities that were lacking in a majority of the justices in *Dennis*.[51]

\* \* \*

IN OUR NATIONAL CONSCIOUSNESS, the indelible symbol of this era was Joseph McCarthy. Things did not end well for him. Like so many others, President Eisenhower tried to steer clear of McCarthy. As he told his friends, he refused to "get into the gutter with that guy."[52] But then McCarthy went too far. He attacked the former general's Army. McCarthy made the mistake of launching a series of highly publicized investigations intended to expose alleged Communist infiltration of the military.

Ironically, the instruments of McCarthy's destruction were his own lieutenants, David Schine and Roy Cohn, key members of his congressional staff. Schine had been drafted into the Army. Cohn ordered Schine's commander to grant Schine privileged treatment. The uproar that followed led to the Army-McCarthy hearings. Technically, the issue in the hearings was whether Cohn and McCarthy had attempted to intimidate Schine's commander, but no one had any doubt that the real issue was whether the hearings would bring McCarthy down. Knowing this would be a climactic confrontation, Senator Lyndon Johnson arranged for every moment of the hearings to be televised in the hope that, given enough rope, McCarthy would hang himself. It seemed every eye in America was locked onto the unfolding drama.

McCarthy made a spectacle of himself. As Roy Cohn later recalled, "with his easily erupting temper, his menacing monotone, his unsmiling mien, his perpetual five-o'clock shadow," McCarthy was "the perfect stock villain."[53] Seated across from McCarthy was Joseph Welch, a sixty-three-year-old Boston lawyer who had been retained to represent the Army. Welch had a keen mind, a folksy manner, and incisive instincts. He had originally intended to bring with him to Washington two young associates, Jim St. Clair, who twenty years later would represent President Richard Nixon in the Watergate investigation, and Fred Fisher. But when Fisher informed Welch that as a law student he had belonged to the radical National Lawyers

Guild, Welch sent him back to Boston. He did not want anything to divert attention from the task at hand.

The critical moment of the hearings occurred during Welch's cross-examination of Roy Cohn. In a voice dripping with malevolence, McCarthy interrupted Welsh and announced that Welch "has in his law firm a young man named Fisher . . . who has been for a number of years a member of an organization which was named, oh, years and years ago, as the legal bulwark of the Communist party."[54] Welch's response, seen live by millions on television, was withering: "Until this moment, Senator, I think I never really gauged your cruelty or your recklessness. . . . Let us not assassinate this lad further. . . . You have done enough. Have you no sense of decency, sir, at long last? Have you left no sense of decency?"[55] Welch then rose and walked from the room, which exploded in applause. It was the moment that finally and indelibly exposed Joseph McCarthy for what he was: a vicious bully willing to destroy anyone who stood in his way.

In the weeks after the hearings, McCarthy's popularity plummeted. The *Christian Science Monitor* pointedly observed that despite all of his investigations and accusations, McCarthy had not produced the conviction of a single spy or uncovered a single Communist working in a classified defense position.

On June 11, 1954, a seventy-four-year-old Republican senator, Ralph Flanders of Vermont, acting in direct defiance of the Republican leadership, introduced a resolution to censure McCarthy. Before doing so, however, Flanders walked up to McCarthy on the Senate floor and personally handed him a written invitation to attend the Senate session at which he would present the resolution. Flanders's resolution charged that McCarthy had engaged in conduct "unbecoming a member of the United States Senate."[56]

Even the Democrats were uneasy. The resolution risked upsetting the Senate's long-standing tradition of "live and let live." Over the next several months, the matter percolated slowly through the Senate process. Finally, on September 27, 1954, a six-member committee unanimously recommended that McCarthy be "condemned"—the word had been changed from "censured"—for "contemptuous" and "reprehensible" conduct.[57]

McCarthy roared that he was the "victim" of a Communist conspiracy and that the Communist Party "has now extended its tentacles even to . . . the United States Senate." After two weeks of harsh debate, the Senate adopted the resolution by a vote of 67 to 22. Every Democrat who was present voted for censure; the Republicans were evenly divided. Six weeks later, in the 1954 election, the Democrats regained control of both houses of Congress, and candidates tied to McCarthy were defeated throughout the nation. Two years later, an abandoned, bitter, and chronically alcoholic Joseph McCarthy died of cirrhosis of the liver at the age of forty-nine.

McCARTHY'S RISE AND FALL spanned five inglorious years. The era of what we loosely call "McCarthyism" lasted well over a decade. During all of that time, in which tens of thousands of innocent individuals had their reputations, careers, and personal lives destroyed, most civil libertarians, most lawyers, most public officials, and most others who should have known better, including the justices of the Supreme Court, dithered over what to do. What made this possible?

Certainly, at the height of the Cold War, a small, highly disciplined cohort of dedicated Communists, working in secret with agents of the Soviet Union, sought to harm the United States. We know from recently available KGB files that this network included 200 to 400 people. I do not mean to make light of this danger or of the perilous state of the world. But the danger these individuals presented was not the subversion of the American people. It was the danger of espionage and sabotage. The appropriate way for a democratic government to address that danger is not to broadly stifle public discourse or foster a climate of repression. It is to focus precisely on the unlawful conduct and to use appropriate *law enforcement* tools to identify, punish, and deter lawbreakers. This is the essential distinction between a free society and a police state.

Partisan exploitation caused the leap from a reasoned fear of espionage and sabotage to an unreasoned fear of disloyalty. With the Iron Curtain, the fall of China, the Korean War, and the fear of "weapons of mass destruction" raining down on American cities, public hysteria lurked just beneath the surface. It was a natural breeding ground for opportunistic politicians. For anti–New Deal Republicans trying to claw their way back into power, it was the opportunity of a lifetime, and they seized it.

As former Attorney General Francis Biddle observed at the time, power in America now depends upon public opinion. The struggle for freedom is therefore no longer a struggle against an "oppressive tyrant," but a struggle against "the people themselves, who, in fear of an imagined peril" may demand the repression of others. Fear, Biddle observed, "is an infection that spreads quickly."[58] During the McCarthy era, Americans were exhorted to fear not only Soviet agents but "un-Americanism." And we responded to the exhortation. We grew fearful not only about our national security, but about subversion of our religious, moral, and national values. Fanned by unprincipled and cunning politicians, fear of an insidious enemy led Americans to distrust other Americans and to confuse panic-peddling with patriotism.

For fifty years, Joseph McCarthy's name has evoked associations of fear, meanness, irresponsibility, and cruelty. He is the quintessential American goblin. Recently, a not so subtle campaign has been launched to rehabilitate McCarthy as a loyal American who did our nation a great service.[59]

This version of history runs essentially as follows: After the United States and the Soviet Union became mortal enemies in the late 1940s, many public employees, labor leaders, educators, lawyers, journalists, and writers who had once seemed reasonable security risks could no longer be trusted. After all, anyone who had once had a connection to Communism, however remote or indirect, *might* be disloyal. It was essential to ferret them out and remove them from positions of influence. But the Democrats would not investigate their "fellow liberals" to determine whether they might be closet Reds. It was therefore necessary for HUAC, Richard Nixon, and Joseph McCarthy to do it for them.

To be sure, even the revisionists concede that McCarthy lied, bullied, abused, and humiliated innocent individuals. But what McCarthy contributed, they argue, was a fearless, stubborn, unyielding insistence on pursuing an important inquiry in the face of blind obstructionism. Confronted by a concerted liberal effort to sweep under the carpet the Democratic failure to protect our national security, McCarthy was an essential lightning rod. Even if he was wrong in the details, the argument goes, he was right in the big things.

This is wrong, and dangerously so. The goal of preserving the nation's security from unlawful espionage, sabotage, and foreign influence is certainly legitimate—indeed, compelling—and there were well-justified concerns about these matters during the Cold War. But a democracy is about means as well as ends. As the Supreme Court has recognized in protecting our fundamental rights, not only must the ends be compelling, but the *means must be necessary*. It disserves our history to say that the Red-hunters meant well, but merely went about it the wrong way. Their methods violated the most basic norms and the most essential values of the American constitutional system.

CHAPTER VI

# The Vietnam War
## "To Expose, Disrupt, and Otherwise Neutralize"

❦

THE Vietnam War triggered one of the most turbulent periods in American history. It raised old—and new—questions about the nature and depth of the American commitment to civil liberties in wartime. Opposition to the war came from many quarters and employed a broad range of tactics, including prayer vigils, teach-ins, mass public demonstrations, nonviolent civil disobedience, and bombings. Over more than a decade of conflict, the war provoked bitter dissent and furious repression. In an era marked by the 1968 Chicago Democratic Convention, the Kent State shootings, the Pentagon Papers, and the Days of Rage, many Americans believed that their nation was, quite literally, coming apart.

It is important to recall how this all came about. After struggling for centuries to free themselves from Chinese domination, the people of Vietnam came under French control in the mid nineteenth century. At the end of World War II, a nationalistic Vietnamese movement gained strength. From 1946 to 1954, the Communist Vietminh, led by Ho Chi Minh, waged a fierce guerilla war against the French, culminating in the climactic French defeat at Dienbienphu. The 1954 Geneva Accords divided Vietnam. The Democratic Republic of Vietnam, in the North, was led by Ho Chi Minh. The government the French had installed in the South was controlled by Ngo Dinh Diem.

The United States supported Diem as part of its global effort to contain the spread of Communism. The Vietcong, made up of remnants of the Vietminh in the South, continued its fight to overthrow Diem and unify Vietnam. By the time John F. Kennedy became president in 1961, Vietnam was a shambles. With considerable misgivings, Kennedy ordered four hundred Special Forces troops and other military advisers to Vietnam in order to prop up the failing South Vietnamese army. By December 1961, the number of American troops in Vietnam had increased to 3,164. By a year later, that number had more than tripled. Military leaders assured the president that success was imminent, but the military situation continued to deteriorate. By the end of 1963, the United States had over 16,000 soldiers in Vietnam.

Over the next several years, under President Lyndon Johnson, the United States poured ever more armaments and men into South Vietnam. By the end of 1965, the number of American troops had increased to 184,000; by the end of 1966, to 385,000; by the end of 1967, to more than 500,000. By the time the United States finally withdrew from Vietnam in 1973, more than 50,000 Americans had died there.

WAR CRITICS POSED FUNDAMENTAL questions about America's political, military, and strategic aims in Vietnam. They asked whether the United States was right to pursue unilateral military action in Vietnam and questioned whether it was moral for the United States to inflict such suffering on the Vietnamese people in order to achieve its own military and strategic goals.

A major challenge for those who opposed the war was to criticize the nation's policy without providing, or seeming to provide, "aid and comfort to the enemy." Like protesters in other wars, opponents of the war in Vietnam were vilified as traitors or dupes who (intentionally or unintentionally) encouraged and emboldened the enemy. Lyndon Johnson charged war opponents with harming American interests by raising false hopes among the enemy that the United

States would weaken and disengage from the conflict. Senator Thomas Dodd of Connecticut castigated antiwar demonstrations as "tantamount to open insurrection" and Georgia Senator Richard Russell accused dissenters of disloyalty because "[e]very protest will cause the Communists to believe they can win if they hold on a little longer."[1]

By mid-1966, public approval of Johnson's handling of the war had fallen below 50 percent, and one in three Americans thought intervention in Vietnam had been a mistake. In April 1967, hundreds of thousands of antiwar demonstrators marched in rallies across the nation. But by this time, after several years of peaceful protest, the radical elements of the antiwar movement began to lose patience with efforts to change the government's policy by building public opinion. They had learned from the civil rights movement that there was power in polarization, and that polarization required confrontation. The refrain "We Won't Go" began to echo across college campuses, and over the next several years more than 25,000 men were indicted for refusing induction.

In October 1967, 50,000 antiwar demonstrators convened at the Lincoln Memorial and marched across the Potomac to the Pentagon. Several thousand protesters broke through lines set up by federal troops and refused to leave the Pentagon grounds. After a lengthy standoff, hundreds of heavily armed soldiers formed a wedge and sliced through the demonstrators, who were sitting, arm in arm, in rows. The troops used tear gas, rifle butts, and cudgels to scatter and beat the protesters. By the end of the night, 647 demonstrators had been arrested and 47 hospitalized. Lyndon Johnson began referring to protesters as "storm troopers" and publicly charged that the antiwar movement was linked to Communist subversion.

"Stop the Draft" protests occurred in thirty cities, leading to more than 600 arrests. The next twelve months saw the continued escalation of the war, the assassinations of Martin Luther King, Jr., and Robert F. Kennedy, the withdrawal of Lyndon Johnson from the campaign for the Democratic presidential nomination, the nationally televised riots at the Chicago Democratic Convention,* and the election of Richard Nixon as president of the United States.

Antiwar protests intensified in violence as the decade drew to a fractious end. From the fall of 1969 to the spring of 1970, at least 250 bombings, about one per day, were directed at ROTC buildings, draft boards, induction centers, and federal offices. The goal of these bombings was to "bring the war home." At Kent State University, after an ROTC building was burned, national guardsmen shot and killed four students who were protesting their presence on campus. This triggered student protests on more than half the nation's campuses. Within a few days, 1.5 million students walked out of class, shutting down a fifth of the nation's colleges and universities. It was the most massive antigovernment protest in the history of American higher education. Thirty ROTC buildings were burned or bombed in the first week of May, and National Guard units were mobilized in sixteen states.

THE JOHNSON AND NIXON ADMINISTRATIONS were shocked by the magnitude and intensity of the opposition to the war. After the events at Kent State, "a sense of panic enveloped Richard Nixon and the men around him."[2] Henry Kissinger recalled that "the fear of another round of demonstrations permeated all the thinking about Vietnam."[3] Understandably, both administrations wanted desperately to

---

*Theodore White's description of the scene in Chicago is worth quoting at length: "Dusk has now closed and in the dark [there is a] triple-ranked police formation, lined up quietly in varying shades of blue, their billy-clubs held at rest across their thighs. . . . [The demonstrators] yell to the cops, 'Hey, Hey, Go Away.' . . . [Then, like] a fist jolting, like a piston expoding from its chamber, comes a hurtling column of police. . . . And as the scene clears, there are . . . police clubbing youngsters, police dragging youngsters, police rushing them by the elbows, their heels dragging, to patrol wagons. . . . It is a scene from . . . the Russian Revolution. . . . There are splotches of blood. . . . [Demonstrators] in the front . . . rank kneel, with arms folded across their breasts. They take up a song, 'America the Beautiful.' . . . A commotion expodes in the front rank; one sees the clubs coming down. . . . There is much blood now. . . . The chants change . . . to 'The Whole World Is Watching.'" Theodore H. White, *The Making of the President, 1968* 369–73 (Atheneum 1969).

suppress or at least defuse their critics. The most natural solution was to put them in jail.

As we have seen, this response would hardly have been unprecedented. Adams, Lincoln, and Wilson had certainly laid the foundation for this response. But neither Johnson nor Nixon seriously considered prosecuting their critics for seditious libel. Their restraint in this regard reflected a fundamental change in America's political and constitutional culture. By 1968, it was impossible to imagine the United States prosecuting American citizens merely for opposing a war. Unlike Matthew Lyon, Clement Vallandigham, and Eugene Debs, Eugene McCarthy was never prosecuted or even threatened with such a prospect. Gradually, over the course of two centuries, America's understanding of free speech and its commitment to free and open public debate had changed profoundly.

This is not to say that Johnson and Nixon did not want to silence their critics. On the contrary, both presidents, and especially Nixon, prosecuted protesters for a wide variety of activities related to their opposition to the war, including trespass, flag desecration, draft-card burning, and conspiracy. But these were indirect and relatively ineffective methods of stifling dissent. More effective was the government's use of massive programs of surveillance, infiltration, and harassment in order to disrupt and incapacitate the antiwar movement.

Longtime FBI Director J. Edgar Hoover first honed his extraordinary organizational and surveillance skills during World War I, when he focused the new Bureau of Investigation on spying on antiwar protesters. Over the next half century, Hoover developed ever more aggressive methods of intelligence gathering. In some instances, his actions were authorized; in others, he disobeyed direct orders to terminate his activities and took it upon himself to protect the nation from "subversion."

In the 1950s, Hoover initiated a secret counterintelligence program (COINTELPRO) against the Communist Party of the United

States. He instituted this program without the knowledge or authorization of either the attorney general or the president. His goal was to go beyond surveillance to active disruption and harassment. The FBI promoted the publication of information that would embarrass members of the CPUSA, fostered animosity among party members by fabricating rumors of betrayal, secretly arranged for the party to be denied access to meeting places, and even set organized crime against the CPUSA.

As antiwar protests escalated in the 1960s, President Johnson prodded Hoover to expand his activities. At the 1964 Democratic National Convention, the FBI secretly kept tabs on "dissident" groups within the Democratic Party and informed the president of their plans. In early 1965, it began wiretapping Students for a Democratic Society and the Student Nonviolent Coordinating Committee. Several months later, Johnson directed Hoover to investigate "subversive" involvement in the antiwar movement. Both Johnson and Hoover were confident that the investigation would prove that Communists were actively engaged in inciting and organizing opposition to the war, but the report found otherwise.

Undaunted, the FBI expanded its surveillance of antiwar activities. A teach-in in Philadelphia resulted in a forty-one-page FBI intelligence report, incorporating the remarks of ministers, professors, and other speakers. This report, compiled by undercover informants, was distributed widely to military intelligence, the State Department, and the Internal Security Division of the Justice Department. President Johnson also requested and received FBI reports on antiwar senators, congressmen, journalists, and academics. At his direction, the FBI investigated the philosopher Hannah Arendt, newsman David Brinkley, and columnist Joseph Kraft, among many others.

In 1968, the FBI turned its COINTELPRO tactics against the antiwar movement. The key directive stated that its goal was to "expose, disrupt and otherwise neutralize" antiwar organizations. The FBI instructed its agents to frustrate "every effort of these groups . . . to recruit new . . . members," disrupt their activities, spread misinformation about their meetings, exploit "organizational and personal conflicts," and promote suspicion, distrust, and dissension among their leaders. Hoover exhorted his agents to act with "imagination and enthusiasm."[4]

In its campaign to destabilize the antiwar movement, the FBI sent anonymous letters to employers, landlords, parents, and schools accusing antiwar protesters of drug abuse, homosexuality, and treason. It distributed bogus campus newspapers defaming peace activists, sent fraudulent letters to supporters of antiwar political candidates to sabotage their campaigns, spread false rumors that antiwar leaders were embezzling funds or cooperating with the FBI, incited local police departments to harass antiwar activists for minor offenses, and disrupted peaceful demonstrations.

THE FBI WAS NOT THE ONLY government agency directed to undermine the antiwar movement. In 1966, the Central Intelligence Agency (CIA) began reading international mail sent to or from individuals involved in the antiwar movement. Over the next few years, the CIA turned over to the FBI information resulting from more than 20,000 such mail openings, including material of a highly personal nature. The CIA also engaged in domestic spying. In 1967, it began monitoring a broad array of antiwar organizations and activities, compiling information on more than 12,000 individuals, particularly those active on college campuses. The most drastic domestic CIA program, Operation CHAOS, became a repository for huge quantities of information about the lawful political activities of American citizens, ultimately accumulating material on more than 300,000 people. Much of this information was routinely shared with the FBI and the White House. These programs clearly violated the CIA's legislative charter, which expressly prohibits the CIA from undertaking any "internal security" role.

Army intelligence ran its own domestic spying operation. Although the initial goal was to enable the Army to plan for possible domestic disorders, the program expanded quickly. Army intelligence assigned 1,500 undercover agents to collect information about virtually every group seeking significant change in the United States. The Army gathered information on more than 100,000 opponents of the Vietnam War, including Senator Adlai Stevenson III, Congressman Abner Mikva, Georgia State Senator Julian Bond, Martin Luther King, Jr., and folksinger Joan Baez. Among the organizations the Army investigated were the American Civil Liberties Union, Americans for Democratic Action, the Anti-Defamation League, the American Friends Service Committee, and *Ramparts* magazine. Army intelligence monitored private communications, infiltrated antiwar organizations, participated in antiwar protests and demonstrations, and posed as press representatives. The Army gathered information about the private political, financial, and sex lives of tens of thousands of American citizens and then disseminated that information to a broad range of government agencies, including local police, the FBI, the CIA, and the National Security Agency (NSA).

In 1969, at the behest of the White House, the NSA began intercepting telephone communications involving the antiwar movement. Because the NSA was authorized by law to engage in intelligence activities only *outside* the United States, this program was clearly illegal. To avoid exposure, the NSA devised separate filing systems for these intercepts and fraudulently classified them "Top Secret."

When Richard Nixon assumed the presidency in January 1969, he inherited a formidable apparatus to implement a program of political repression. His administration took full advantage of this machinery. From the outset, Nixon pressed the FBI to expand its domestic surveillance activities. In 1969, Attorney General John Mitchell directed the FBI to investigate individuals who participated in antiwar protests, provide information about the income sources of antiwar groups, and report the identities of all speakers at antiwar demonstrations. FBI reports on these matters were disseminated to the White House, the CIA, the State Department, the military intelligence agencies, the Secret Service, and the Department of Justice.

The Nixon administration prodded the FBI to expand COINTEL-PRO and pushed the CIA to intensify its domestic surveillance activities. The CIA began furnishing the FBI with more than 1,000 domestic intelligence reports each month. This information was gathered by undercover agents, break-ins, illegal wiretaps, and mail openings. The CIA was fully aware of the illegality of these activities. In passing one report on to the White House, CIA Director Richard Helms noted, "[T]his is an area not within the charter of this Agency, so I need not emphasize how extremely sensitive this makes the paper."[5]

The Nixon White House also enlisted the Internal Revenue Service on a massive scale. In 1969, it informed the IRS of the president's concern that tax-exempt funds might be supporting antiwar groups. Eight days later, the IRS established the Activist Organizations Committee to "collect relevant information on organizations predominantly dissident . . . in nature and on people prominently identified with these organizations."[6] This committee was later renamed the Special Service Staff (SSS) to mask its real purpose.

By 1974, the SSS had compiled files on 2,873 organizations and 8,585 individuals. The IRS routinely furnished this information (including lists of contributors to antiwar organizations) to the FBI, the Secret Service, Army intelligence, and the White House. The goal was to cripple critics of the administration through the use of targeted tax audits and tax investigations. The SSS investigated such individuals as the columnist Joseph Alsop, the journalist Jimmy Breslin, New York City Mayor John Lindsay, actress Shirley MacLaine, and New York Senator Charles Goodell. The organizations it investigated included the American Jewish Committee, the National Organization for Women, the National Council of Churches, and the Americans for Democratic Action. This program was kept strictly secret because of its "political sensitivity."[7]

In 1970, the White House began compiling an "enemies list" under the direction of Charles Colson, special assistant to the president. Some two hundred people and eighteen organizations were targeted for "special" government attention. Among those on the list were former Attorney General Ramsey Clark and New York Congresswomen Bella Abzug and Shirley Chisholm; Democratic Senators Edward Kennedy, Edmund Muskie, and Walter Mondale; the presidents of Harvard, Yale, the Ford Foundation, and the Rand Corporation; and the journalists James Reston, Marvin Kalb, and Daniel Schorr.

A month after the Kent State killings, Nixon moved to centralize domestic intelligence in the Oval Office. At his request, White House assistant Tom Charles Huston proposed a new White House unit to oversee the investigation of political dissent. In July 1970, Huston prepared a memorandum, which came to be known as the Huston Plan, recommending intensified electronic surveillance, monitoring of international communications, "mail coverage" (that is, opening and reading mail), and the expanded use of undercover informants and "surreptitious entry." It also proposed the creation of a central agency on domestic intelligence, with representatives from the White House, the FBI, the CIA, the NSA, and the military. The Huston Plan has been fairly characterized as a "blueprint for a police state in America."[8] Although J. Edgar Hoover vetoed the plan because it threatened his dominance, many elements of the plan were surreptitiously put into operation.

THE GOVERNMENT'S SECRET MACHINATIONS to "expose, disrupt and otherwise neutralize" the antiwar movement were not known to the press or the public until March 8, 1971, when an antiwar group— the Citizens' Commission to Investigate the FBI—broke into an FBI office in Media, Pennsylvania, and stole approximately 1,000 confidential documents. One of the documents, dated September 16, 1970, was mysteriously captioned "COINTELPRO–New Left." The first public intimation of the existence of this covert program, this document recommended intensified FBI interviewing of dissenters to "enhance the paranoia" and underscore the fear that "there is an FBI agent behind every mailbox."[9]

President Nixon's response to these disclosures was to warn that any further disclosure "could endanger the lives or cause other serious harm to persons engaged in investigation activities on behalf of the United States."[10] The *Washington Post* countered that these revelations showed that the FBI had been implementing a form "of internal security appropriate for the Secret Police of the Soviet Union." The *Post* argued that "the American public needs to know what the FBI is doing" and "needs to think long and hard about whether internal security rests especially upon official surveillance and the suppression of dissent or upon the traditional freedom of every citizen to speak his mind on any subject, whether others consider what he says wise or foolish, patriotic or subversive, conservative or radical."[11]

Over the next several weeks, as more COINTELPRO activities came to light, several major newspapers and congressmen called for J. Edgar Hoover's resignation. Under intense public pressure, Hoover announced on April 28, 1971, that he had officially terminated COINTELPRO. At that time, the FBI had some 2,000 agents engaged in domestic intelligence activities, and they were supervising an additional 1,700 domestic intelligence informants and 1,400 "confidential" sources.

After the public disclosure of these activities, Congress authorized investigating committees to probe more deeply. One Senate committee made the following findings:[12]

The Government has often undertaken the secret surveillance of citizens on the basis of their political beliefs, even when those beliefs posed no threat of violence or illegal acts. . . . The Government, operating primarily through secret informants, . . . has swept in vast amounts of information about the personal lives, views, and associations of American citizens. Investigations of groups deemed potentially dangerous—and even of groups suspected of associating with potentially dangerous organizations—have continued for decades, despite the fact that those groups did not engage in unlawful activity. . . . FBI headquarters alone has developed over 500,000 domestic intelligence files. . . .

Another Senate committee concluded that the surveillance had served no legitimate purpose but had seriously infringed the rights of American citizens.[13] In 1976, President Gerald Ford formally prohibited the CIA from using electronic or physical surveillance to collect information about the domestic activities of Americans and banned the NSA from intercepting any communication made within, from, or to the United States.

That same year, Attorney General Edward Levi imposed new restrictions on the investigative activities of the FBI. In these "guidelines," Levi prohibited the FBI from investigating, discrediting, or disrupting any group or individual on the basis of protected First Amendment activity and from monitoring protected First Amendment activity in the absence of "specific and articulable facts" justifying a criminal investigation. The Levi guidelines were a critical step forward in protecting the rights of Americans against overzealous and misguided government officials. They represented good government at its best. Without regard to whether these limitations were required by the Constitution, and without waiting for legislative action, Levi promulgated these regulations as a matter of sound public policy. As Levi recognized, the protection of civil liberties demands not only compliance with the Constitution, but also thoughtful, restrained use of government power.

Two years later, Congress enacted the Foreign Intelligence Surveillance Act (FISA) of 1978, which was designed to prevent similar abuses in the future. The act placed clear limits on how and when the government may lawfully undertake foreign intelligence investigations. As we shall see in Chapter VII, twenty-five years later the disregard of FISA by the administration of George W. Bush would become a pivotal issue in the war on terrorism.

\* \* \*

WERE THE ACTIVITIES IMPLICATED in COINTELPRO, the Huston Plan, and the Army, CIA, and NSA intelligence programs unconstitutional? Some plainly were. It is settled law, for example, that the government cannot constitutionally break into a person's home, open her mail, bug her office, or tap her telephone without probable cause and a warrant. Such searches clearly violate the Fourth Amendment.

During the Vietnam War, the Nixon administration argued that in order to protect the national security the president could wiretap American citizens on American soil *without* complying with the probable cause and warrant requirements of the Fourth Amendment. In 1972, in *United States v. United States District Court* (the *Keith* case),[14] the Supreme Court *unanimously* rejected this claim, holding that even in national security investigations the president has no lawful authority to conduct electronic surveillance of American citizens on American soil without a search warrant based upon a judicial finding of probable cause.

The constitutionality of other activities employed by the government in this era is less certain. Consider government surveillance of public meetings and demonstrations. Suppose an antiwar group sponsors a public event at which speakers attack the morality of a war. May FBI agents photograph and record the names of those in attendance? Under current law, this surveillance would not violate the Fourth Amendment. The Supreme Court has held that individuals have no "reasonable expectation of privacy" in not being observed when they are voluntarily in a public place. Hence, there is no "search" within the meaning of the Constitution.[15]

This practice would clearly violate the Levi guidelines, however, and might violate the First Amendment. The First and Fourth amendments protect different values. The former protects free expression, association, and religion; the latter protects one's general sense of privacy. The argument that such surveillance may violate the First Amendment, even if it doesn't violate the Fourth, finds support in Supreme Court decisions protecting the privacy of one's associations. In *NAACP v. Alabama*,[16] for example, the Court held in the late 1950s that Alabama could not constitutionally compel the NAACP to disclose its membership lists, because such disclosure might deter individuals from exercising their First Amendment rights. The Court made clear that the freedoms of speech, association, and religion are protected "not only against heavy-handed frontal attack, but also from being stifled by more subtle governmental interference."[17]

Government surveillance of antiwar protests might not be quite as chilling as the situation faced by NAACP members in Alabama at the height of the civil rights movement. But the knowledge that government agents (whether undercover or in uniform) may be taking names and photographs at protest rallies, and reporting the identities of protesters to the FBI, the IRS, the INS, and local police, would surely deter some people from exercising their First Amendment rights. Unless the government has a clear, legitimate, and even-handed justification for engaging in such surveillance, it should be held to violate the First Amendment.*

What of the use of informers and secret agents? The Court has held that the government's use of undercover agents to deceive individuals into revealing information or granting informers access to nonpublic meetings or places is not a "search" within the meaning of the Fourth Amendment. Thus, if an undercover police officer dresses up like a meter man and deceives you into letting him enter your home, there is no violation of the Fourth Amendment. The Court's rationale is that in day-to-day life we naturally "assume the risk" that those with whom we deal are not who they purport to be.

---

*If the government has a clear, legitimate, and evenhanded justification for being present at the public event, its conduct may be warranted. For example, the government has a responsibility to provide reasonable police protection at mass public demonstrations. The presence of the police for that purpose is constitutionally permissible. But this would not justify recording names or taking photographs of individuals engaged in constitutionally protected First Amendment activity.

Whatever the (in my view dubious) merits of this reasoning in the Fourth Amendment context,[18] it should *not* govern the use of deceit to infiltrate and otherwise spy upon a political or religious organization. If your fellow protester—an undercover FBI agent—tricks you into inviting her to participate in your organization's planning meeting or giving her a copy of your group's membership list, this poses a serious First Amendment question. For the government intentionally to cause such organizations to fear that their members may be government spies would undermine the mutual trust that is essential to effective political and religious association. This practice should be held to violate the First Amendment unless the government has reasonable grounds to believe that the political or religious organization is involved in *criminal* activity, and the investigation is narrowly tailored to that end.[19]

DURING THE VIETNAM WAR, the Supreme Court decided several important First Amendment cases, addressing such issues as flag desecration, draft-card burning, and the use of profanity in political debate. Two of the Court's decisions in this era are especially worthy of note.

In 1967, Secretary of Defense Robert McNamara secretly commissioned the compilation of a "History of U.S. Decision-Making Process on Vietnam Policy, 1945–1967." Although McNamara had been a key architect of the nation's policy in Vietnam, by 1967 he had begun to have doubts. His objective in ordering the report "was to bequeath to scholars the raw material from which they could reexamine the events of the time."[20] It took two years to complete the project—a work of 7,000 pages in forty-seven volumes. When McNamara read the completed report, he commented, "[Y]ou know, they could hang people for what's in there."[21]

Although much of what was in the study was common knowledge, it also shed important new light on key aspects of America's involvement in Vietnam. It documented, for example, that at the end of World War II President Truman had rejected urgent appeals from

Ho Chi Minh for American assistance; that President Kennedy's "advisers" in Vietnam had not merely advised the South Vietnamese military but had also participated in military operations; that the Gulf of Tonkin resolution, which had authorized a major escalation of American involvement in Vietnam, had been rammed through Congress under false pretenses; and that the U.S. government had concealed from the American people the fact that extensive bombing of North Vietnam had done little to impair the Communists' military capacity, but had killed tens of thousands of innocent Vietnamese civilians.[22]

In the spring of 1970, Daniel Ellsberg, a former Defense Department official who had turned against the war, gave a copy of the "Pentagon Papers" to the *New York Times*.* On June 13, the *Times* began publishing excerpts from the Papers. The next day, Attorney General John Mitchell sent a telegram to Arthur Sulzberger, publisher of the *Times*, stating that the June 13 and 14 issues of the *Times* contained information bearing "a top-secret classification." Mitchell added that "publication of this information" was "directly prohibited" by the Espionage Act of 1917 and that further publication would "cause irreparable injury to the defense interests of the United States." He therefore requested that the *Times* "publish no further information of this character and advise" him that it had "made arrangements for the return of these documents to the Department of Defense."[23]

---

*Born in Chicago in 1931, Ellsberg attended Harvard, studied economics at Cambridge, and then joined the Marines. Several years later, after earning his Ph.D. from Harvard, he accepted a position with the Rand Corporation, one of the nation's most high-powered defense research centers. During the Kennedy years, he took a position in the Defense Department under Secretary of Defense McNamara. A committed hawk, Ellsberg was dedicated to the American policy in Vietnam. In mid-1965, he volunteered to serve in Vietnam as a State Department representative. As he came to know the Vietnamese people, his understanding of the war began to change. He came to appreciate the suffering caused by the war and the inaccuracy of the information provided the American public. After returning to Rand, he began reading the Pentagon Papers. In March 1971 he decided to bring the Pentagon Papers to the attention of the American public. After deleting the sections he thought sensitive to national security concerns, he turned the Papers over to the *New York Times*.

Two hours later, the *Times* transmitted a response, which it released publicly: "The *Times* must respectfully decline the request of the Attorney General, believing that it is in the interest of the people of this country to be informed of the material contained in this series of articles." The *Times* added that if the government sought to enjoin any further publication of the material, it would contest the government's position, but would "abide by the final decision of the court."[24]

Events escalated quickly. On Tuesday, June 15, the U.S. government filed a complaint for injunction against the *New York Times* in the federal district court in Manhattan. Judge Murray Gurfein granted the government's request for a temporary restraining order on the ground that "any temporary harm that may result from not publishing during the pendency of the application for a preliminary injunction is far outweighed by the irreparable harm that could be done to the interests of the United States government if it should ultimately prevail" in the case.[25] This was the *first* time in the almost two-hundred-year history of the United States that a federal judge had restrained a newspaper from publishing information relevant to public debate.

When Ellsberg saw that the June 16 issue of the *New York Times* did not include the next installment in the series, but instead reported the *Times's* decision to obey Judge Gurfein's injunction, he delivered another copy of the Pentagon Papers to the *Washington Post*. On Thursday, June 17, the *Washington Post's* publisher, Katharine Graham, gave the directive: "Go ahead."[26] Once again, the United States sought and obtained a restraining order.

Over the next few days, the two cases rapidly worked their way up to the Supreme Court of the United States. On Friday, June 25, the Supreme Court agreed to review the *New York Times* and *Washington Post* cases together and to hold an unprecedented Saturday morning session in order to hear oral arguments. On Wednesday, June 30, the Court announced its decision.[27] Reflecting the extraordinary nature of the case, each Justice wrote an opinion. Six justices held that the government had not met its "heavy burden of showing justification" for a prior restraint on the press.[28] The Court therefore ruled that the *Times* and the *Post* were free to resume publication of the Pentagon Papers.*

Justice Potter Stewart's opinion best captures the view of the Court: "We are asked . . . to prevent the publication by two newspapers of material that the Executive Branch insists should not, in the national interest, be published. I am convinced that the Executive is correct with respect to some of the documents involved. But I cannot say that disclosure of any of them will surely result in direct, immediate, and irreparable damage to our Nation or its people."[29]

The publication of the Pentagon Papers was a major event in the history of American journalism. A voluminous, "top secret" study of the Vietnam War, prepared within the recesses of the Department of Defense, that "revealed that the American people had been systematically misled by their elected and appointed leaders," had been made available to the public "through an unprecedented breach of security." Even an old Washington hand like Secretary of Defense Clark Clifford commented that he had "never seen anything like it."[30]

A fundamental question posed by the Pentagon Papers controversy is *who* should decide whether it is in the national interest for classified information to be made public. In the first instance, it would seem that our *elected officials*, who are charged with the responsibility of protecting the national security, must have the authority to decide such matters. But we know that our elected offi-

---

*The concept of prior restraint is deeply imbedded in the history of the First Amendment. Historically, censorship took the form of licensing. No one could publish a book without first obtaining a license from the government. If an individual published without obtaining a license, he could be punished even if a license would have been issued. Injunctions operate in much the same way. If a publication is enjoined, and a newspaper violates the injunction, it can be punished for violating the injunction even if the injunction should not have been granted. In this sense, licensing requirements and injunctions are different from ordinary criminal laws. A speaker who is prosecuted for violating a criminal law may argue in his defense that the law is unconstitutional. Licensing requirements and injunctions, on the other hand, cannot be challenged by violating them. As a result, they can be even more restrictive than criminal prohibitions, and thus constitute "prior restraints."

cials may sometimes have mixed motives for keeping things secret. They may be concerned not only with protecting the national security, but also with hiding their own mistakes and wrongdoing. To give them the *final* say about confidentiality thus risks depriving the American people of potentially critical information about the conduct of their elected officials.

In the Pentagon Papers case, the Supreme Court embraced the view that although elected officials have broad authority to keep information secret,* once such information gets in the hands of the press, the government has only limited authority to prevent its further dissemination. This is obviously an awkward compromise. It is one we shall explore more fully in Chapter VII, when we consider the war on terrorism.

The Vietnam War labored on for two dreary years after publication of the Pentagon Papers, but the disclosures helped shape American public opinion about the war, the nation's use of military force to direct world events, and the appropriate authority of presidents relative to Congress in such matters. Even more important, the Pentagon Papers fostered a greater public awareness of the dangers of government secrecy and a deeper and more probing skepticism about the candor of our national leaders.

Most important, though, the Pentagon Papers controversy changed both the nation's understanding of the First Amendment and the Supreme Court's conception of its responsibilities under the Constitution. The decision was a bold, confident, and courageous

---

*After the Supreme Court's decision, Daniel Ellsberg turned himself in to the FBI. He was promptly indicted on felony charges carrying a possible total sentence of 125 years in prison. The indictment charged that Ellsberg had stolen the lawful property of the United States and given documents related to the national security to persons not authorized to receive them. As events turned out, the courts never had to decide whether Ellsberg could constitutionally be convicted of these offenses. In September 1971, a group of individuals (the "plumbers"), acting under orders from the White House, burglarized the offices of Daniel Ellsberg's psychiatrist in order to obtain information that could be used to embarrass Ellsberg. In 1973, the judge presiding over the prosecution learned of this burglary and dismissed all charges against Ellsberg because of "unprecedented" government misconduct.

assertion of judicial independence in the face of emphatic (and disin-genuous) executive claims of national security. It showed the nation what an independent federal judiciary can and *should* do.

THE OTHER MAJOR SUPREME COURT decision during this era did not arise out of the war. In *Brandenburg v. Ohio*,[31] which involved the prosecution of a Klansman for inciting racial violence, the Court revisited its earlier decisions about subversive advocacy. As we have seen, in its World War I–era decisions, such as *Schenck* and *Debs*, the Court held that dissenters could be criminally punished if their speech had a "tendency" to interfere with the war effort. Twenty-five years later, in *Dennis*, the Court replaced the bad tendency standard with a diluted version of the clear-and-present-danger test.

In *Brandenburg*, in a unanimous opinion, the Court held that "the constitutional guarantees of free speech and free press do not permit a State to forbid or proscribe" even express advocacy of "law viola-tion except where such advocacy" is likely to incite "imminent law-less action."[32] Thus, half a century after *Schenck*, the Court finally and unambiguously embraced the Holmes-Brandeis version of clear and present danger. With this development, the Court effectively overruled *Schenck*, *Frohwerk*, *Debs*, *Abrams*, and *Dennis*. The *Branden-burg* formulation represented a bold new approach. It provides broad constitutional protection to dissent that calls the government sharply to account—even in time of war.

The combination of *Pentagon Papers* and *Brandenburg* made clear that the Court had learned over fifty years of experience that it is impossible to excise from public debate those views that are thought to be "dangerous" without undermining free speech more generally. The Court had learned that although each generation's effort to sup-press *its* idea of "dangerous" speech seemed justified at the time, each proved with the benefit of hindsight to have been an overwrought, excessive, and dangerous response to the problems facing the nation. The Court had learned that even well-intentioned citizens, legisla-tors, presidents, and judges have a natural tendency to want to suppress ideas they find offensive, inflate the potential dangers of such expression, and underestimate the dangers of suppression. As Judge Learned Hand had wisely observed in *Masses*, this insight is no "scholastic subterfuge," but a "hard bought acquisition in the fight for freedom."

# CHAPTER VII

# The War on Terrorism
# "Not a Blank Check"

❧❧

THE terrorist attacks of September 11, 2001, shocked the American people. Images of the collapsing towers of the World Trade Center left the nation in a profound state of fear, fury, grief, and uncertainty. Anxious that September 11 may have been but the first wave of attacks, Americans expected and, indeed, demanded that their government take immediate and decisive steps to protect them.

In the aftermath of September 11, the government's response had both positive and negative elements. President George W. Bush earned high marks for immediately cautioning the public against hostile reactions to Muslims and Muslim-Americans. The contrast with Wilson's rhetoric about German-Americans and Roosevelt's treatment of Japanese-Americans was striking. This is a good example of lessons learned.

Moreover, as of this writing, there have been no direct federal criminal prosecutions of any individuals for antiwar dissent. This is a far cry from our past experience. It shows, again, how far we have come. American values, politics, and law have now reached a point where such prosecutions seem almost unthinkable. A reasonable analogy to the prosecutions of Matthew Lyon in 1798, Clement Vallandigham in 1863, and Eugene Debs in 1918 would have been the prosecution of Howard Dean in 2004 for his opposition to the Iraq

War. The very implausibility of this prospect is testament to our nation's progress.

On the other hand, like previous wartime leaders, members of the Bush administration have gone out of their way to tar their political opponents as "disloyal." Shortly after September 11, President Bush warned, in a phrase strikingly reminiscent of Adams, Wilson, and Nixon, "You are either with us or with the terrorists." Attorney General John Ashcroft went even further, castigating those who challenged the necessity or constitutionality of the government's demand for restrictions of civil liberties: "To those who scare peace-loving people with phantoms of lost liberty, my message is this: Your tactics only aid terrorists—for they erode our national unity and diminish our resolve. They give ammunition to America's enemies."[1]

Moreover, as in earlier episodes, the Bush administration has often sought to excite rather than calm public fears. As former ambassador James Goodby observed, under George Bush fear has too often been "the underlying theme of domestic and foreign policy." The "bottom line" has been " 'You are scared—trust us.' "[2] A frightened public was too easily led into understanding September 11 as the first stage of a "war." Declaring a "war" on terrorism was more than a rhetorical device to rally the public. It also enabled the administration to claim the extraordinary powers reserved to the executive in wartime.

The president's further declaration that the threat of international terrorism is not only a "war," but a war that will last *indefinitely*, added to the sense of gravity. Of course, it is impossible to know whether there will be a serious threat of international terrorism five, ten, or twenty years from now. But if Bush is right that this war will slog on in perpetuity, that is all the more reason to be *scrupulous* in scrutinizing proposed restrictions of civil liberties. The fear of perpetual war can be seen as a reason to strip away all "unnecessary" civil liberties, but the opposite is true. A saving "grace" of America's past excesses is that they were usually of short duration. Once the crisis passed, the nation returned to equilibrium. A war of indefinite duration, however, seriously increases the risk that "emergency" restrictions will become a permanent feature of American life.

IN THE WAKE OF SEPTEMBER 11, the United States faced grave and uncertain dangers. Bush, like Lincoln and Roosevelt before him, claimed far-reaching powers to address the crisis. In principle, this is sensible, even essential. The president can act more quickly and more effectively in an emergency than either Congress or the courts, and every president who has faced such a crisis has aggressively asserted executive authority. This is a proper response, but that authority must be exercised with due regard for both our civil liberties and our separation of powers, which rest at the very heart of the American government.

Immediately after September 11, Americans were more than willing to accept significant encroachments on their freedoms in order to forestall further attacks. To reinforce this willingness, the Bush administration repeatedly declared that the terrorists had taken "advantage of the vulnerability of an open society" and that the government therefore needed to restrict our freedoms.[3] Some of these restrictions were modest in scope and addressed serious deficiencies in the nation's intelligence apparatus. Others were more problematic.

The most questionable measures included secret detention of thousands of noncitizens; secret deportation proceedings; secret and indefinite detention of American citizens; expanded surveillance of political and religious groups and activities; warrantless interception of telephone calls and e-mail communications; and denial of habeas corpus to "enemy combatants" detained at Guantánamo Bay.

The centerpiece of the Bush administration's initial antiterrorism strategy was the USA PATRIOT Act,[4] an exceedingly complex statute drafted by the Justice Department and pushed through Congress only six weeks after September 11. Attorney General John Ashcroft and other administration officials tarred anyone who questioned the proposed legislation as "soft on terrorism," and Congress adopted the act in an atmosphere of urgency that precluded any serious deliberation.

Indeed, no more than a handful of congressmen even read the legislation before it was voted into law. Although civil liberties organizations identified several significant flaws in the act, even members of Congress known to be "strong voices in favor of civil liberties" were reluctant to object.[5]

The result was a statute that has fairly been characterized as opportunistic. The PATRIOT Act failed to require adequate executive branch accountability, undermined traditional checks and balances, and ignored the principle that government restrictions of civil liberties should be narrowly tailored. On the other hand, the act was neither as draconian as many prior wartime statutes nor as repressive as some civil libertarians charged.

In a curious way, the Bush administration, and especially Attorney General Ashcroft, oversold the act, suggesting that it was *more* drastic than it really was. Presumably, this strategy was designed to reassure the public that the administration was "on the case." This puffery, combined with the act's deliberately inflammatory name, baited civil liberties organizations into furiously criticizing the act, sometimes exaggerating the extent to which it threatened core constitutional values. This enabled them to rally their base, thus serving their interests as well as those of the administration.

Over time, it became increasingly clear that the most objectionable provisions of the act were relatively narrow. Unfortunately, when Congress finally had an opportunity to correct those deficiencies when it reenacted the act in early 2006, it largely acquiesced in the administration's insistence that *any* change in the PATRIOT Act would endanger the nation.

ALTHOUGH CONGRESS READILY acceded to the Bush administration's demand for the PATRIOT Act in 2001, it soon grew more skeptical about further calls to limit civil liberties. When Attorney General Ashcroft announced his intention to institute a TIPS program (Terrorism Information and Prevention System), which would have exhorted citizens to monitor and report on other citizens who seemed "suspicious," members of Congress objected, leading Ashcroft to withdraw the proposal.

Similarly, Congress blocked funding for Bush's proposed Total Information Awareness program, which was designed to develop a vast surveillance system and database of personal and commercial information in order to detect "suspicious" behavior patterns among American citizens. Even leading Republicans balked at this proposal. Republican Senator Charles Grassley of Iowa, for example, objected that TIA posed a "chilling" threat to civil liberties.[6]

In January 2003, the Justice Department floated plans for PATRIOT Act II, entitled the Domestic Security Enhancement Act of 2003. This legislation would have reduced judicial oversight over surveillance, created an extensive DNA database, lifted existing judicial restraints on local police spying on religious and political organizations, and authorized the federal government to keep secret the identity of *anyone* detained in a terror investigation—including American citizens. PATRIOT Act II met with howls of public, press, and bipartisan congressional opposition, and the Bush administration buried the proposal.

Thus, although the initial response of Congress and the public was almost blindly to support the president's demand for additional powers, once fears began to subside, the response was more clear-eyed. As the law professor and journalist Jeffrey Rosen wrote roughly a year after September 11, "a principled, bipartisan libertarian constituency" emerged that was willing to defend civil liberties "even in the face of popular fears" and aggressive executive plans to expand its authority.[7]

As we have seen, detention is often a critical issue in wartime. The Alien Friends Act of 1798, Lincoln's suspensions of habeas corpus, and the World War II internment all posed serious questions about the legality of wartime detention. Not surprisingly, the war on terrorism has triggered its own conflicts over this issue. Was it constitutional, for example, for the government to round up noncitizens in the United States after September 11 and hold them for several months, without a hearing, because they had "possible" terrorist connections? Was it lawful for the government to imprison in Guantánamo Bay more than a thousand alleged "enemy combatants," captured in Afghanistan, without granting them hearings or access to habeas corpus to challenge the legality of their detention? Was it permissible for the government to seize American citizens and hold them incommunicado, indefinitely, and without a hearing, because they were *alleged* enemy combatants?

Although the Supreme Court has not addressed the first of these questions, it squarely rejected the contentions of the Bush administration in the other two. In *Rasul v. Bush*,[8] the Court held in 2004 that federal courts have habeas corpus jurisdiction to review the legality of the confinement of the Guantánamo Bay detainees. This issue was especially acute in light of the circumstances in Afghanistan. Ordinarily, soldiers wear uniforms. This reduces the likelihood that bystanders will mistakenly be swept up as enemy soldiers. In Afghanistan, however, local fighters—both the Taliban and those who fought alongside American troops—did not wear uniforms. It was thus inevitable that some noncombatants would be captured during the conflict. In *Rasul*, the Court rebuffed the arguments of the Bush administration and held that the Guantánamo Bay detainees could invoke the writ of habeas corpus to contest in federal court whether they had fairly been determined to be enemy combatants.*

In *Hamdi v. Rumsfeld*,[9] decided on the same day as *Rasul*, the Court went even further. Yaser Hamdi, an American citizen, was seized in Afghanistan by the Northern Alliance (an American ally) and turned over to the U.S. military. In April 2002, Hamdi was covertly

---

*In September 2006, Congress enacted new legislation sharply limiting the access of the Guantánamo Bay detainees to habeas corpus. This new law directly poses the question whether this constitutes an unconstitutional "suspension" of the writ of habeas corpus, or whether it is outside the scope of the "suspension" clause because the detainees are technically not on American soil.

shipped to a military brig in South Carolina. The Bush administration maintained that Hamdi was an "enemy combatant" and that it could therefore detain him indefinitely, without access to counsel, and without any formal charge or proceeding.

In an eight-to-one decision (Justice Clarence Thomas was the lone dissenter), the Court held that this violated Hamdi's right to due process of law. In her plurality opinion, Justice Sandra Day O'Connor declared that "a citizen-detainee seeking to challenge his classification as an enemy combatant must receive notice of the factual basis for his classification, and a fair opportunity to rebut the Government's factual assertion before a neutral decisionmaker." O'Connor explained, "It is during our most challenging and uncertain moments that our Nation's commitment to due process is most severely tested, and it is in those times that we must preserve our commitment at home to the principles for which we fight abroad." In rejecting the government's assertion that the Court should play "a heavily circumscribed role" in reviewing the actions of the executive in wartime, O'Connor pointedly observed that "a state of war is not a blank check for the President when it comes to the rights of the Nation's citizens."*[10]

Even more troubling was the administration's position in *Rumsfeld v. Padilla*.[11] An American-born citizen, José Padilla was seized not on a battlefield, but at O'Hare Airport. Federal authorities allegedly suspected him of plotting to set off a "dirty" bomb. Instead of arresting Padilla and charging him with a crime, they hustled him off to a military brig in order to prevent him from communicating with anyone. They informed no one of his whereabouts—not his family, neighbors, coworkers, or friends—and held him incommunicado, without access to counsel or courts, and without any hearing to determine the legality of his detention, for more than *three years*.

Bush defended this action on the ground that as "commander in

*After this decision, the Bush administration released Hamdi rather than give him a hearing, on condition that he renounce his U.S. citizenship and promise to leave the country and never return.

chief" of the Army and Navy he had "inherent" constitutional authority to seize an American citizen, on American soil, and hold him incommunicado, indefinitely, without a hearing, without counsel, and without informing anyone of his whereabouts, because someone in the executive branch had decided that he was something called an "enemy combatant."

In my judgment, this is one of the most reckless assertions of executive authority in American history. The Alien Friends Act of 1798 did not authorize the detention of citizens and did not authorize secret incarceration; Lincoln's suspensions of habeas corpus granted detainees trials before military tribunals and did not involve secret detentions; and even the World War II internment was a public act that did not hold anyone incommunicado. With the wave of his hand, Bush made an American citizen *disappear*. This is the closest we have ever come to what might fairly be described as a "Gestapo-like tactic."

When the constitutionality of Padilla's detention was finally on the verge of Supreme Court review, the administration abruptly ended his forty-two-month confinement as an enemy combatant and indicted him for criminal conspiracy, on charges wholly unrelated to the alleged dirty-bomb plot. This sudden shift was clearly designed to moot Padilla's case and prevent the Court from ruling on the legality of his detention.

It is important to note that the American people learned of Padilla's detention *only* because the government slipped up in processing him by bringing him briefly into the criminal justice system, where he was assigned a lawyer. But for that slipup, José Padilla would simply have disappeared from the face of the earth. To this day, we have no way of knowing how many other American citizens, if any, remain in secret custody.

A RELATED ISSUE CONCERNS the procedures under which the United States will *criminally* prosecute those who are charged with committing terrorist acts against the United States. On November 13, 2001, President Bush issued an executive order providing that noncitizens charged with such offenses would be tried by military commissions.

Ordinarily, individuals (both citizens and noncitizens) charged with criminal offenses against the United States must be tried in federal court. The Uniform Code of Military Justice (UCMJ), however, authorizes the president to use military tribunals to prosecute members of the U.S. military for certain criminal offenses. In most respects, the UCMJ requires these tribunals to use the same rules of procedure and evidence as those used in federal court. The UCMJ also authorizes the president to use military commissions to try individuals (both citizens and noncitizens) for violations of the *laws of war*.* Military commissions have been used throughout American history for this purpose, and the Supreme Court has upheld the constitutionality of the practice.

The UCMJ provides further that, so far as is practicable, military commissions that try individuals for violating the laws of war must use the same rules of procedure and evidence that the UCMJ specifies for other military tribunals. The 2001 executive order departed from those procedures in several significant respects. Specifically, the executive order authorized the government to use against the defendant (a) classified information, without revealing such evidence to the defendant or his civilian counsel; (b) coerced confessions of the defendant, if not unreliable; and (c) hearsay evidence, if not unreliable. President Bush argued that these departures from the standards of proof used in all criminal prosecutions in federal court and all other military tribunals were justified in light of the special circumstances of the war on terrorism.

* Although there is some ambiguity about what we mean by "war" in this setting, it is reasonable to assume that those who planned and executed the September 11 attacks violated the laws of war, which have been held to apply to non-state actors in some circumstances. The UCMJ also authorizes the president to use military commissions to try individuals for crimes committed in occupied territory.

In the spring of 2006, the Supreme Court, in a five-to-three decision, held in *Hamdan v. Rumsfeld*[12] that the president had no constitutional authority to establish these military commissions. The case involved Salim Ahmed Hamdan, a Yemeni national. During the hostilities in Afghanistan, the Afghan militia captured Hamdan and turned him over to the U.S. military. In 2003, President Bush deemed Hamdan eligible to be tried by a military commission for conspiracy to participate in the commission of terrorist acts against the United States, in part because he was Osama bin Ladin's driver.

The Court in *Hamdan* explained that Congress had authorized criminal prosecutions through two and only two procedures: criminal prosecutions in federal court and military prosecutions subject to the UCMJ. Although the government could prosecute Hamdan in a military proceeding governed by the UCMJ, the military commissions established in the 2001 executive order departed without legal authority from the UCMJ. Because the procedures established for the Bush military commissions were inconsistent with those Congress had authorized, the Executive could not lawfully use them to try Hamdan. The Court conceded that Hamdan might be "a dangerous individual," but insisted that in undertaking to subject him to criminal punishment the president cannot simply make up the rules as he goes along, but must "comply with the Rule of Law."*[13]

The core principle relied upon by the Court in *Hamdan* was the constitutional separation of powers. Without deciding whether Congress and the Executive could enact *legislation* embodying some or all of the elements of the 2001 executive order, the justices made clear that the president could not unilaterally disregard the UCMJ.

In the aftermath of *Hamdan*, the Bush administration proposed new federal legislation that would essentially enact into law the 2001 executive order. The result was the Military Commissions Act of 2006. Because of objections from most Democrats and a few key

---

* The Court also held that the procedures authorized for the military commissions violated the provisions of the Geneva Conventions.

Republicans, including Senators John McCain, John Warner, and Lindsey Graham, Congress rejected the secret use of classified evidence and limited the use of the more extreme forms of interrogation, but authorized the government to use both coerced confessions and otherwise inadmissible hearsay against the defendants in these proceedings, as long as the evidence is not "unreliable."

The legislation allowing military commissions to use coerced confessions and hearsay is most unfortunate. It flies in the face not only of long-standing standards of American justice, but also of specific constitutional rights. The Fifth Amendment expressly provides that no person "shall be compelled in any criminal case to be a witness against himself." This guarantee has long been understood to mean that the United States may not constitutionally use a coerced confession against a criminal defendant. It makes no difference whether the confession is "reliable." It is easy to understand why the president wants to be able to coerce terrorists to confess. But the privilege against compelled self-incrimination has governed the trials of mass murderers, assassins, and war criminals throughout American history. There is no compelling necessity for the United States suddenly to abandon our commitment to this value.

The use of otherwise inadmissible hearsay is equally troubling. Like the 2001 executive order, the 2006 legislation was designed to enable the government to introduce into evidence *ex parte* statements made by captured enemy combatants during the course of interrogation. Suppose, for example, witness W was seized in Afghanistan, transferred to Guantánamo, and interrogated there by military officials. Suppose he made statements implicating defendant D in terrorist acts. Ordinarily, if the government wants to introduce W's statement against D, it must call W as a witness, so W will have to testify under oath, before the jury, subject to cross-examination by D's counsel. The Military Commissions Act of 2006, however, authorizes the government simply to introduce W's hearsay statement against D.

The admission of such evidence is forbidden by the federal rules of evidence and by the laws of all fifty states, and with good reason. The

2006 law sweeps aside the defendant's constitutional right to confront and cross-examine the witnesses against him, a right that has aptly been described as "the greatest legal engine ever invented for the discovery of truth." Indeed, the Sixth Amendment expressly provides that in "all criminal prosecutions, the accused shall enjoy the right . . . to be confronted with the witnesses against him."

In a 2004 opinion written by Justice Antonin Scalia, the Supreme Court held that the procedure envisioned by the Military Commissions Act of 2006 squarely violates the Sixth Amendment. In *Crawford v. Washington*,[14] Justice Scalia observed that the right to confront one's accusers dates back at least to Roman times, and that the framers of the Sixth Amendment clearly intended to forbid the admission against a criminal defendant of any such statement of a witness who does not testify at trial unless (a) he is unavailable to testify in person *and* (b) the defendant had a prior opportunity to cross-examine him.

Scalia recalled that one of the most notorious instances of procedural abuse in Anglo-American history, one with which the framers of our Constitution were intimately familiar, occurred in the 1603 trial of Sir Walter Raleigh for treason. Scalia described the incident as follows:

Lord Cobham, Raleigh's alleged accomplice, had implicated him in an examination before the Privy Council. . . . At Raleigh's trial, [Cobham's statement was] read to the jury. Raleigh argued that Cobham had lied to save himself. . . . Suspecting that Cobham would recant, Raleigh demanded that the judges call him to appear, arguing . . . "Call my accuser before my face." The judges refused and, despite Raleigh's protestations that he was being tried "by the Spanish Inquisition," the jury convicted, and Raleigh was sentenced to death. One of Raleigh's trial judges later lamented that "the justice of England has never been so degraded and injured as by the condemnation of Sir Walter Raleigh."[15]

What, though, of the possibility that such evidence might not be "unreliable"? Surely, as the Bush administration has argued, evidence that is not "unreliable" should not be inadmissible. Justice Scalia unequivocally rejected this reasoning: "Admitting statements deemed reliable by a judge is fundamentally at odds with the right of confrontation. . . . Dispensing with confrontation because testimony is obviously reliable is akin to dispensing with jury trial because a defendant is obviously guilty. This is not what the Sixth Amendment prescribes."[16]

Of course, respect for the constitutional rights of the individual will make it more difficult for us to convict accused terrorists. So, too, will the inconvenience of a trial. But if we are going to succeed in the war on terrorism, we must demonstrate to those around the world who doubt us that the United States stands for something important. We will not succeed in this struggle if we abandon our most fundamental values.

What made this legislation especially troubling is that it was enacted in haste just before the congressional recess preceding the 2006 election. In a tone reminiscent of the Federalists in 1798 and the Red baiters during the Cold War, Republican leaders unabashedly politicized a serious constitutional issue, as House Majority Leader John Boehner characterized Democrats who opposed the law as "dangerous" and Speaker of the House Dennis Hastert charged Democrats with sacrificing the national security in order "to protect the rights of terrorists."[17]

ANOTHER IMPORTANT CIVIL LIBERTIES issue in the war on terrorism concerns government surveillance. To combat espionage, sabotage, and terrorism, the nation needs information about who is planning what with whom. But in seeking this information, the government may butt up against constitutional rights. As ever, the challenge is to strike an appropriate balance between national security and individual liberty.

As we saw in Chapter VI, after the FBI's COINTELPRO came to

light in the 1970s, Attorney General Edward Levi promulgated a series of guidelines restricting the FBI's authority to investigate political and religious activities. The Levi guidelines prohibited the Bureau from investigating any group or individual on the basis of protected First Amendment activity or investigating any organization engaged in protected First Amendment activity in the absence of "specific and articulable" evidence of criminal conduct.

On May 30, 2002, Attorney General John Ashcroft effectively dismantled the Levi guidelines and once again authorized FBI agents to monitor political and religious activities without *any* showing that unlawful conduct might be afoot.[18] The most immediate implication of this change was that the Bureau was authorized for the first time in twenty-five years to spy on public political and religious activities.

Now, it may seem only sensible that federal agents should be able to attend and monitor public events in the same manner as members of the public. After all, if *you* can attend public demonstrations and religious services, why shouldn't FBI officers do so as well? But it isn't so simple. As we have seen, individuals planning to participate in an antiwar rally will be less likely to do so if they know FBI agents are taking names. Such surveillance, whether open or surreptitious, can have a deadly effect on First Amendment freedoms.

An essential reality about free speech is that individuals know that their own participation in public debate is unlikely to have an appreciable impact on national policy. Thus, if they fear that marching in a demonstration or signing a petition might land them in a government file, they may decide that the better part of wisdom is *not* to express their views. If many individuals independently make this decision, the *overall* effect might be seriously to distort the thought process of the community. Indeed, it is because of our concern with this "chilling" effect that we traditionally use secret ballots for voting. The same principle applies whenever government surveillance threatens the anonymity of free expression. By eviscerating the Levi guidelines, the Bush administration acted in direct disregard of this principle.

* * *

SECTION 215 OF THE PATRIOT Act poses a related concern. This provision authorizes government officials investigating terrorism to demand records about private individuals from businesses, hospitals, universities, libraries, and other organizations without *any* showing of probable cause or even reasonable grounds to believe that the individuals are engaged in terrorist or other unlawful acts.

At first blush, you might think this should violate the Fourth Amendment. Surely, it is an unreasonable search for the government to order your bank or hospital to disclose information about your finances or health without *any* showing of justification. But, as noted earlier, the Supreme Court has held that there is no "search" within the meaning of the Fourth Amendment if there is no "reasonable expectation of privacy." For example, if you walk down the street wearing a blue shirt, and a police officer follows you because she is investigating a crime committed by a person wearing a blue shirt, she has not "searched" you. Because you have voluntarily exposed both your shirt and your movements to public view, you have no "reasonable expectation of privacy" in this information.

What does this have to do with your bank and hospital records? Building on the logic of the blue shirt hypothetical, the Court ruled in the 1970s that you have no "reasonable expectation of privacy" in information you voluntarily expose to strangers—including employees of your bank, hospital, university, Internet provider, bookstore, and library.[19] By revealing this information to strangers, you have indicated your indifference to the privacy of the information. Hence, orders issued under Section 215 do not constitute "searches" within the meaning of the Fourth Amendment. Perhaps you find this unsettling. You should. It doesn't make much sense. But it is settled law.

As we've already seen, though, that a law doesn't violate the Fourth Amendment doesn't mean it doesn't violate the First. The issue under Section 215 with respect to libraries and bookstores is similar to that posed by government surveillance of political activities. If FBI agents can create an investigative file on you because you buy or borrow a book about terrorist practices or the history of terrorism, and you know that file might turn up sometime in the future when you apply for a government job, you might think twice before purchasing such a book or checking it out of your library.

Reasonable people can and do differ over whether the application of Section 215 to libraries and bookstores violates the First Amendment. But that is not the only question. The Constitution sets a *minimum* baseline for our liberties. It does not define their outer limits. That a practice does not violate the Constitution does not make it good public policy. We rely not only on the Constitution, but on common sense and a decent respect for the freedoms of the American people to protect our liberties. This is evident in an endless list of laws, regulations, and policies that go far beyond constitutional requirements in protecting individual rights, ranging from the Levi guidelines to the Civil Rights Act of 1964, from Congress's rejection of the "press censorship provision" in the 1917 Espionage Act to tax exemptions for religious organizations, from statutory privileges for journalists to the Voting Rights Act of 1965. Even if Section 215 is not unconstitutional, it is bad public policy—certainly, as applied to bookstores and libraries.

Although many responsible groups and individuals voiced this concern about Section 215, and although a reasonable suspicion standard for government inquiries into the reading material of American citizens would hardly cripple the war on terrorism, President Bush adamantly opposed any appreciable change in Section 215. As a result, although Congress made some changes in this provision when it reenacted the PATRIOT Act in 2006, it left its core intact. As in its repeal of the Levi guidelines, the Bush administration's intransigence failed to take seriously its responsibility to protect not only America's security, but its freedoms as well.

ANOTHER SET OF ISSUES IN THE WAR on terrorism arose out of President Bush's secret authorization of National Security Agency surveillance of international telephone calls and emails. To understand these issues, we need some context.

By the late 1960s, it was settled that, by analogy to reading mail, wiretapping telephone calls invades "reasonable expectations of privacy" and thus constitutes a "search" within the meaning of the Fourth Amendment.[20] The Supreme Court therefore held that before government officials can wiretap a phone call they first must obtain a search warrant based upon a judicial finding of probable cause.

In the early 1970s, however, the Nixon administration argued that different rules should govern *national security* investigations. Specifically, the Nixon administration maintained that in order to protect the nation from attempts to "subvert the existing structure of the government,"[21] the president must be free to wiretap in such investigations *without* obtaining a warrant.

In 1972, in *United States v. United States District Court* (the *Keith* case),[22] the Supreme Court unanimously rejected this argument. *Keith* involved a prosecution for conspiracy to blow up a CIA office. The Court held that even in national security investigations the president has no constitutional authority to wiretap American citizens on American soil without a judicially issued search warrant based on probable cause.

The Court acknowledged that the president has a constitutional responsibility to protect the nation, but cautioned that "history abundantly documents the tendency of government" to abuse its authority and "to view with suspicion those who most fervently dispute its policies."[23] Moreover, because executive branch officials are charged with keeping the nation safe, they are not "neutral and detached" arbiters in deciding whether there is probable cause to search. Thus, the Fourth Amendment requires "a prior judicial judgment" before government investigators may use "constitutionally sensitive means in pursuing their tasks."[24]

The Nixon administration maintained, however, that the "special circumstances" of national security investigations necessitate an *exception* to the warrant requirement. It contended that requiring a warrant would "obstruct the president in the discharge of his constitutional duty to protect" the nation, that courts have "neither the knowledge nor the techniques necessary to determine whether there was probable cause to believe that surveillance was necessary to protect national security," and that disclosure to a judge of the highly secret information involved in national security investigations would create a risk of leaks and "serious potential dangers to the national security." The Court rejected each of these arguments, holding that even in national security investigations the government must comply with the warrant and probable-cause requirements of the Fourth Amendment.[25]

*Keith* resolved the issue of a national security exemption from the Fourth Amendment. But the Court in *Keith* put aside, as not before it, the applicability of the Fourth Amendment to government surveillance of "foreign powers or their agents." Although the reasoning of *Keith* would seem logically to apply to foreign as well as domestic security investigations, *Keith* left the matter unresolved.

Several years later, Congress addressed this question from a legislative perspective in the Foreign Intelligence Surveillance Act of 1978 (FISA).[26] The most important legislation arising out of the surveillance abuses of the Vietnam era, FISA struck a careful balance between civil liberties and national security in the realm of foreign intelligence. In explaining the need for the act, the Senate Judiciary Committee observed that this "legislation is in large measure a response to the revelations that warrantless electronic surveillance . . . has been seriously abused."[27]

Congress expressly considered and rejected the argument that the president should be free to engage in foreign intelligence surveillance of American citizens on American soil without complying with the probable cause and warrant requirements. But because such surveillance involves unique challenges, Congress established a special court—the Foreign Intelligence Surveillance Court—to oversee foreign intelligence warrants. Congress also empowered the attorney general to authorize foreign intelligence surveillance in exceptional circumstances for a period of up to twenty-four hours *before* obtaining a warrant from the FISA court. Congress emphasized, however, that any electronic surveillance not authorized by statute is *unlawful* and that FISA set forth the *exclusive* means by which foreign intelligence surveillance could lawfully be conducted. The act was signed into law by President Jimmy Carter, who praised the legislation as necessary to protect both the national security and individual liberty.

IN JANUARY 2006, THE *NEW YORK TIMES* reported that, several months after September 11, President Bush had secretly authorized the National Security Agency to conduct foreign electronic surveillance of American citizens on American soil without probable cause and without obtaining a warrant from the FISA court.[28] This covert directive probably violated the Fourth Amendment and almost certainly violated FISA.

Although we do not know, as of this writing, the precise contours of the NSA program, Attorney General Alberto Gonzales explained shortly after its disclosure that it was directed at telephone and email communications between people inside the United States and persons outside the United States and was employed whenever the NSA had "a reasonable basis to conclude that one party to the communication is a member of al Qaeda, affiliated with al Qaeda, or a member of an organization affiliated with al Qaeda, or working in support of al Qaeda."[29] President Bush added that the program was "reviewed approximately every 45 days" by officials in the NSA and the Department of Justice to ensure it was "being properly used."[30] According to the *New York Times* reporter James Risen, by 2006 the NSA was "eavesdropping on as many as five hundred people in the United States at any given time and it potentially had access to the phone calls and emails of millions more."[31]

The Bush administration maintained that this program does not violate the Constitution because there is a "foreign intelligence exemption" from the Fourth Amendment. As we saw, in 1972 the Supreme Court unanimously rejected the Nixon administration's claim that there is a national security exemption from the Fourth Amendment, but left open the possibility of a foreign intelligence exemption. Although the reasoning of *Keith* seems logically to govern foreign intelligence as well as national security investigations, this remains an open question.[32]

But whether or not the NSA program violates the Fourth Amendment, it almost certainly violates FISA, which *expressly* prohibits such surveillance in the absence of probable cause and a warrant. Defenders of the NSA program have advanced two arguments to support their contention that the program does not violate FISA.

First, they argue that the Authorization for Use of Military Force (AUMF), which was enacted by Congress three days after 9/11 and authorized the president to use all "necessary and reasonable force" against those who had attacked the United States on 9/11, freed the president from the constraints of FISA.[33] This is implausible. Not only did the AUMF say nothing about surveillance of American citizens, but FISA expressly anticipated this situation. FISA provides that in the event of a *declaration of war* the president may disregard FISA's requirements for a period of *fifteen days*, during which he can, if necessary, propose legislation to amend FISA.[34] Because the AUMF cannot conceivably be *more* than a declaration of war, it clearly did not authorize Bush to disregard FISA for what is now almost *five years*. If the president didn't like FISA, his proper remedy was to urge Congress to change it.*

Second, defenders of the NSA program argue that FISA is unconstitutional insofar as it limits the president's inherent constitutional authority to protect the nation. Invoking Article II, Section 2 of the

---

*Indeed, in *Hamdan* the Supreme Court expressly rejected the Bush administration's argument that the AUMF implicitly authorized the president to establish military commissions that did not comply with the UCMJ: "While we assume that the AUMF activated the President's war powers, and that those powers include the authority to convene military commissions in appropriate circumstances, there is nothing in the text or legislative history of the AUMF even hinting that Congress intended to expand or alter the authorization set forth in [the] UCMJ." 128 S. Ct. 2749 (2006). Moreover, the NSA surveillance issue is even clearer in this regard, because of the specific provision in FISA dealing with declarations of war.

Constitution, which provides that the president shall be "the Commander in Chief of the Army and Navy of the United States," they maintain that the president has power to protect the national security—even if he acts in direct contravention of federal law. This, too, is unpersuasive.

The Constitution vests much, perhaps most, of the power and responsibility to protect the national security in Congress, not in the president. Article I, Section 8, for example, assigns to Congress the authority to declare war, raise and support the Army and Navy, call forth the state militias to suppress insurrections and repel invasions, make rules for the governance and regulation of the Army and Navy, and make rules concerning captures on land and sea. The suggestion that the Constitution makes the president the supreme ruler in matters of national defense is simply false. Indeed, and this is *critical*, although the Framers recognized the need for a single commander to lead the Army and Navy, they were deeply wary of granting too much authority to the president, even (perhaps especially) in wartime. They fully understood and appreciated the dangers of an overreaching executive.

Thus, as commander in chief, the president may implement a broad range of measures to protect the nation, but those measures must be constitutional, lawful, and reasonably related to protecting the national security. As the Court held in *Hamdi* and *Hamdan*, even as commander in chief, the president is not above the law. The Constitution, after all, is founded on the principle of separation of powers. As Justice Robert Jackson observed more than fifty years ago, the Constitution makes the president commander in chief of the Army and Navy, not commander in chief of the nation,[35] and as Justice Sandra Day O'Connor stressed in *Hamdi*, the commander-in-chief role does not give the president a "blank check" to run roughshod over the rule of law.

Of course, the president may take steps to learn the enemy's plans, and he may even authorize surveillance of American citizens on

American soil, but he may not do so in ways that violate either the Fourth Amendment or duly enacted laws that regulate such surveillance. As Congress noted when it enacted FISA, "even if the President has the inherent authority *in the absence of legislation* to authorize warrantless electronic surveillance for foreign intelligence purposes, Congress has the power to regulate the conduct of such surveillance by legislating a reasonable procedure, which then becomes the exclusive means by which such surveillance may be conducted."[36]

Within this framework, some matters may be so central to the role of commander in chief that they must be understood as committed *exclusively* to the president. For example, as Lincoln demonstrated in the early days of the Civil War, the president has the inherent authority to repel an invasion, without first convening Congress to seek a declaration of war. Similarly, *military* decisions, such as whether to appoint X or Y a general, whether to invade Iraq from the north or the south, or whether to send in the Army or the Marines, properly belong to the commander in chief. They are the types of command decisions with which Congress, as the general lawmaking body, ordinarily should not, and may not, meddle. But there is no reason in logic, experience, or constitutional history to suppose that the decision to institute a draft, impose taxes in order to wage a war more effectively, detain American citizens without a hearing, or wiretap American citizens on American soil should rest *exclusively* with the president.

The Supreme Court has *never* held an act of Congress unconstitutional on the theory that it impermissibly limits the president's authority as commander in chief. On several occasions, however, it has held that the commander in chief must conform his decisions to the requirements of the law. During the Half War with France, for example, the Court held unconstitutional an executive order of President John Adams ordering the seizure of ships sailing *from* France, because Congress had authorized only the seizure of ships sailing *to* France.[37]

Almost 150 years later, during the Korean War, the Court held in the *Steel Seizure* case[38] that President Harry Truman could not constitutionally seize control of steel mills that had ceased production due to a labor dispute, even though steel production was essential to the war effort. The Court emphasized that Congress had considered and declined to enact legislation that would have authorized such action by the president, and explained that whatever may be the authority of the commander in chief over "day-to-day fighting in a theater of war," measures involving the operation of the economy are the responsibility of "the Nation's lawmakers, not . . . its military authorities."[39] As Justice Jackson stated in his oft-quoted concurring opinion, "When the President takes measures incompatible with the expressed . . . will of Congress, his power is at its lowest ebb." A president's claim to such power, he added, "must be scrutinized with caution, for what is at stake is the equilibrium established by our constitutional system."[40]

The NSA spy program presents an even *weaker* case for the president than those earlier disputes, for in the NSA situation Congress expressly *prohibited* the president's action, whereas in the earlier episodes Congress had merely refused to authorize it. As we have seen, the Supreme Court held in *Hamdi* that even as commander in chief President Bush could not constitutionally detain an American citizen indefinitely without a hearing. In rejecting Bush's claim that he could unilaterally decide such matters, Justice O'Connor insisted that the Constitution "envisions a role for all three branches when individual liberties are at stake."[41] And in *Hamdan*, the Court expressly held that, even assuming the president has "independent power, absent congressional authorization, to convene military commissions," he nevertheless "may not disregard limitations that Congress has, in proper exercise of its own war powers, placed on his powers."[42]

My point is not that the president is subordinate to Congress, but that he must act in *coordination* with Congress in striking the proper balance between national security and civil liberties, and this is especially so when there is a law on the books expressly addressing the question.* If one takes seriously the Bush administration's extraordinary claims about the commander-in-chief power, then the president did not need Congress to enact the PATRIOT Act. If the president can unilaterally (and secretly) authorize the NSA to spy on American citizens, he can unilaterally (and secretly) grant himself all the authority Congress granted him in the PATRIOT Act. Under the Bush doctrine, we don't need a Congress in wartime. All we need is a commander in chief.

THE NSA CONTROVERSY POSES many intriguing questions. Perhaps most obviously, why didn't the Bush administration simply run the NSA surveillance program through the FISA court? After all, that court was designed to deal with ultrasecret foreign intelligence surveillance and it had issued warrants in response to more than 95 percent of the government's applications.

After the existence of the NSA program came to light, Attorney General Gonzales argued that because the NSA needs to act quickly it cannot take the time to obtain warrants before initiating its surveillance. This makes no sense. Only weeks before the president authorized the NSA spy program, he sought and obtained from Congress an amendment of FISA extending the time period during which foreign intelligence surveillance could proceed *without* a FISA warrant from twenty-four to seventy-two hours.[43] If even seventy-two hours was inadequate, he could certainly have sought a further amendment of FISA. But he didn't.

Frankly, it is difficult to escape the inference that the *real* reason Bush chose to circumvent the FISA court had nothing to do with

---

*The president's defenders argued that because prior presidents, including Lincoln, Wilson, and Franklin D. Roosevelt, authorized mail openings and the interception of telegraph messages, Bush could do the same. But there are important differences. First, the prior episodes preceded the widespread abuse of wartime surveillance that occurred during the Vietnam War. It was only after that experience that the nation fully recognized the dangers of such surveillance. Second, because of technological changes, the potential impact of unregulated electronic surveillance is much greater today than ever before. Third, and most important, Lincoln, Wilson, and Roosevelt acted in conformity with, rather than in contravention of, existing law.

expedition, and everything to do with probable cause. Even the FISA court cannot issue a warrant without probable cause. The NSA spy program, however, is not limited to circumstances of probable cause. According to Gonzales, the president authorized the NSA to intercept phone calls and emails whenever it has reason to believe that a party to a communication has *some* connection to al Qaeda. This is a far cry from probable cause. (It is more like wiretapping everyone in Tony Soprano's phone book or, perhaps more accurately, everyone in the phone books of everyone in Tony Soprano's phone book.) The FISA court would have dismissed such applications out of hand.

But this doesn't explain why the president didn't propose legislation to *authorize* the FISA court to issue warrants on less than probable cause. Perhaps he believed that the technology employed in the NSA spy program is so novel and so secret that any effort to authorize its use through legislation would have tipped off the terrorists and destroyed the effectiveness of the program. This seems unlikely. Terrorists undoubtedly assume that we do our best to intercept their communications. As one commentator observed, no one in the administration ever "explained why any terrorist would be so naïve as to assume that his electronic communication was impossible to intercept."[44]

Moreover, many provisions of the PATRIOT Act were subject to the same logic. For example, if terrorists know that Congress has authorized sneak-and-peek searches,* they will take precautions to avoid them. But that didn't stop the Bush administration from asking Congress to authorize such searches.

Finally, whatever secrecy surrounds the NSA program must concern the technology, not the policy question of whether the president should be authorized to engage in such surveillance. That

---

*Ordinarily, when government officers search someone's home pursuant to a warrant, they must leave notice that a search has occurred. Sneak-and-peek searches empower the government to search without immediately notifying the target that his premises have been searched. This enables the investigation to proceed without notifying the target that he is under investigation.

policy question could readily have been addressed by Congress *without* disclosing the underlying technology.

The most credible explanation for the administration's behavior was that it feared that the NSA program was over the line. Indeed, it appears that even Attorney General John Ashcroft voiced concerns about the legality of the program.[45] And after the program was publicly exposed, Ashcroft's successor, Alberto Gonzales, acknowledged that the administration had "had discussions with . . . certain members of Congress . . . as to whether or not FISA could be amended" to authorize the NSA program, but was "advised that that would be difficult, if not impossible."[46] Moreover, even if Congress had approved the program, it would surely have triggered a vigorous constitutional challenge, the outcome of which would have been uncertain. The "easier" course was for the president *secretly* to order the NSA to act. After all, if no one outside the administration knew of the program's existence, who could object?

PRESIDENT BUSH'S RESPONSE TO THE *New York Times*'s disclosure of the NSA spy program was to decry the revelation as "shameful" and to order an investigation to identify the sources of the leak.[47] This raises another question: Can the government constitutionally punish the government employees who revealed this program to the *New York Times*?

We should proceed on two alternate hypotheses. First, assume the NSA program is *lawful*, because (a) it does not violate the Fourth Amendment *and* (b) FISA violates the president's inherent constitutional authority as commander in chief. In this scenario, the government will likely prevail. Its argument is straightforward: The United States is entitled to keep secret practices, policies, and information related to the national security. Government employees have no right to override the government's judgment by deciding on their own to disclose such information to the public. In this circumstance, the government will analogize the NSA situation to one in which the government breaks the enemy's secret code and a government employee leaks that information to the public and, hence, the enemy.

Second, if the NSA program is *unlawful*, because (a) it violates the Fourth Amendment *or* (b) it violates FISA and FISA does not violate the president's authority as commander in chief, then the terminology changes. The sources are no longer "leakers" but "whistleblowers." In this scenario, the sources are on stronger ground. In general, the government should not be able to punish its employees for disclosing its own *wrongdoing*. The government is, after all, accountable to the public. In a self-governing society, citizens need to know when their representatives violate the law.

The government will argue, however, that public employees should *never* disclose classified programs, practices, or information to the public, even if they believe them to be unlawful. Well-intentioned whistleblowers might be wrong in their assessment of a program's legality, and by leaking the information they might seriously damage the national security. The government will maintain that in dealing with *classified* information government employees must err on the side of protecting the national security, and that the sources of the NSA disclosure must therefore be punished, even if the program is unlawful. Only in this way, they will argue, can the government effectively deter future leakers from playing craps with the national security.

From a constitutional standpoint, this is unexplored terrain. In my judgment, the whistleblowers should prevail on this issue if the NSA program is unlawful. In terms of deterrence, it should be sufficient for the government to punish those who disclose classified programs that are *not* unlawful. When the program is in fact unlawful, the public's need to know outweighs the government's interest in secrecy.

An intermediate position might allow the government to punish those who disclose even unlawful programs if (a) the whistleblowers knew or should have known that the government regards the program as critical to the national security and that disclosure would seriously undermine the national security, *and* (b) there were reasonable procedures in place through which the sources could have questioned the legality of the program, without going to the press, and they failed to use those procedures.* If such procedures exist and the government employee complies with them, he should not be punishable for then disclosing an *unlawful* program.

A RELATED QUESTION IS WHETHER the government can constitutionally punish the *New York Times* for publishing the NSA information.‡ Senator Jim Bunning and Congressman Peter King accused the *Times* of "treason," and Republicans in the House of Representatives passed a resolution condemning the *Times* for "putting the lives of Americans in danger." Although no newspaper has *ever* been criminally prosecuted for publishing information about the activities of the federal government, the Bush administration expressly raised the specter of such a prosecution. Attorney General Gonzales and some of the administration's supporters argued that in publishing this story the *New York Times* and its reporters violated a provision of the 1917 Espionage Act, which provides in part that anyone in unauthorized possession "of information relating to the national defense, which information the possessor has reason to believe could be used to the injury of the United States," who willfully communicates it to any person not entitled to receive it, "shall be fined under this title or imprisoned not more than 10 years, or both."[48]

For at least three reasons, such threats are largely empty. First,

*The Intelligence Community Whistleblower Protection Act of 1998 sets forth a limited mechanism to enable whistleblowers dealing with classified information to raise their concerns with agency officials or members of congressional oversight committees. The act covers whistleblowers who want to report (1) a serious abuse or violation of law; (2) a false statement to, or willful withholding of information from, Congress; or (3) a reprisal in response to an employee's reporting of an urgent matter.

‡The Bush administration has also threatened to prosecute the *Washington Post* for its disclosure of the government's secret detention camps for enemy combatants in Eastern Europe. See Dana Priest, *CIA Holds Terror Suspects in Secret Prisons*, Washington Post A1 (Nov 2, 2005). It is noteworthy that both the *New York Times* and the *Washington Post* won the Pulitzer Prize for journalism for publishing these stories. It is also noteworthy that the *New York Times* sat on the NSA surveillance story for a year before finally publishing it, at the request of the Bush administration.

this provision was never intended to be used against the press. As we saw in Chapter III, when the Espionage Act was proposed by Woodrow Wilson, it included the "press censorship" section that would expressly have made it a crime for the press to publish information that the president had declared to be "of such character that it is or might be useful to the enemy." Congress overwhelmingly rejected that proposal, with members of both parties characterizing it as "un-American" and "an instrument of tyranny."

Second, if the Espionage Act had been intended to apply to journalists, it would violate the First Amendment. Laws regulating speech must be precisely tailored to prohibit only speech that may constitutionally be proscribed. This requirement addresses the concern that overbroad laws will chill the willingness of individuals to speak freely. Because the Espionage Act was enacted in 1917—before the Supreme Court had interpreted the First Amendment—it does not incorporate *any* of the safeguards the Court has since held the Constitution requires. For example, the provision is not limited only to published accounts that pose a "clear and present danger" of serious harm to the nation. For this reason, any prosecution of the press under this section should be dismissed out of hand by the judiciary.

Third, if Congress today enacted legislation that incorporated the requirements of the First Amendment, it could not constitutionally apply to articles like those published by the *New York Times* about the NSA surveillance program. Such a statute would have to be limited to articles that, first, do not disclose information of legitimate public interest and, second, pose a clear and present danger. Nobody could seriously deny that the legality of secret NSA surveillance of American citizens on American soil is a matter of legitimate public interest. Moreover, the Bush administration has made no credible showing that the disclosure of this program created a clear and present danger of serious harm to the national security.

Indeed, the Bush administration knew full well that the *Times* was aware of the NSA surveillance program for many months *before* the *Times* published the story. If the danger of disclosure was truly "clear," "present," and "grave," why didn't the administration seek an injunction against publication? Certainly, as in the *Pentagon Papers* case more than thirty-five years earlier, the *Times* would have withheld publication in the face of such an injunction. Moreover, as in the *Pentagon Papers* case, the government could have litigated an injunction without revealing to the public the secret information at issue. But in all the time the Bush administration knew that the *Times* was considering publication, it did not seek an injunction against publication.

The reason seems obvious. The lawyers in the administration *knew* they could not prove a danger sufficiently "clear," "present," and "grave" to justify an injunction. Rather than test the matter in a court of law, the administration sat on its hands and allowed the story to be published. Then, after the fact, it accused the *Times* of disloyalty and embarked on a campaign to intimidate the press with threats of a criminal prosecution.

I don't mean to suggest that the government has no interest in keeping military secrets or that it may never punish the press for publishing classified information.* To the contrary, the government may take many steps to keep such information secret, including (in appropriate circumstances) firing and even prosecuting public employees who unlawfully leak such information. Moreover, in narrowly defined circumstances, the government can constitutionally punish the press for disclosing classified national security information. Such a prosecution might be consistent with the First Amendment, for example, if a newspaper revealed that the government had secretly broken an important al Qaeda code, thus causing that group to change its cipher. But the *New York Times*'s revelation of the NSA spy

---

*A factor that seriously complicates these situations is the *overuse* of classification. If programs or documents were classified only when their disclosure would truly be harmful to the national security, then classification might be a useful proxy for serious danger. Unfortunately, the process of classification is inadequately regulated and government officials tend to resolve doubt by overclassification. As a consequence, government officials routinely leak classified information when it serves their partisan purposes, and the mere fact of classification therefore cannot serve as a useful measure of whether publication would seriously harm the national interest.

program disclosed potentially serious government wrongdoing. Such revelations are essential to effective self-governance and are at the very core of the First Amendment.

UP TO THIS POINT, WE HAVE focused on whether the NSA surveillance program was lawful. But there is another question: *Should* it be lawful? Perhaps we should amend FISA to authorize the program and interpret the Fourth Amendment to recognize a "foreign terrorist exemption." Why should anyone care that the NSA spies on Americans in this manner? If you're not a terrorist, what difference does it make that the NSA may be monitoring your phone calls and reading your emails?

This is not a rhetorical question. In the eighteenth century, when the Framers recognized the "right of the people to be secure in their persons, houses, papers, and effects against unreasonable searches," a "search" was a physical invasion of one's person or property. It was, by definition, disruptive, humiliating, and invasive of private property. With the advent of electronic bugging and wiretapping, courts found themselves in a quandary. Electronic surveillance can be undertaken in secret, so it is neither disruptive nor humiliating. And because it can be implemented without entering your house or seizing your effects, it needn't implicate your property rights.

For these reasons, the Supreme Court held for forty years that electronic surveillance did *not* constitute a "search" within the meaning of the Fourth Amendment.[49] Unlike traditional searches, the government could therefore use such surveillance without complying with the probable cause and warrant requirements.

It wasn't until 1967 that the Court finally held that the Fourth Amendment protects "the right of the people to be secure" not only against disruption, humiliation, and invasion of their property rights, but also against pure invasions of *privacy*, even if the other three factors are absent.[50] This was a huge leap.* In effect, the Court

---

*The closest historical analogy was the reading of private mail while in transit, which was clearly regarded as a "search." But in the mail situation it could be argued that either the sender or the recipient, or both, had a property right in the tangible object.

held that a wiretap, in which a government official surreptitiously listens to a telephone call by splicing into the telephone company's line, constitutes a "search" within the meaning of the Fourth Amendment, and that such a search is constitutionally permissible only if the government first secures a warrant based upon a judicial finding of probable cause.

The debate over NSA spying has caused some people to wonder, "What's the big deal about electronic surveillance, anyway?" After all, if the government surreptitiously listens to your phone calls or reads your emails, you're not disturbed, you're not humiliated, and there's no interference with your property. Indeed, you may not even be aware it's happening. If you haven't done anything wrong, and have nothing to hide, why should you care? Perhaps the Court shouldn't have extended the Fourth Amendment to electronic surveillance.

The response, of course, is that we value our privacy. But *why*? Even if a government official (or a government computer) learns who you're dating or what movie you saw last week, the government has no interest in such mundane matters. Such stuff is just the miscellaneous debris the government has to wade through in order to find what it's looking for—terrorists. So, even if all the other stuff gets heard, read, and recorded, why should you care? It's not enough to say, "It invades my privacy." You have to explain why that *matters*.

Here are three possible answers. If they're not persuasive, perhaps we shouldn't fret about NSA spying or, indeed, about electronic surveillance generally. First, perhaps privacy matters because it is important for you to be free to lead your life without the government constantly peering over your shoulder. This is a point about the ordinariness of life. Perhaps being watched, and knowing you're being watched, undermines your *sense* of freedom. Perhaps being free means knowing you're not being watched by the government, without a good reason.

But why would you *care* about being watched if you're not a criminal and the only thing the watchers care about is whether you are? If you're engaging in unlawful acts, then you have no right to hide your illegal behavior, and if you're not engaging in unlawful acts, then you have nothing to fear from surveillance.

This brings me to my second answer. Perhaps we shouldn't be so quick to assume that the only thing the watchers care about is criminal acts. Once the government gathers information about you (for example, what you read, who your friends are, what organizations you join), it then has the *capacity* to use that information in ways that have nothing to do with terrorists. Certainly, we have seen this throughout our history. As the Supreme Court cautioned in *Keith*, "history abundantly documents the tendency of government" to abuse its authority and "to view with suspicion those who most fervently dispute its policies." Information is power, and power can (and usually will) be abused. Perhaps freedom includes the ability to take risks, make mistakes, and even occasionally step out of line without being called to account. Imagine if every phone call and every email were permanently preserved in a government database that could be accessed at any time by those who will decide, perhaps many years from now, whether to hire you for a government job, oppose you for elective office, allow you to practice law, or audit your taxes. Might the knowledge that such information is being collected and stored affect even your lawful behavior?

Third, maybe privacy matters because in a self-governing society we must vigilantly reinforce the sense of independence of the individual. For a self-governing society to function, citizens must feel they are the *governors*, not the subjects. It may be difficult to feel like the governor when your government monitors your every move. Perhaps limiting government surveillance is essential to democracy itself. Certainly, life in the former Soviet Union, with its pervasive government surveillance, illustrates how such monitoring can crush the openness, the spontaneity, and the life out of a society. If we do that to ourselves, perhaps we will be worse than the terrorists.

TO SAY THAT THE NSA SURVEILLANCE program is unlawful and possibly unconstitutional does not mean that there might not be some means to enable our government effectively to protect us through electronic surveillance. Post-September 11, we face a challenge that is unique in American history. It is a challenge we must confront realistically. For the first time in our national experience, a small group of state-less individuals has both the willingness and the capacity (either now or in the not-too-distant future) to use chemical, biological, nuclear, or other weapons to kill thousands, perhaps tens or even hundreds of thousands, of Americans.

Although the magnitude of this danger pales in comparison to the danger posed by the Soviet Union at the height of the Cold War, there is a critical difference: The Soviets (and we) could be deterred from using our weapons. Once both sides developed massive arsenals that could not be destroyed in a "first strike," the policy of Mutually Assured Destruction ("MAD") effectively ensured that neither side would attack the other. In the current situation, however, given the nature and beliefs of the "enemy," we appear for the moment to have no realistic ability to deter further attacks. Prevention, therefore, is essential.

There are many ways to pursue prevention. But because effective prevention in this setting requires us to search constantly for the proverbial "needle in a haystack," information is critical. That inevitably leads us back to surveillance. One way to protect ourselves against further terrorist attacks is to find the terrorists and disrupt their plans *before* they can act. This is presumably the goal of the President's NSA surveillance program. It is not the goal of the program that is problematic, but the way the program was put into place and the means by which it pursues the goal. Even if the program had been authorized by Congress, it would be problematic because it enables the government to monitor the communications of American citizens without either a warrant or probable cause to believe that a participant in the communication is hatching a terrorist plot. Such monitoring invades the privacy of potentially vast numbers of individuals who have done nothing wrong, risks government misuse of the information obtained, chills the openness of communication, places government in the position of "Big Brother," undermines the sense of individual autonomy that is essential to self-governance, and grants the Executive vast power to implement surveillance without judicial and congressional oversight.

Is it possible to envision a policy that might enable the government to engage in some variation of this sort of surveillance and at the same time satisfy legitimate civil libertarian concerns? In his recent book, *Not a Suicide Pact*, Judge Richard Posner offers an interesting suggestion: "Suppose that the National Security Agency's listening devices gathered the entire world's electronic communications traffic, digitized it, and stored it in databases, where it was machine-searched for clues to terrorist activity, but the search programs were designed to hide from intelligence officers all data that contained no clues to terrorist plans or activity."[51] Might it be possible to embrace some more limited version of this proposal? Suppose, for example, the NSA were authorized by legislation to intercept (in the sense described by Judge Posner) any international electronic communication for which it has reasonable grounds to believe that a participant in the communication may be associated with a terrorist organization. (The terms, of course, would need to be defined.) All such information would be digitized and stored (for a limited period of time, after which it would be destroyed), but could not be examined by any intelligence officer without probable cause. Probable cause could be determined either in the conventional manner (with a warrant from the FISA court) or through the use of an algorithm that enables computers that search the database to determine probable cause based on words, phrases, personal connections, etc. In a sense, this is like a drug-sniffing dog, where the algorithm is the dog.

It is easy to imagine such algorithms. For example, it would be quite possible (I would imagine) to develop an algorithm that would determine based on the content and nature of messages whether there is probable cause to believe that a particular individual is a lawyer, or a doctor, or a psychotherapist. (How often does she use phrases like "*res ipsa loquitur*," "malpractice insurance," or "borderline personality"?) Presumably, it would also be possible to develop an algorithm for terrorists. The FISA court would have review and approve or disapprove the use of such algorithms after hearing expert testimony. Moreover, such a program could be designed to reduce the risks of abuse by forbidding the government to use the information other than for national security purposes and by requiring periodic reports to the FISA court, congressional watchdog committees, departmental inspectors general, and neutral agencies such as the General Accountability Office.

Such a program might both substantially increase the ability of the government to identify terrorists (relative to a conventional probable cause regime) and substantially reduce the dangers of invasion of privacy and government abuse (relative to the NSA surveillance program). For many reasons, such a program may prove infeasible, but it is worth considering.*

AS REFLECTED IN THE NSA CONTROVERSY, another issue arising out of the war on terrorism concerns the unprecedented secrecy of the Bush

---

* Judge Posner rejects two of the safeguards I suggest—limiting the program to international communications and insisting on "reasonable suspicion" for the initial monitoring:

> If two terrorists inside the United States communicate with each other, the interest in intercepting their communications is as great as when one of them is overseas. And, as important, it is not possible to discover who the terrorists are if before intercepting their communications you must have reasonable grounds to believe that at least one party to a communication is a terrorist. What I think national security requires is a two-stage process. In the first, computer search programs search the world's entire daily electronic traffic (to the extent feasible) for messages that are suspicious because of names or word clusters in the message, social security numbers or other personal identifying information besides names, the origin or destination of the message, and other suspicious characteristics. These messages, a minute fraction of all those screened by the search programs, would be listened to or read (as the case may be) by (human) intelligence officers. Computer screening is not a search, because a computer is not sentient. But listening to or reading private messages is, and . . . a properly configured search program might be sufficiently reliable to furnish reasonable suspicion or probable cause to read a message flagged by the computer program.

See http://uchicagolaw.typepad.com/faculty/2006/09/not_a_suicide_p_1.html.

administration. Overbroad government assertions of secrecy cripple informed public debate. It is impossible for citizens responsibly to consider the merits of public policy decisions if they are kept in the dark about the actions of their elected officials. As Senator Daniel Patrick Moynihan once observed, "secrecy is the ultimate form of regulation because people don't even know they are being regulated."[52]

Excessive secrecy has been a consistent and disturbing theme of the Bush administration, including its refusal to disclose the names of those it detained after September 11, its crabbed interpretation of the Freedom of Information Act,* its decision to close deportation proceedings from public scrutiny, its redaction of vast quantities of "sensitive" information from tens of thousands of government documents and Web sites, its secret NSA surveillance program, and its creation of secret prisons in Eastern Europe for alleged terrorists.[53]

Some measure of secrecy is, of course, essential to the effective functioning of government, especially in wartime. But the Bush administration's obsessive secrecy has constrained meaningful oversight by Congress, the press, and the public, directly undermining the vitality of democratic governance. As the legal scholar Stephen Schulhofer has noted, one cannot escape the inference that the cloak of secrecy imposed by the Bush administration has "less to do with the war on terrorism" than with its desire "to insulate executive action from public scrutiny."[54] Such an approach to governance weakens our democratic institutions and renders "the country less secure in the long run."[55]

THERE ARE THOSE WHO SAY that the war on terrorism has led to the most repressive period in American history. Those who say this know nothing of American history. Some of the measures enacted by the Bush administration are highly problematic. Some, such as the government's extraordinary assertion of authority over José Padilla, are

---

*Enacted in 1966, the Freedom of Information Act (FOIA), 5 U.S.C. § 552, establishes the public's right to obtain information from federal government agencies.

shocking. But, on the whole, it is important to recognize that there has been no suspension of the writ of habeas corpus, no mass internment of American Muslims, no broadside effort to prohibit criticism of the war, and no "witch hunt" to ferret out al Qaeda sympathizers in the United States. Perhaps it is too low a bar to boast that we haven't done those things. But those are the things we've done in the past. That we haven't done them in the present is a real measure of progress.

This is not to say, of course, that all is well. Many of the Bush administration's restrictions of civil liberties—such as the NSA surveillance program, the evisceration of the Levi guidelines, and the detention of both noncitizens and citizens without meeting the demands of due process—must be condemned as unnecessary, excessive, and dangerous to a free society. An important lesson of the war on terrorism is that a critical way to preserve our civil liberties is to fiercely contest even *modest* restrictions as they arise. Determining where the battle lines are drawn is half the battle. This is an *essential* strategy for those who hope to forestall a repeat of the worst abuses of the past.

One final aspect of the war on terrorism requires attention, though it is largely beyond the purview of *War and Liberty*. In the international arena, where American civil liberties have little reach, the Bush administration has frequently acted in flagrant disregard of both international law and a decent respect for human rights. By authorizing secret prisons, abusive interrogation techniques, and rendition; by treating the detainees in Guantánamo Bay as "unlawful combatants" rather than as prisoners of war (even though there may be a *technical* rationale for doing so); and by disregarding the most elemental demands of due process, President Bush has betrayed American values and failed to convey to the world our commitment to the "human decencies" for which we say we are fighting.[56] This is not only a missed opportunity, but a tragic failure of leadership in a struggle that may be more about moral values than military power.

CONCLUSION

# A Culture of Civil Liberties

✤

A S Justice Robert Jackson observed more than half a century
ago, "it is easy, by giving way to passion, intolerance and suspicions of wartime, to reduce our liberties to a shadow, often in
answer to exaggerated claims of security."[1] As we have seen, the
United States has a long and unfortunate history of overreacting to
the dangers of wartime. Time and again, we have allowed fear to
get the better of us. Some measure of fear, of course, is inevitable—
even healthy—in time of war. Without fear, it would be difficult for
a nation to make the sacrifices war demands. An essential challenge to democracy is to channel fear so it plays a constructive
rather than a destructive role.

The central thesis of *War and Liberty* is that although each of these
episodes presented a distinct challenge, in each we went too far in
restricting our liberties. Of course, this cannot be proved with the
exactitude of a mathematical formula. As with any counterfactual,
we cannot know for certain what would have happened if Lincoln
had not suspended the writ of habeas corpus, Wilson had not prosecuted those who protested World War I, or McCarthy had not raged
against Communist subversion. Perhaps the Confederate States of
America would still be with us; perhaps we would have lost World
War I; perhaps the Berlin Wall would still be standing. Perhaps. But it

is difficult to believe, with the benefit of hindsight, and with a deeper understanding of these events, that any of these consequences would have resulted.

Certainly, we know that in the first six of these episodes the nation came, after the fact, to regret its actions. These after-the-fact judgments should not be controversial. They are sound conclusions based on comprehensive information about the actions and motives of the participants. Indeed, it should hardly surprise us that a nation swept up in war fever would lose its sense of composure. The fear, anger, and patriotism engendered during a war inevitably undermine the capacity of individuals and institutions to make clearheaded judgments about risk, fairness, and danger. We all know this as a matter of personal experience. It is difficult to make calm, balanced decisions in a state of personal anxiety, outrage, or passion.

The challenge of remaining levelheaded is even greater at the national than the individual level, for as the powerful emotions triggered by war cascade through a community, they grow ever more intense. Suspicion feeds suspicion; fear breeds fear. We see spies and saboteurs around every corner; rumors run rampant. As the political scientist John Keane has observed, "fear eats the soul of democracy."[2] After World War I, Judge Charles Amidon recalled that in Espionage Act prosecutions otherwise "sober, intelligent" men serving as jurors responded "with the savagery of wild animals."[3] Terms like "contagion" aptly capture the phenomenon.

Moreover, as we grow fearful, we naturally insist that our leaders protect us, and elected officials, often distressed themselves, quickly respond. It is logical to seek safety in the face of danger, especially when we can mitigate the threat to ourselves by disadvantaging others. This enables us both to secure our own safety and vent our anger at those we may already loathe. If we have to put some secessionists or anarchists or Japs or Reds in jail in order to increase our sense of security, so be it. Indeed, all the better. This is not theory. It is the unimpeachable lesson of history.

In light of the inevitable pressures of wartime, is there anything we can do to prevent the recurrence of such excesses in the future? Are we doomed to repeat this pattern over and over again?

BEFORE ADDRESSING THAT QUESTION, I would like to pose two preliminary issues. First, does the fear created in wartime in fact cause us to *overreact*? Fear is an appropriate response to danger. It can sharpen our focus, draw attention to prior misjudgments (perhaps we failed to protect ourselves adequately against the risk of attack before Pearl Harbor and/or 9/11), and enable us to protect ourselves better in the future. But we are concerned here not with fear in that limited sense, but with fear that runs out of control and that impairs rather than informs sound decision making.

Even in its most instinctive form, fear is risk averse. We are more likely to flee from a shadow that may be an attacker than to move closer to determine whether it is in fact an attacker. This is a natural and sensible response. The risk of harm to us of being "wrong" if we flee is much less than the risk of harm of being "wrong" if we inspect. What concerns us here, however, is *excessive* fear—fear that is pathological and leads to irrational decisions—decisions that would *not* be made by individuals with equal knowledge in a state of calm.

Faced with the dilemma of the shadow, we would all endorse the decision to flee, even if we were evaluating the dilemma from a distance. But the decisions to adopt the Sedition Act of 1918, or the Japanese internment, or the McCarran Internal Security Act of 1950 were *not* decisions we would ratify in a state of calm. They were severe *overreactions* based on exaggerated and ill-informed fear.

Second, how seriously should we take these wartime restrictions of civil liberties? Even if we have overreacted, is this an important mistake, or is it merely an incidental consequence of the grand sweep of war? Civil libertarians often argue that once constitutional rights are compromised, they are lost forever. If that were true, it would surely be a compelling reason to avoid *any* unnecessary limitation of our freedoms. If rights, once lost, are never regained, then civil liberties would be in a permanent downward spiral. But that is not the case. In fact, after each of the first six of these episodes (we cannot yet judge the war on terrorism), the nation's commitment to civil liberties rebounded, usually rather quickly, sometimes more robustly than before. In that sense, then, the worst-case scenario—that rights once lost are not regained—has not come to pass. As long as wars are reasonably time-bound, this phenomenon *lessens* the long-term dangers of limiting our freedoms in wartime.

But this does not mean that wartime deprivations of civil liberties are unimportant. For government unjustifiably to deny an individual her freedom—whether freedom of speech, freedom of religion, or freedom from detention—for a year, or several years, is a matter of moment both to the individual and to the nation. For government to tell an individual she may not oppose a war or leave an internment camp is a serious intrusion on individual liberty.

It is often argued, however, that given the sacrifices we ask citizens (especially soldiers) to make in time of war, it is a small price to ask others to surrender some part of their peacetime liberties to help win a war. As the Supreme Court argued in *Korematsu*, "hardships are part of war, and war is an aggregation of hardships."[4] This is a seductive but dangerous argument. To fight a war successfully, it is necessary for soldiers to risk their lives. But it is not necessarily "necessary" for others to surrender their freedoms. That necessity must be demonstrated, not merely presumed. And this is especially true when, as is almost always the case, the individuals whose rights are sacrificed are not those who make the laws, but minorities, dissenters, and noncitizens. In those circumstances, "we" are making a decision to sacrifice "their" rights—not a very prudent way to balance the competing interests.

This argument is particularly misguided when the freedom of speech is at issue. A critical function of free speech in wartime is to help the nation make wise decisions about how to conduct the war, whether our leaders are leading well, whether to end the war, and so on. If free speech is essential to self-governance in ordinary times, it is even more critical when citizens must decide whether to let the South secede, withdraw our troops from Vietnam, or commit additional troops to Iraq. Those questions *cannot* be put in suspension during a war.

The nation's commitment to the freedom of speech is not only about the personal liberties of those who are silenced; it is also about the operation of democracy itself. To the extent government silences dissent, in wartime or otherwise, it warps the thinking process of the community and undermines self-government. Free and open debate can help save the nation from tragic blunders and crippling pathologies. Thus, even though wartime restraints of free speech may be time-bound and may not carry over once peace is restored, they can have profound implications both for the individual and for the nation during the crisis itself.

So, CAN WE DO BETTER? SURELY, YES. For one thing, despite the fear that has swept the nation in these periods, *some* individuals managed to maintain a sense of perspective and recognized that the demand to abandon civil liberties was unwarranted. Examples include, among many others, Congressman Albert Gallatin in 1798; Judge Hand during World War I; Attorney General Biddle during World War II; Joseph Welch and Senator Herbert Lehman during the Cold War; Justices Black and Douglas in *Dennis*; and so on. If these individuals could see clearly despite the fog of war, others can as well.

Moreover, although *War and Liberty* focuses on instances in which we succumbed to wartime hysteria, those examples do not tell the whole story. Many proposals for the suppression of civil liberties were rejected during these eras, because individuals in positions of authority understood them to be unwise. For example, as oppressive as the Sedition Act of 1798 may have been, it was less severe than other proposals Congress rejected at the time. Similarly, Congress enacted a significantly less restrictive version of the Espionage Act of 1917 than that proposed by Woodrow Wilson. And although Wilson was prepared to go quite far in suppressing dissent, he rejected calls to suspend the writ of habeas corpus. Ultimately, it is a matter of degree. For the nation to "do better" does not mean that we will strike the "perfect" balance between liberty and security, but that we will be less quick to abandon liberty than we have been in the past.

I am also confident we can do better in the future because we have made progress in the past. Of course, such progress is impossible to prove with certainty. Each situation is distinct, and no one can confidently predict that the United States will never reenact some version of the Sedition Act of 1798 or undergo another era like the period of McCarthyism. Indeed, if the United States had been hit with six terrorist attacks on the scale of September 11 within a single month in 2001, who knows what measures we might have embraced?

Nonetheless, I am confident that the major restrictions of civil liberties discussed in *War and Liberty* would be *less* thinkable today than they were in 1798, 1861, 1917, 1942, 1950, or 1969. In terms of both the evolution of constitutional doctrine and the development of a national consciousness about civil liberties, we have made demonstrable progress. In the past, the United States imprisoned such national leaders as Matthew Lyon, Clement Vallandigham, and Eugene Debs for criticizing a war. But in 2004 it was inconceivable that the Bush administration would prosecute Howard Dean, even though his criticisms of the war in Iraq were every bit as inflammatory as the criticisms of Lyon, Vallandigham, and Debs. This is a profound and hard-bought achievement. We should neither take it for granted, nor underestimate its significance. It is a testament to the strength of American democracy.

How, THEN, DO WE GET IT "right" in the future? The most daunting obstacle to a more measured response is that by the time we realize we are in the midst of a crisis, it may already be too late. As in other contexts, the time to prepare for a crisis is *before* rather than after it strikes.

A critical determinant of how our nation responds to the stresses of wartime is the attitude of the public. Citizens in a self-governing society are responsible for their own actions and the actions of their government. They cannot expect public officials to act calmly and judiciously without regard to their own response. As Judge Learned Hand reflected in 1944:

> I often wonder whether we do not rest our hopes too much upon constitutions, upon laws and upon courts. These are false hopes; believe me, these are false hopes. Liberty lies in the hearts of men and women; when it dies there, no constitution, no law, no court can save it.[5]

In some of these episodes, the public responded remarkably well. In 1800, Americans voted the Federalists out of power. The election of Thomas Jefferson and the demise of the Federalist Party were, in no small part, a direct rebuke to the Federalists for the Sedition Act of 1798. Similarly, during the Civil War many Republicans raised their voices against the more egregious attempts of military commanders to suppress the Copperhead opposition. One of the most impressive features of the controversy over Clement Vallandigham's arrest and banishment was that Republicans as well as Democrats condemned the government's actions. More recently, public objections during the war on terrorism put a halt to TIPS, TIA, PATRIOT Act II, and efforts of the Bush administration to use extreme methods of "interrogation."

More often, however, the public has either failed to protest the suppression of civil liberties or vociferously demanded it. In World War I and the Cold War, for example, most members of the public were either swept up in the frenzy or, at the very least, cowed into submission. With few exceptions, even the traditional bulwarks of civil liberties—the legal profession, higher education, the press, and civil libertarians—were unwilling to confront the storm of public accusation and condemnation. Fearful of losing clients, contributions, subscribers, votes, status, respect, and employment, even those who should have known better bowed to the fearsome pressure to be "loyal."

Because the protection of liberty ultimately "lies in the hearts of men and women," it is essential for citizens to understand and internalize the value of civil liberties. They must appreciate why those liberties matter, and why *they* must protect them. They must understand that in wartime even well-meaning individuals can be swept along by the mentality of the mob.

Of course, it is not easy to resist the temptation to restrict civil liberties. Such actions make us feel safer—indeed, may make us safer. To withstand the perils of war fever, a nation needs not only the legal protection of civil liberties, but a *culture of civil liberties*. We can see this clearly in Iraq. When we attempt to install democracy in Iraq, we must not only provide voting booths, but we must also instill a new set of attitudes and values that make self-governance possible. In our own nation, this is a constant process. The preservation of liberty requires citizens to rise above their most basic instincts. This must be learned and then relearned with each generation.

To the extent the United States has made progress over time, it is largely because we have come increasingly to celebrate and take pride in our commitment to civil liberties. Inspired by such events as America's role in World War II, the Supreme Court's 1954 decision holding racial segregation unconstitutional, and the achievements of the civil rights movement, Americans have embraced an almost romantic vision of what makes our nation unique. Although there are continuing disagreements over such issues as abortion, pornography, and same-sex marriage, the aspiration of Americans to be fair, tolerant of others, and respectful of constitutional liberties may be more deeply embedded in our culture today than at any time in our history.

Educational institutions, government agencies, foundations, the media, the legal profession, and civil liberties organizations can all help cultivate an environment in which citizens are more open-minded, skeptical, critical of their political leaders, tolerant of dissent, and protective of the freedoms of *all* individuals. Above all, as Judge Hand observed, the "spirit of liberty is the spirit which is not too sure that it is right."[6] These are values and capacities that can be learned, ingrained, and exercised over time. The task is ultimately "an educational one."[7]

One of the greatest threats to the continuing affirmation and evolution of a culture of civil liberties in the United States is the modern day McCarthys of the media whose often irresponsible rants appeal to the worst rather than the best in the American people. The Bill O'Reillys, Rush Limbaughs, and Ann Coulters of the current generation debase public discourse and endanger democratic values. That they have a right to speak their piece goes without saying. The challenge for Americans is to be sufficiently thoughtful, informed, and discerning to separate the wheat from the chaff.*

ALTHOUGH THE PERSPECTIVE and disposition of the public are critical in determining the nation's response to wartime, it eventually falls to the federal government to enact and enforce laws, implement poli-

---

* In December 2005, I had a run-in with O'Reilly that illustrates the concern. I was invited to appear on his cable television show *The O'Reilly Factor* to debate the question: "Is dissent disloyal." After the producer and I discussed the issue, O'Reilly (according to the producer) decided to redefine the question: "Can an American who wants the United States to lose the war in Iraq be patriotic?" This is, of course, a loaded question. It implies that those who oppose the war in Iraq want the United States to lose and, worse, want American soldiers to die (as O'Reilly later actually charged). Accepting his rather peculiar framing of the question (it is, after all, his show), I argued that a patriotic citizen could in principle want his nation to lose a war—if the war is unjust and if "losing" means that fewer soldiers and civilians will die for no good reason. For example, patriotic Italians in World War II could well have hoped Italy would lose the war, the quicker, the better.

To cover the weakness of his position, O'Reilly began spewing such ugly invectives as "despicable," "traitor," and "disloyal" (not at me, but at those he imagined might want the United States to lose the war in Iraq). His evident purpose was to inflame his audience against this imaginary enemy. What is the consequence of such demagoguery? As always, it is to foster rage rather than reflection. After the show, I was inundated with emails capturing the anger I believe O'Reilly deliberately incited. The emails charged that I was "un-American" and fumed that I should "be convicted of treason," "move out of the U.S.A.," and watch out for GIs who might "take the law into their own hands." By inciting such rage, O'Reilly and others like him dishonor their profession. This is not democratic deliberation. It is dividing Americans against Americans just for the sport of it. For political "commentators" to exploit people's fears in a time of war for nothing more than their own ratings is a pretty good definition of "unpatriotic."

cies, and interpret the Constitution. How well have the three branches of government fulfilled these responsibilities, and how can they do better in the future?

Over the years, Congress has enacted the Sedition Act of 1798, the Sedition Act of 1918, and the McCarran Internal Security Act of 1950. This is a questionable record of legislative achievement. On the other hand, as we have seen, Congress has not reflexively enacted every piece of repressive legislation ever proposed. To the contrary, Congress is quite capable of exercising restraint. Too often, however, it has either failed to exercise a check on public demands or moved beyond anything the public demanded.

This is understandable. Congressmen are not invulnerable to stampeding fear. They, too, may panic in the face of a crisis. Moreover, and apart from their own emotions, elected officials are by nature responsive to the wants of voters and are likely to act quickly and decisively when citizens are in a state of panic. Indeed, once fear overwhelms the public, there is no sure or easy way to defuse it. Even conscientious efforts to reassure people by explaining that they are "overreacting" may only exacerbate their anxiety. In such circumstances, the most effective way to alleviate the public's fear may be to demonstrate that their government is taking action, whether or not that action is likely otherwise to be effective. Sometimes this may calm the public, but the very fact that the government takes drastic action also affirms the legitimacy of the fear. And, of course, the precise *nature* of the "drastic" action is critical. It is one thing to announce a tripling of the defense budget and quite another to jail or deport hundreds or even thousands of innocent people in order to salve the public's anxiety.

Some members of Congress have courageously stood fast and insisted that the nation do the right thing, rather than what the public demands or what seems expedient or opportunistic. But such individuals have been the exception. More often, Congress has reflexively responded to wartime fear with thoughtless and sometimes savage legislation. Too often, members of Congress have exploited the public's anxieties to serve their narrow, partisan interests.

There are several steps Congress could take to break, or at least alleviate, this pattern. It could adopt certain "rules" or protocols, for example, to guide it whenever it considers wartime legislation that would restrict civil liberties. An obvious peril in wartime is that Congress will act precipitously in response to public hysteria. To prevent this, Congress could adopt a rule prohibiting it from enacting such legislation without full and fair deliberation. A clear rule against precipitate action, a sort of mandatory "cooling off" period, would afford Congress a fuller opportunity to consider the more questionable features of the proposed law. The debate over the Espionage Act of 1917 provides a useful example of an instance in which full deliberation resulted in a more thoughtful and more carefully crafted piece of legislation.

Another such protocol might require any wartime legislation limiting civil liberties to contain a "sunset" provision. Because such legislation will often be warped by the effects of a crisis mind-set, it should automatically be reconsidered within a relatively short time. Interestingly, both the Sedition Act of 1798 and the PATRIOT Act of 2001 incorporated this device. The Sedition Act of 1798 was by its own terms to expire on March 3, 1801, the date of the next president's inauguration, and the PATRIOT Act included a four-year sunset requirement for at least some of its provisions. This was a sound idea, but four years is too long. Most wars do not last that long and, in any event, enormous damage can be done in four years. To be effective, such provisions should require reconsideration within no more than one year of enactment, and regularly thereafter.

As WE HAVE SEEN, presidents have at best a mixed record in wartime. Some have paid little heed to the protection of civil liberties; others have demonstrated some care in attempting to balance freedom and security. Perhaps the most important step future presidents can take to improve the response of the executive branch is to ensure that every administration has within its highest councils individuals who will ardently and credibly defend civil liberties. As the legal scholar Cass Sunstein has explained, when the members of a group share a common set of premises, deliberation within that group usually results in an outcome that is more extreme than the group's "pre-deliberation tendencies."[8] In other words, a presidential cabinet consisting only of individuals with the same general ideology is likely to wind up endorsing extreme positions. This is especially likely, and especially dangerous, in wartime, when emotions are most raw. In such circumstances, even a single dissenter can play a significant role.

One of my most serious concerns about the administration of President George W. Bush is the absence of *any* senior official representing civil libertarian views. Such a person may sometimes or even often lose the policy debate, but an administration *without* such a voice is much more likely to embrace extreme positions than one that fosters genuine internal deliberation.

One other lesson for the executive is worth noting. There is invariably a tendency in wartime, even more than in normal times, for the executive to become overly secretive. To some degree, increased secrecy is both natural and proper. But when taken to excess, secrecy can be used to evade accountability. In a self-governing system committed to the separation of powers, excessive secrecy is a recipe for disaster. The American system of government depends on a reasonable degree of transparency, congressional oversight, and public awareness in order to check the threat of an overreaching executive. Presidents must understand and accept that there is a difference between using secrecy to protect the nation and using secrecy to protect themselves. They must understand that they have a responsibility not only to protect us from our enemies, but also to respect and preserve our constitutional system. Too often, presidents have failed in that responsibility.

Congress can and must police and reinforce this presidential responsibility by insisting upon meaningful oversight of executive action. This is the very essence of the separation of powers. As we have seen during the war on terrorism, such oversight is undermined when both houses of Congress and the presidency are controlled by the same political party. In such circumstances, the separation of powers is directly undermined by partisan self-interest, posing a serious danger to American democracy. At these moments, the American people must be especially vigilant to protect their own rights.

WHAT IS THE APPROPRIATE ROLE of courts in wartime? To what extent can—and should—the Constitution, as interpreted and applied by the judiciary, restrain the pressures for wartime sacrifice of constitutional rights? Justice Jackson described the form in which these questions typically reach the Supreme Court: "Measures [ordinarily] violative of constitutional rights are claimed to be necessary to security, in the judgment of officials who are best in a position to know, but the necessity is not provable by ordinary evidence and the court is in no position to determine the necessity for itself. What should it do then?"[9]

After two centuries of wrestling with this question, we seem to have achieved consensus on two key propositions: The Constitution applies in time of war, but the special demands of war may affect the application of the Constitution. We have thus rejected the more extreme positions—that the Constitution is irrelevant in wartime and that wartime is irrelevant to the application of the Constitution.

What this means in practice is that in applying the applicable constitutional standard in any particular area of the law, whether it be clear and present danger, "due process of law," or "unreasonable" search and seizure, it is appropriate for courts to take the special circumstances of wartime into account in determining whether the government has sufficient justification to limit the constitutional right at issue. What it does *not* mean, however, is that courts should abdicate their responsibilities in the face of assertions of national security or military necessity.

Some commentators contend that this stance accords courts excessive authority in time of war. In their view, because war presents unique challenges and dangers, the ordinary standards of judicial review should be suspended. After all, when national security is at stake, the danger to the nation is particularly grave, and if judges err in their assessment of the risks and prohibit the government from acting when action is necessary, the consequences could be catastrophic. Moreover, judges are not particularly well situated to make judgments about the demands of national security, for such judgments often involve matters of unusual complexity and secrecy. Courts are therefore more likely to flounder in dealing with such matters than when they address more run-of-the-mill disputes. When grave issues of national security are at stake, we should be more willing to tolerate the risks of unconstrained executive power. Or so the argument goes.

There is some merit in these concerns, but not much. The comparative advantage of courts over the executive and legislative branches in interpreting and enforcing constitutional rights is evident. Responsiveness to the electorate is essential to the day-to-day workings of democracy, but as the Framers of the Constitution well understood, that responsiveness can also lead the government too readily to sacrifice fundamental liberties, particularly when it can do so without jeopardizing the rights of the majority. Judges with life tenure and a professional attention to the preservation of our constitutional freedoms are much more likely to protect civil liberties than the elected branches of government. As the journalist Anthony Lewis has observed, "the distinctive American contribution to the philosophy of government has been the role of judges as protectors of freedom."*[10]

---

*The Framers were well aware of this: "The independence of the judges is equally requisite to guard the Constitution and the rights of individuals from the effects of those ill humors which the arts of designing men, or the influence of particular conjunctures, sometimes disseminate among the people themselves, and which, though they speedily give place to better information and more deliberate reflection, have a tendency in the meantime to occasion dangerous innovations in the government, and serious oppressions of the minor party in the community." Federalist No. 78, in Garry Wills, ed, *The Federalist Papers by Alexander Hamilton, James Madison & John Jay* 397 (Bantam 1982).

Of course, the central question is not how to protect constitutional rights in wartime, but how to protect those rights *without preventing the government from responding effectively to a crisis*. If courts were irresponsibly aggressive in construing individual rights in wartime, if they were inclined to cripple the nation's capacity to wage war effectively, if they regarded the Constitution "as a suicide pact,"[11] it would certainly make sense to empower the elected branches to override their judgments. But nothing could be further from the truth. Throughout our history, judges have erred on the side of deference in times of crisis. Like other citizens, judges do not want the nation to lose a war, and they certainly do not want to be responsible for a tragedy. As Chief Justice William Rehnquist observed, "judges, like other citizens, do not wish to hinder a nation's 'war effort.' "[12] Moreover, as we have seen, judges, like other citizens, are not immune to the fears and anxieties of the moment. This makes them even more prone—indeed, too prone—to err on the side of deference.

Not surprisingly, then, in *Schenck, Korematsu, Dennis*, and other wartime decisions, the Supreme Court has applied constitutional standards in a way that accords the president and Congress the benefit of the doubt. Although Congress and the president have often *underprotected* civil liberties in wartime, there is not a single instance in which the Supreme Court has *overprotected* those liberties in a way that caused *any* demonstrable harm to the national security. The argument that courts cannot be trusted because they will unduly shackle our nation's ability to fight is simply unfounded. There is no reason in logic or national experience to believe that courts would give *excessive* protection to constitutional rights in a way that would jeopardize the national security.

On the other hand, as we have seen, history is replete with instances in which we have excessively suppressed civil liberties without any compelling or even reasonable justification. The problem is not too much judicial enforcement of civil liberties in wartime, but too *little*. Although some judges have proved themselves courageous,

independent, and confident in our nation's commitment to civil liberties, too many have been too timid, too much "company men," or too
easily cowed by the clamorous atmosphere around them. And
although the Supreme Court has sometimes taken a strong stance in
defense of civil liberties in the face of exaggerated claims of military
necessity, as in *Pentagon Papers* and *Hamdi*, in most instances the justices have yielded too readily to executive demands that they not
stand in the way.

Moreover, even if justices became much more insistent in their
protection of individual liberties in wartime, the potential "danger"
would not be so dire. There are many ways to achieve a desired level
of security. If one measure is unavailable, others can be pursued.
Suppose, for example, the Supreme Court had invalidated the Sedition Act of 1798, the Espionage Act of 1917, or the internment of
individuals of Japanese descent. Even if such decisions would have
hampered the protection of national security, the government could
easily have attained the same overall *level* of safety by, for example,
increasing the penalties for particular crimes, such as draft evasion
or espionage, or committing greater resources to ferreting out spies
and saboteurs.

In a world of limited resources, the government must always
choose between different means of achieving its objectives. Should it
expand the number of investigators? Upgrade its technology? Invest
more in security at our borders? What the Constitution does is to take
off the table the suppression of civil liberties as an "easy" means of
achieving, or purporting to achieve, the government's legitimate
goals. It does this for good reason. Laws punishing dissent, detaining
noncitizens, or wiretapping people without probable cause are especially appealing to public officials because they are relatively inex-
pensive, cater to a witch-hunt mentality, create the illusion of
decisive action, burden only those who already are viewed with contempt, and enable public officials to silence their critics in the guise of
serving the national interest. The Constitution commands that such
measures should be a last, rather than a first, resort.

* * *

Having said all this, we still must ask whether anything courts do in these periods matters. It is often said that, as a practical matter, presidents do what they please in wartime. Attorney General Biddle once observed that "the Constitution has not greatly bothered any wartime President,"[13] and Chief Justice Rehnquist suggested that "there is no reason to think that future wartime presidents will act differently from Lincoln, Wilson, or Roosevelt."[14]

The record, however, is more complex than this suggests. Although presidents may think of themselves as bound more by political than by constitutional constraints in time of war, the two are often linked. Lincoln did not propose a Sedition Act, Wilson rejected calls to suspend the writ of habeas corpus, and Bush did not impose a federal loyalty program on Muslim-Americans. Even in wartime, presidents have not attempted to restrict civil liberties in the face of *settled* Supreme Court precedent. Although presidents often push the envelope when the law is unclear, they do not defy established constitutional doctrine.

What this suggests is that in periods of relative calm the Court should consciously construct constitutional doctrines that will provide firm guidance for later periods of stress. Perhaps the best example of this in modern constitutional law is the Court's 1969 decision in *Brandenburg*, in which the Court redefined fifty years of jurisprudence in order to adopt a clear and unambiguous statement of the doctrine governing issues at the very heart of the First Amendment.

As we have learned by long experience, if the nation is to preserve civil liberties in the face of war fever, the Court must articulate clear constitutional rules that are not easily circumvented or manipulated by prosecutors, jurors, presidents, or even future Supreme Court justices. Malleable principles, open-ended balances, and vague standards may serve well in periods of tranquility, but they will fail us just at the point when we need the Constitution most. In effect, the Court must establish firm principles that may sometimes overprotect civil liberties in ordinary times in order to ensure that we adequately protect them in times of great stress.

Finally, it is often repeated as a form of conventional wisdom that the Supreme Court will not decide a case against the government on an issue of military security during a period of national emergency. The decisions most often cited in support of this proposition are *Korematsu* and *Dennis*. The distinguished political scientist Clinton Rossiter once observed that "the government of the United States, in the case of military necessity," can be "just as much a dictatorship, after its own fashion, as any other government on earth." The Supreme Court, he added, "will not and cannot be expected to get in the way of this power."[15]

This does not give the Court its due. There are many counterexamples. During World War II, the Court upheld the rights of dissenters in a series of deportation and denaturalization proceedings.[16] In 1943, at the very height of the war, the Court held that the government could not constitutionally compel children in public schools to pledge allegiance to the American flag,[17] and less than a year after Pearl Harbor the Court held that civilians in Hawaii could not be tried by military tribunals.[18] During the Korean War, the Court rejected President Truman's effort to seize the steel industry,[19] and in a series of decisions after 1957 the Court helped usher out the era of McCarthyism.[20] During the Vietnam War, in decisions like *Pentagon Papers* and *Keith*, the Court confidently rejected national security claims by the executive and vigorously enforced both First and Fourth amendment freedoms. Most recently, the Court's decisions in *Rasul*, *Hamdi*, and *Hamdan* emphatically rejected some of the more extreme positions of the Bush administration.

These more recent decisions suggest that the justices themselves have learned the lessons of history. Demands for judicial deference to executive branch judgments have credibility only insofar as that deference proves warranted. Over time, however, the executive has repeatedly overstated its claims and exaggerated its reasons for restricting civil liberties in wartime. The justices have learned that they cannot give the president a "blank check" if they want to meet their constitutional responsibilities and do not want their own legacies to be marked by decisions like *Dennis* and *Korematsu*.

So, although it is true that the Court tends to be careful in wartime not to overstep its bounds, it is also true that the Court has a long, if uneven, record of fulfilling its responsibility to protect individual liberties even in time of war. And because the Congress and the president have consistently deferred to the Court's interpretation of the Constitution, these decisions have had a significant impact on how the United States responds to the exigencies of wartime.

IT IS, OF COURSE, MUCH EASIER to look back on past crises and find our predecessors wanting than it is to make wise judgments when we ourselves are in the eye of the storm. But that challenge now falls to this generation of Americans. Freedom can endanger security, but it is also the fundamental source of American strength. As Justice Louis Brandeis explained in 1927, "those who won our independence . . . knew that . . . fear breeds repression" and that "courage is the secret of liberty."[21] Those are the two most central lessons for Americans to bear in mind.

To strike the right balance, we need political leaders who know right from wrong; federal judges who will stand fast against the furies of their age; members of the bar and the academy who will help us see the issues clearly; a thoughtful, responsible, and independent press; members of Congress who will jealously safeguard the separation of powers and insist on executive transparency and accountability; justices of the Supreme Court with the wisdom to know excess when they see it and the courage to preserve liberty when it is imperiled; and, perhaps most of all, an informed and tolerant public who will value not only their own liberties, but the liberties of others.

# Notes

✥

## CHAPTER I

1. Address of John Adams to Special Session of Congress, May 16, 1797, in 2 *Journal of the Senate* 358–60 (Gales and Seaton 1820).

2. John Adams, *Message from the President of the United States to Both Houses of Congress, Delivered on March 19, 1798,* in *American State Papers* 4 (Wright and Richardson, 1798).

3. 8 *Annals of Congress* 1484 (Gales and Seaton 1851).

4. Id at 1342.

5. Id at 2071–72.

6. Letter from John Adams to the Inhabitants of Arlington and Bandate, Vermont, June 25, 1798, in Charles Francis Adams, ed, 9 *The Works of John Adams* 202 (Little, Brown 1854).

7. John C. Miller, *Crisis in Freedom: The Alien and Sedition Acts* 41 (Little, Brown 1951).

8. The act authorized the president "to order all such aliens as he shall judge dangerous to the peace and safety of the United States, or shall have reasonable grounds to suspect are concerned in any treasonable or secret machinations against the government thereof, to depart out of the territory of the United States, within such time as shall be expressed in such order. . . ." An Act Respecting Alien Enemies, 5th Cong, 2d Sess, in 1 *Public Statutes at Large* 577–78 (Little, Brown 1845).

9. 8 *Annals of Congress* at 1995 (cited in note 3).

10. Id at 1989.

11. Letter from James Madison to Thomas Jefferson, May 20, 1798, in Richard

N. Rosenfield, *American Aurora* 128 (St. Martin's 1997); Letter from Thomas Jefferson to James Madison, May 31, 1798, id at 136.

12. Richmond Examiner (June 21, 1798), excerpted in Miller, *Crisis in Freedom* at 32–33 (cited in note 7); Joseph Hopkinson, *What Is Our Situation? And What Our Prospects? A Few Pages for Americans, by an American* 29 (1798).

13. Henry Cabot Lodge, ed, 7 *The Works of Alexander Hamilton* 377 (Putnam 1904).

14. Letter from John Adams to the Mayor, Aldermen, and Citizens of Philadelphia, in Adams, ed, 9 *Works of John Adams* at 182 (cited in note 6); John Adams, *Answer: To the Citizens of Newark, in the State of New Jersey*, Gazette of the United States 2 (May 2, 1798).

15. Miller, *Crisis in Freedom* at 29 (cited in note 7).

16. Aurora (Sept 11, 1795).

17. Gazette of the United States 3 (May 14, 1800).

18. Jeffrey L. Pasley, "The Tyranny of Printers: Newspaper Politics in the Early American Republic" 72 (Virginia 2001); *Original Communications*, Gazette of the United States 3 (May 26, 1792).

19. An Act for the Punishment of Certain Crimes Against the United States, 5th Cong, 2d Sess, ch 74 (1798).

20. 8 *Annals of Congress* at 2110 (cited in note 3); id at 2164.

21. 2 *Abridgement of the Debates of Congress* 257 (Appleton 1857); *Communications*, Massachusetts Mercury 2 (June 12, 1798); 8 *Annals of Congress* at 2093–94 (cited in note 3).

22. Id at 2096–98.

23. Id at 2109.

24. Id at 2162.

25. Id at 2146.

26. Id at 2160; id at 2142.

27. Benjamin Franklin, *An Account of the Supremest Court of Judicature in Pennsylvania, viz. The Court of the Press* (Sept 12, 1789), in Albert Henry Smyth, ed, 10 *The Writings of Benjamin Franklin* 37 (Macmillan 1907).

28. Geoffrey R. Stone, Louis M. Seidman, Cass R. Sunstein, Mark V. Tushnet, Pamela S. Karlan, *The First Amendment* at 3–5 (Aspen 2d ed 2003); T. B. Howell, ed, 14 *State Trials* 1128 (Hansard 1816).

29. James F. Stephen, 2 *A History of the Criminal Law of England* 350 (Macmillan 1883).

30. Fredrick Seaton Siebert, *Freedom of the Press in England, 1476–1776* 269 (Illinois 1952).

31. James Madison, *The Virginia Report of 1799–1800*, in Leonard W. Levy, *Emergence of a Free Press* 198–212 (Oxford 1985); James Madison, *Address of the General Assembly to the People of the Commonwealth of Virginia, January*

*23, 1799,* in Gaillard Hunt, ed, 6 *The Writings of James Madison* 339 (Putnam 1906).

32. Francis Wharton, *State Trials of the United States* 333–34 (Carey and Hart 1849).

33. Wharton, *State Trials* at 335–37 (cited in note 32).

34. Aurora 4 (Nov 1, 1798); Letter from Thomas Jefferson to John Taylor, Nov 26, 1798, in Andrew A. Lipscomb and Albert Ellery Bergh, eds, 10 *The Writings of Thomas Jefferson* 63 (Thomas Jefferson Memorial Association 1905).

35. Wharton, *State Trials* at 661, 664 (cited in note 32).

36. Id at 665.

37. Id at 668.

38. Thomas Cooper, *An Account of the Trial of Thomas Cooper, of Northumberland; on a Charge of Libel Against the President of the United States* 39 (Bioren 1800).

39. Id at 675–76, 679.

40. Miller, *Crisis in Freedom* at 213 (cited in note 7); id at 214.

41. Wharton, *State Trials* at 688–90 (cited in note 32).

42. Wharton, *State Trials* at 692–95 (cited in note 32).

43. Worthington Chauncey Ford, ed, *Thomas Jefferson and James Thomson Callender* 23–24 (Historical Printing Club 1897).

44. John P. Foley, 10 *The Jefferson Cyclopedia: A Comprehensive Collection of the Views of Thomas Jefferson* 368 (Funk and Wagnalls 1900).

45. Thomas Jefferson, *First Inaugural Address* (1801), reprinted in Melvin I. Urofsky, 1 *Documents of American Constitutional and Legal History* 171–74 (Knopf 1989).

46. Miller, *Crisis in Freedom* at 231 (cited in note 7).

47. Cong Globe, 26th Cong, 1st Sess 411 (1840). See 26 HR 80, 26th Cong, 1st Sess, Doc 86 (1840).

48. 376 US 254 (1964).

49. Id at 273, 276.

50. *Gertz v. Robert Welch, Inc,* 418 US 323, 339 (1974).

51. Id at 339–40.

## CHAPTER II

1. Dwight L. Dumond, *The Secession Movement, 1860–1861* 104 (Macmillan 1931).

2. Letter from Abraham Lincoln to John B. Fry, Aug 15, 1860, in Roy P. Basler, ed, 4 *The Collected Works of Abraham Lincoln* 95 (Rutgers 1953).

3. *The Terrors of Submission,* Charleston Mercury 1 (Oct 11, 1860).

4. John W. Burgess, 1 *The Civil War and the Constitution, 1859–1865* 80 (Charles Scribner 1901).

5. James Buchanan, *Fourth Annual Message, Dec 3, 1860,* in James D. Richardson, ed, 5 *A Compilation of the Messages and Papers of the Presidents, 1789–1897* 626, 635 (Government Printing Office 1897).

6. *Going to Go,* New-York Tribune 4 (Nov 9, 1860).

7. James M. McPherson, *Battle Cry of Freedom: The Civil War Era* 256 (Oxford 1988).

8. *Harris v. Nelson,* 394 US 286, 290–91 (1969).

9. See James G. Randall, 1 *Lincoln the President: Springfield to Gettysberg* 288–91 (Vail-Ballou 1946).

10. Letter from Lyman Trumbull to Abraham Lincoln, Apr 21, 1861, excerpted in Mark E. Neely Jr., *The Fate of Liberty: Abraham Lincoln and Civil Liberties* 6 (Oxford 1991); Letter from Orville Hickman Browning to Abraham Lincoln, Apr 22, 1861, excerpted id; John G. Nicolay and John Hay, 4 *Abraham Lincoln: A History* 151 (Century 1914).

11. *Dred Scott v. Sandford,* 60 US 393 (1857).

12. 17 F Cases 144 (D Md 1861).

13. 8 US (4 Cranch) 95, 101 (1807) ("If at any time the public safety should require the suspension of the powers vested by [the Habeas corpus Act] in the courts of the United States, it is for the legislature to say so.").

14. Joseph Story, 3 *Commentaries on the Constitution* § 676 (Hilliard Gray 1833) ("The power is given to congress to suspend the writ of habeas corpus.").

15. *Merryman,* 17 F Cases at 148.

16. *Ex parte Merryman,* 17 F Cases 144 (Cir Ct Md 1861).

17. *Merryman,* 15 F Cases at 147–48.

18. Carl Sandburg, 2 *Abraham Lincoln: The War Years* 280 (Harcourt, Brace 1939).

19. Cong Globe, 37th Cong, 2d Sess 329 (Jan 14, 1862).

20. Abraham Lincoln, *Final Emancipation Proclamation,* Sept 22, 1862, in *Abraham Lincoln: Speeches and Writings, 1859–1865* 424 (Library of America 1989).

21. Cong Globe App, 37th Cong, 2d Sess 242 (June 3, 1962).

22. J. Matthew Gallman, *North Fights the Civil War: The Home Front* 128 (Ivan R. Dee 1994).

23. McPherson, *Battle Cry of Freedom* at 609 (cited in note 7).

24. Robert E. Sterling, *Civil War Draft Resistance in the Middle West* 96–97 (unpublished PhD Dissertation, Northern Illinois University 1975), excerpted in McPherson, *Battle Cry of Freedom* at 493 (cited in note 7).

25. Abraham Lincoln, *Proclamation Suspending the Writ of Habeas Corpus,* Sept 24, 1862, in Roy P. Basler, ed, 5 *The Collected Works of Abraham Lincoln* 436–37 (Rutgers 1953).

26. Sandburg, 2 *Abraham Lincoln* at 154–55 (cited in note 18).

27. Abraham Lincoln, *Message to Congress in Special Session*, July 4, 1861, in *Abraham Lincoln: Speeches and Writings* at 250–53 (cited in note 20).

28. Letter from Abraham Lincoln to Erastus Corning and Others, June 12, 1863, id at 456–57.

29. Id at 457.

30. Id at 458; Abraham Lincoln, *Reply to Ohio Democrats*, June 29, 1863, id at 467.

31. Daniel Farber, *Lincoln's Constitution* 161 (Chicago 2003).

32. Neely, *Fate of Liberty* at 60 (cited in note 10); see id at 58–61.

33. Abraham Lincoln, Memorandum: Military Arrests, May 17, 1861, in 4 *Collected Works of Abraham Lincoln* at 372 (cited in note 2).

34. Letter from Abraham Lincoln to John M. Schofield, July 13, 1863, in Basler, ed, 6 *The Collected Works of Abraham Lincoln* 326 (Rutgers 1953).

35. Report of Major-General Ambrose E. Burnside, Nov 13, 1865, in 1:23:1 *The War of the Rebellion: A Compilation of the Official Records of the Union and Confederate Armies* 12 (Government Printing Office 1902).

36. *The Trial of Hon. Clement L. Vallandigham by a Military Commission* 7 (Rickey and Carroll 1863).

37. Id. at 11–12.

38. Mount Vernon Democratic Banner (May 9, 1863), excerpted in Frank L. Klement, *The Limits of Dissent: Clement L. Vallandigham and the Civil War* 154 (Fordham 1998).

39. *Ex parte Vallandigham*, 28 F Cases 874, 875 (Cir Ct Ohio 1863).

40. Id at 921–22.

41. *The Arrest of Vallandigham*, Albany Argus 2 (May 8, 1863), excerpted in Kent Curtis, *Free Speech "The People's Darling Privilege"* 320 (Duke 2000); 320 (cited in note 71); *The Military Discretion*, Detroit Free Press 2 (June 10, 1863).

42. *Ohio Democratic State Convention*, Cincinnati Daily Commercial 2 (June 12, 1863).

43. *Vallandigham*, New-York Daily Tribune 4 (May 15, 1863); *The Voice of Reason*, National Intelligencer 3 (May 16, 1863) (reprinted from New York Evening Post), excerpted in Michael Kent Curtis, *Free Speech* 326 (cited in note 41); *From the Bedford (Rep.) Standard*, Detroit Free Press 2 (May 27, 1863); *Senator Trumbull's Chicago Speech*, Cincinnati Daily Commercial 2 (June 11, 1863).

44. John G. Nicolay and John Hay, 7 *Abraham Lincoln: A History* 338 (Century 1914).

45. Abraham Lincoln, *Reply to the Ohio Democratic Convention*, June 29, 1868, in *Abraham Lincoln: Speeches and Writings* at 468 (cited in note 20).

46. Klement, *Limits of Dissent* at 178–79 (cited in note 38).

47. *The Anti-Democratic Press Opposed the Arrest of Mr. Vallandigham*, Crisis 5 (May 27, 1863).

48. Nicolay and Hay, 7 *Abraham Lincoln* at 340 (cited in note 44).

49. Klement, *Limits of* Dissent at 181 (cited in note 38); *The Great Demonstration at Albany*, Cincinnati Daily Enquirer 1 (May 23, 1863); letter from Erastus Corning to Abraham Lincoln, May 29, 1863, excerpted in Klement, *Limits of Dissent* at 181 (cited in note 38). See id at 178–81; Robert S. Harper, *Lincoln and the Press* 246–48 (McGraw-Hill 1951).

50. Letter from Abraham Lincoln to Erastus Corning and Others, June 12, 1863, in *Abraham Lincoln: Speeches and Writings* at 459–60 (cited in note 20).

51. Id.

52. Id at 460.

53. Id at 468–69 (emphasis added).

54. *The News and President Lincoln*, New York Daily News 4 (May 23, 1864).

55. *The Conscription: The President Ill Advised*, New York Evening Express 2 (Aug 12, 1863); Harper, *Lincoln and the Press* at 270 (cited in note 48); Chicago Times (Mar 20, 1864), excerpted id at 263.

56. Springfield Gazette, excerpted in *The President and His Critics*, Cincinnati Gazette 1 (Nov 29, 1862).

57. 71 US (4 Wall) 2 (1866).

58. Id at 127.

59. Id at 120–21.

60. Neely, *Fate of Liberty* at 235 (cited in note 10).

61. Harold M. Hyman, *A More Perfect Union: The Impact of the Civil War and Reconstruction on the Constitution* 101 (Knopf 1973).

**CHAPTER III**

1. Woodrow Wilson, Address to Joint Session of Congress, Apr 2, 1917, in Arthur S. Link, ed, 41 *The Papers of Woodrow Wilson* 520–21 (Princeton 1983).

2. 65th Cong, 1st Sess, in 55 Cong Rec S 214 (Apr 4, 1917).

3. 65th Cong, Spec Sess, in 55 Cong Rec S 104 (Apr 2, 1917).

4. Paul L. Murphy, *World War I and the Origin of Civil Liberties in the United States* 53 (Norton 1979).

5. Woodrow Wilson, Third Annual Message to Congress, Dec 7, 1917, in Albert Shaw, ed, 1 *The Messages and Papers of Woodrow Wilson* 150–51 (Review of Reviews 1924).

6. New York Sun (July 14, 1914), excerpted in Richard Polenberg, *Fighting Faiths: The Abrams Case, the Supreme Court, and Free Speech* 22 (Viking 1987).

7. Emma Goldman, *Anarchism: What It Really Stands For*, in Emma Goldman, *Anarchism and Other Essays* 56 (Mother Earth 2d ed 1911).

8. Emma Goldman, *The Promoters of War Mania*, Mother Earth (Mar 1917).

9. HR 291 tit I § 4, 65th Cong, 1st Sess, in 55 Cong Rec H 1695 (May 2, 1917).

10. Report of the Committee on the Judiciary, HR Report No 30, 65th Cong, 1st Sess 9 (1917). See 54 Cong Rec S 3606–07 (Feb 19, 1917) (discussing the use of the word "disaffection").

11. HR 291 § 1100, 65th Cong, 1st Sess, in 55 Cong Rec H 1595 (Apr 30, 1917).

12. Resolutions of the American Newspaper Publishers' Association, 65th Cong, 1st Sess (Apr 25, 1917), in 55 Cong Rec S 1861 (May 5, 1917).

13. 65th Cong, 1st Sess in 55 Cong Rec H 1590–91 (Apr 30, 1917).

14. Thomas F. Carroll, *Freedom of Speech and of the Press in War Time: The Espionage Act*, 17 Mich L Rev 621, 628 (1919).

15. 65th Cong, 1st Sess, in 55 Cong Rec S 2097 (May 11, 1917).

16. 65th Cong, 1st Sess, in 55 Cong Rec H 1594 (Apr 30, 1917).

17. Id at 1773 (May 3, 1917).

18. Id at 1773.

19. *Wilson Demands Press Censorship*, New York Times 1 (May 23, 1917) (quoting a letter from Woodrow Wilson to Representative Webb).

20. 65th Cong, 1st Sess, in 55 Cong Rec H 3134 (May 31, 1917).

21. 65th Cong, 1st Sess, in 55 Cong Rec S 2062 (May 10, 1917).

22. 65th Cong, 1st Sess, in 55 Cong Rec H 1779 (May 3, 1917).

23. 65th Cong, 1st Sess, in 55 Cong Rec H 1604 (Apr 30, 1917) (noting that the opinion of the solicitor of the Post Office Department would "prevail without a trial").

24. Conf Rep No 65, on HR 291, 65th Cong, 1st Sess, in 55 Cong Rec H 3124, 3129 (May 29, 1917); 65th Cong, 1st Sess, in 55 Cong Rec H 3306 (June 7, 1917).

25. Hearings on 291 before the House Committee on the Judiciary, 65th Cong, 1st Sess 36–43 (Apr 9 and 12, 1917).

26. 65th Cong, 1st Sess, in 55 Cong Rec H 1594 (Apr 30, 1917) (Rep Webb).

27. See Espionage Act of 1917, 40 Stat at 219.

28. 65th Cong, 1st Sess, in 55 Cong Rec H 1594–95 (Apr 30, 1917).

29. Thomas Gregory, *Suggestions of Attorney General Gregory to Executive Committee in Relation to the Department of Justice*, 4 ABA J 305, 306 (1918).

30. New York Times 3 (Nov 21, 1917). See Robert J. Goldstein, *Political Repression in Modern America: From 1870 to the Present* 108 (Schenckman 1978).

31. Schofield, *Freedom of the Press in the United States*, 9 Am Soc Society Papers and Proceedings 67, 73, 83–88 (1914).

32. Judge Bourquin's opinion in *United States v. Hall* is reported in 65th Cong, 2d Sess, 56 Cong Rec S 4559–60 (Apr 4, 1918).

33. *United States v. Schutte*, 252 F 212, 214 (D ND 1918).

34. 244 F 535 (SD NY 1917).

35. Gerald Gunther, *Learned Hand: The Man and the Judge* 155 (Knopf 1994).

36. *Masses*, 244 F at 539–540.

37. *Masses*, 244 F at 540 (italics added).

38. *Masses Publishing Co v. Patten*, 246 F 24 (2d Cir 1917).

39. 255 F 886 (9th Cir 1919).

40. Id at 887.

41. Id at 887–89.

42. *United States v. Stokes* (unreported) (D Mo 1918), revd 264 F 18 (8th Cir 1920), quoted in Zechariah Chafee, *Free Speech in the United States* 52–53 (Harvard 1941).

43. *"The Spirit of '76,"* 252 F at 947–48 (confiscating the film and prohibiting its presentation without modification).

44. Chafee, *Free Speech* at 52 (cited in note 42).

45. Gregory, 4 ABA J at 306–7, 313, 316 (cited in note 29).

46. 40 Stat 553.

47. Id at 4835.

48. 249 US 47 (1919).

49. Id at 52.

50. 249 US 204 (1919).

51. 249 US 211 (1919).

52. 250 US 616 (1919).

53. Id at 627–28.

54. 250 US at 628.

55. 250 US at 629.

56. Id at 630–31.

57. Harry Kalven Jr., *A Worthy Tradition: Freedom of Speech in America* 147 (Harper and Row 1988).

58. Letter from Thomas Gregory to Woodrow Wilson, Mar 1, 1919, in Harry N. Scheiber, *The Wilson Administration and Civil Liberties* 46 (Cornell 1960).

59. John Dewey, *In Explanation of Our Lapse*, New Republic 13 (1917), reprinted in Jo Ann Boydston, ed, 10 *John Dewey: The Middle Works, 1899–1924* 292 (Southern Illinois 1980).

60. John Dewey, 2 *Characters and Events: Popular Essays in Social and Political Philosophy* 634 (Octagon 1970).

61. John Dewey and James H. Tufts, *Ethics* 401 (Holt 2d ed 1932).

## CHAPTER IV

1. *Johnson v. Eisentrager*, 339 US 763, 772–73 (1950).

2. Alien Registration Act ("Smith Act"), Pub L No 670, 54 Stat 670, 673–76 (1940).

3. Department of Justice, *Annual Report of the Attorney General of the United States for the Year 1942* 14 (Government Printing Office 1942).

4. Department of Justice, *1942 Annual Report* at 15 (cited in note 3); Department of Justice, *1943 Annual Report of the Attorney General of the United States for the Year 1943* 10 (Government Printing Office 1943).

5. 3 CFR EO 9066 (1942). On March 21, 1942, Congress implicitly ratified the executive order by providing that violation of the order of a military commander was unlawful. Act of June 25, 1948, Pub L No 772, 62 Stat 683, 765, codified at 18 USC § 1383 (1974) (repealed by Pub L No 94-412, 90 Stat 1258 (1976)).

6. Erik K. Yamamoto et al, *Race, Rights and Reparation: Law and the Japanese American Internment* 96 (Aspen 2001).

7. Ted Lyons, *Lancer's Column*, Rafu Shimpo 3 (Dec 7, 1941), excerpted in Greg Robinson, *By Order of the President: FDR and the Internment of Japanese Americans* 71 (Harvard 2001); Jerome Frank, *Red-White-and-Blue Herring*, Satevepost (Dec 6, 1941), excerpted in Geoffrey Perrett, *Days of Sadness, Years of Triumph: The American People, 1939–1945* 217 (Wisconsin 1985).

8. Department of Justice, *1942 Annual Report* at 14 (cited in note 3).

9. Ed Cray, *Chief Justice: A Biography of Earl Warren* 115 (Simon and Schuster 1997).

10. Yamamoto et al, *Race, Rights and Reparation* at 97–98 (cited in note 6); Robinson, *By Order of the President* at 84–85 (cited in note 7); Peter Irons, *Justice at War* 26–27, 280–84 (Oxford 1983); Perrett, *Days of Sadness* at 216 (cited in note 7).

11. Commission on Wartime Relocation and Internment of Civilians, *Personal Justice Denied* 67–68 1983); Jacobus tenBroek, Edward N. Barnhart, and Floyd W. Matson, *Prejudice, War and the Constitution* 71–80 (California 1954).

12. Cray, *Chief Justice* at 117 (cited in note 9); Irons, *Justice at War* at 38 ( cited in note 10).

13. San Francisco Examiner (Jan 29, 1942), excerpted in Yamamoto et al, *Race, Rights and Reparation* at 99 (cited in note 6).

14. Cray, *Chief Justice* at 117 (cited in note 9).

15. Id at 118, 121; Irons, *Justice at War* at 29–41 (cited in note 10).

16. Yamamoto et al, *Race, Rights and Reparation* at 100 (cited in note 6).

17. Transcript of meeting in General DeWitt's office, Jan 4, 1942, and testimony before House Naval Affairs Subcommittee, Apr 13, 1943, excerpted in Commission on Wartime Relocation, *Personal Justice Denied* at 65–66 (cited in note 11); Yamamoto et al, *Race, Rights and Reparation* at 99 (cited in note 6); Sidney Fine, *Frank Murphy: Washington Years* 437 (Michigan 1984).

18. Frank J. Taylor, *The People Nobody Wants*, Saturday Evening Post 24, 66 (May 9, 1942), excerpted in *Korematsu v. United States*, 323 US 214, 239 n 12 (1944) (Murphy dissenting).

19. Francis Biddle, *In Brief Authority* 215–17 (Doubleday 1962).

20. Irons, *Justice at War* at 53 (cited in note 10).

21. Biddle, *In Brief Authority* at 218–24 (cited in note 19).

22. Id; Richard Gid Powers, *Secrecy and Power: The Life of J. Edgar Hoover* 249 (Free Press 1987); Irons, *Justice at War* at 23, 28 (cited in note 10).

23. Irons, *Justice at War* at 55-56 (cited in note 10).

24. Cray, *Chief Justice* at 120 (cited in note 9); Irons, *Justice at War* at 72 (cited in note 10).

25. Cray, *Chief Justice* at 120 (cited in note 9).

26. Irons, *Justice at War* at 61 (cited in note 10).

27. Id at 62.

28. Biddle, *In Brief Authority* at 219 (cited in note 19).

29. For a detailed account of how this decision was reached in the White House, see Irons, *Justice at War* at 56–65 (cited in note 10).

30. Robinson, *By Order of the President* at 109–10 (cited in note 7); Irons, *Justice at War* at 51–52 (cited in note 10); Stetson Conn, *The Army and Japanese Evacuation*, in Stetson Conn, Rose C. Engelman, and Byron Fairchild, *Guarding the United States and Its Outposts*, 12 (2) Western Hemisphere Subseries of *The United States Army in World War II* (Office of the Chief of Military History, Dept of the Army 1964), excerpted in Biddle, *In Brief Authority* at 222, 220 n 1 (cited in note 19).

31. Robert H. Jackson, *That Man: An Insider's Portrait of Franklin D. Roosevelt* 59, 68, 74 (Oxford 2003).

32. Biddle, *In Brief Authority* at 219 (cited in note 19).

33. Irons, *Justice at War* at 42 (cited in note 10).

34. 320 US 81 (1943). See also *Yasui v. United States*, 320 US 115 (1943) (also upholding the constitutionality of the curfew order).

35. Fine, *Frank Murphy* at 438 (cited in note 17).

36. *Hirabayashi*, 320 US at 93–95, 99–101 (internal citations omitted).

37. 323 US 214 (1944).

38. Id at 218–20, 223–24 (internal citations omitted).

39. Id at 226.

40. Id at 244–46, 248.

41. Id at 233–35, 241–42 (internal citations omitted).

42. 323 US 283 (1944).

43. Id at 297, 300, 302, 304.

44. Irons, *Justice at War* at 273–77 (cited in note 10).

45. Evacuation Claims Act of 1948, Pub L No 886, 62 Stat 1231.

46. Yamamoto et al, *Race, Rights and Reparation* at 240–41 (cited in note 6).

47. See Irons, *Justice at War* at 72 (cited in note 10).

48. Biddle, *In Brief Authority* at 212, 226 (cited in note 19).

49. Wiley B. Rutledge to Harlan Fiske Stone, June 12, 1943, excerpted in Alpheus Thomas Mason, *Harlan Fiske Stone: Pillar of the Law* 676 (Viking 1956); Fowler V. Harper, *Justice Rutledge and the Bright Constellation* 173 (Bobbs-Merrill 1965).

50. *Justice Black, Champion of Civil Liberties for 34 Years on the Court, Dies at 85*, New York Times 76 (Sept 26, 1971).

51. William O. Douglas, *The Autobiography of William O. Douglas: The Court Years, 1939–1975* 38–39, 279–80 (Random House 1980).

52. Earl Warren, *The Bill of Rights and the Military*, 37 NYU L Rev 181, 191–92 (1962).

53. Earl Warren, *The Memoirs of Earl Warren* 149 (Doubleday 1977).

54. See Cray, *Chief Justice* at 520 (cited in note 9).

55. See Biddle, *In Brief Authority* at 216–19 (cited in note 19); Irons, *Justice at War* at 119 (cited in note 10).

56. John D. Weaver, *Warren: The Man, the Court, the Era* 113 (Little, Brown 1967).

57. Eugene V. Rostow, *The Japanese American Cases—A Disaster*, 54 Yale L J 489, 507, 520 (1945).

58. 3 CFR Proc 4417, An American Promise, Feb 19, 1976.

59. Commission on Wartime Relocation, *Personal Justice Denied* at 5, 8 (cited in note 11).

60. *Korematsu v. United States*, 584 F Supp 1406 (ND Cal 1984).

61. *Korematsu*, 584 F Supp at 1420.

62. *Hirabayashi v. United States*, 828 F2d 591 (9th Cir 1987).

63. *Hirabayashi*, 828 F2d at 598, 603–04.

64. Civil Liberties Act of 1988, Pub L No 100-383, 102 Stat 903, codified at 50 USC App § 1989(b) (1996).

## CHAPTER V

1. Thomas I Emerson and David M Helfeld, *Loyalty Among Government Employees*, 58 Yale L J 1, 17 (1948).

2. David M Oshinsky, *Senator Joseph McCarthy and the American Labor Movement* 52–53 (1976).

3. David Caute, *The Great Fear: The Anti-Communist Purge Under Truman and Eisenhower* 26 (Simon and Schuster 1978).

4. Id at 27.

5. John D Morris, *House Body Maps Exposing of Reds in Labor Unions, Schools, and Films*, New York Times, A1 (Jan 23, 1947).

6. George F Kennan, *The Sources of Soviet Conduct*, Foreign Aff. 566, 582 (July 1947) (written under pseudonym "X").

7. Athan Theoharis, *Seeds of Repression: Harry S. Truman and the Roots of McCarthyism* 55–56 (Quadrangle 1971).

8. Exec Order No 9.835, 12 Fed Reg 1935 (Mar 21, 1947) (entitled "Prescribing Procedures for the Administration of an Employees Loyalty Program in the Executive Branch of the Government").

9. Id.

10. Id at 1938.

11. James MacGregor Burns, *Roosevelt: The Soldier of Freedom* 416 (Harcourt Brace 1970).

12. Exec Order No 9835, 12 Fed Reg 1935 (Mar 21, 1947).

13. Robert J Goldstein, *Political Repression in Modern America: 1870 to the Present* 302 (Schenckman 1978).

14. Caute, *Great Fear* at 276 (cited in note 3).

15. Goldstein, *Political Repression* at 320 (cited in note 13).

16. Thomas C Reeves, *The Life and Times of Joe McCarthy: A Biography* 104–5 (Stein and Day 1982).

17. David H Bennett, *The Party of Fear: From Nativist Movements to the New Right in American History* 296 (North Carolina 1988).

18. Id.

19. Reeves, *Life and Times* at 230–33 (cited in note 16).

20. Robert Griffith, *The Politics of Fear: Joseph R McCarthy and the Senate* 89–90 (Kentucky 1970).

21. Reeves, *Life and Times* at 299 (cited in note 16); *M'Carthy Labels Marshall "Unfit,"* New York Times 3 (Apr. 21, 1950).

22. State Department Employee Loyalty Investigation, Report of the Committee on Foreign Relations Pursuant to S Res 231, S Rep 2108, 81st Cong, 2d Sess 151–52 (1950).

23. William S. White, *Red Charges by M'Carthy Ruled False*, New YorkTimes, 1 (July 18, 1950).

24. Reeves, *Life and Times* at 322 (cited in note 16).

25. Internal Security Act of 1950, 64 Stat 987.

26. Id.

27. Veto Message from the President of the United States, 81st Cong, 2d Sess, in 96 Cong Rec H 15629–32 (Sept. 22, 1950).

28. Id.

29. Griffith, *Politics of Fear* at 115 (cited in note 20).

30. Public Papers of the Presidents of the United States: Harry S. Truman, Containing the Public Messages, Speeches, and Statements of the President, January 1 to December 31, 1950 at 702 (1965) (Address in Kiel Auditorium, St. Louis, Nov. 4, 1950).

31. Reeves, *Life and Times* at 380, 426 (cited in note 16).

32. Robert A Caro, *Master of the Senate: The Years of Lyndon Johnson* 545 (Knopf 2002); Robert Dallek, *An Unfinished Life: John F. Kennedy, 1917–1963* 188 (Little, Brown 2003).

33. Stewart Alsop, *The Center: People and Power in Political Washington* 8 (Harper & Row 1968).

34. Griffith, *Politics of Fear* at 210–11 (cited in note 20); William S White, *Citadel: The Story of the United States Senate* 258 (Harper 1956).

35. Reeves, *Life and Times* at 479–80 (cited in note 16).

36. Id at 485.

37. *Text of Address by Truman Explaining to Nation His Actions in the White Case,* New York Times 26 (Nov 17, 1953).

38. *President's Brother Scores McCarthy,* New York Times 6 (July 25, 1953).

39. Caute, *Great Fear* at 429 (cited in note 3).

40. Act Concerning Sedition, 1918 Conn Pub Acts 312; Act Concerning Public Offenses and Declaring an Emergency, Ind Code Ann § 226 (Michie 1951).

41. Edward L Barrett Jr., *The Tenney Committee: Legislative Investigation of Subversive Activities in California* 68, 301 (Cornell 1951).

42. *Text of President's Speech at Dedication of New Legion Building,* Washington Post 7 (Aug 15, 1951).

43. Madison Capital Times (July 30 and Aug 2, 1951).

44. Goldstein, *Political Repression* at 383–84 (cited in note 13).

45. Normal Mailer, *The White Negro,* excerpted in Massimo Teodori, ed, *The New Left: A Documentary History* 10 (Bobbs-Merrill 1969).

46. 341 US 494 (1951).

47. Id at 508–9.

48. Id at 510–11.

49. Id at 508–9.

50. *Dennis,* 341 US at 581 (Black dissenting).

51. Id at 429.

52. Reeves, *Life and Times* at 474 (cited in note 16); Walter Johnson, *1600 Pennsylvania Avenue: Presidents and the People, 1929–1959* 292 (1960).

53. Roy Cohn, *McCarthy* 208 (1968).

54. Special Senate Investigation on Charges and Countercharges Involving: Secretary of the Army Robert T Stevens, John G Adams, H Struve Hensel

and Senator Joe McCarthy, Roy M Cohn, and Francis P Carr: Hearing Before the Special Subcommittee on Investigations of the Comm On Gov't Operations, 83d Cong 2426–27 (1954).

55. Id. *See also* W. H. Lawrence, *Exchange Bitter*, New York Times 1 (June 10, 1954).
56. 83d Cong., 2d Sess., in 100 Cong. Rec. S 8032–33 (June 11, 1954).
57. Report of the Select Committee to Study Censure Charges Against Joseph R. McCarthy Pursuant to S Res 301, S Rep 2508, 83d Cong., 2d Sess. 30–31, 60–61 (1954).
58. Francis Biddle, *The Fear of Freedom* 2, 7–8, 18–19, 28, 254, 247–49, 253 (1951).
59. Arthur Herman, *Joseph McCarthy: Reexamining the Life and Legacy of America's Most Hated Senator* 100 (Free Press 2000); Ann Coulter, *Slander: Liberal Lies About the American Right* 118 (Three Rivers 2002).

**CHAPTER VI**
1. 89th Cong, 1st Sess, in 111 Cong Rec S 27253 (Oct 18, 1965).
2. Rowland Evans Jr. and Robert D. Novak, *Nixon in the White House: The Frustration of Power* 285 (Random House 1971).
3. Henry Kissinger, *White House Years* 968–69 (Little, Brown 1979).
4. See Intelligence Activities: Senate Resolution 21, Hearings Before the Select Committee to Study Government Operations with Respect to Intelligence Activities of the United States Senate, 94th Cong, 1st Sess, Volume 6: Federal Bureau of Investigations 393 (1976).
5. J. Anthony Lukas, *Nightmare: The Underside of the Nixon Years* 29 (Viking 1976).
6. Athan Theoharis, *Spying on Americans: Political Surveillance from Hoover to the Huston Plan* 188–89 (Temple 1978); Lukas, *Nightmare* at 22 (cited in note 5).
7. Jerry J. Berman and Morton H. Halperin, eds, *The Abuses of the Intelligence Agencies* 90–92 (Center for National Security Studies 1975).
8. David Wise, *The American Police State: The Government Against the People* 154–55 (Random House 1976).
9. Theoharis, *Spying on Americans* at 148–49 (cited in note 6).
10. *Mitchell Issues Plea on F.B.I. Files*, New York Times 24 (Mar 24, 1971).
11. *What Is the FBI Up To?*, Washington Post A20 (Mar 25, 1971).
12. Intelligence Activities and the Rights of Americans: Book II, Final Report of the Select Committee to Study Governmental Operations with Respect to Intelligence Operations, United States Senate, 94th Cong, 2d Sess 71 5–6 (Apr 26, 1976).
13. Army Surveillance of Civilians: A Documentary Analysis by the Staff of the

Subcommittee on Constitutional Rights, Committee on the Judiciary, United States Senate, 92d Cong, 2d Sess 97 (1971).

14. *United States v. United States District Court*, 407 U.S. 297 (1972).

15. *Katz v. United States*, 389 US 347 (1967).

16. 357 US 449 (1958).

17. *Bates v. City of Little Rock*, 361 US 516, 523 (1960). See also *Shelton v. Tucker*, 364 US 479 (1960) (holding unconstitutional a state law requiring teachers to disclose all organizations with which they were affiliated).

18. See Geoffrey R Stone, The Scope of the Fourth Amendment: Privacy and the Police Use of Spies, Secret Agents, and Informers, 1976 Amer Bar. Found Res J 1193.

19. In *Laird Secretary of Defense v. Tatum*, 408 US 1 (1972), the Court declined to rule on the constitutionality of Army domestic intelligence activities, including the monitoring of public meetings, because the complainants lacked "standing." That is, they could not show that information gathered by the Army had actually been used to harm them. The Court held that the mere fact that their First Amendment activities would be "chilled" by the continuation of such activities was not sufficient to allow them to challenge the constitutionality of the surveillance. See *New Alliance Party v. Federal Bureau of Investigation*, 858 F Supp 425 (SD NY 1994) (same with respect to a challenge to FBI surveillance activities).

20. Sanford J. Ungar, *The Papers and the Papers: An Account of the Legal and Political Battle over the Pentagon Papers* 23–27 (Dutton 1972).

21. Halberstam, *The Best and Brightest* 633 (Random House 1972); David Rudenstine, *The Pentagon Papers Case: Rediscovering its Meaning Twenty Years Later*, 12 Cardozo L Rev 1869 (1991).

22. See Ungar, *Papers* at 32–34 (cited in note 20).

23. Ungar, *Papers* at 119–20 (cited in note 20).

24. Max Frankel, *Court Step Likely*, New York Times 1 (June 15, 1971).

25. *United States v. New York Times Co.*, 328 F Supp 324, 325 (SD NY 1971). See Ungar, *Papers* at 124–25 (cited in note 20).

26. Ungar, *Papers* at 139–46 (cited in note 20). See Katharine Graham, *Personal History* 447–51 (Vintage 1997).

27. *New York Times v. United States*, 403 US 713 (1971).

28. Id at 714 (citation omitted).

29. Id at 727, 728, 730 (Stewart concurring).

30. Ungar, *Papers* at 14, 19 (cited in note 20).

31. 395 US 444 (1969).

32. *Brandenburg*, 395 US at 444–45, 447.

**CHAPTER VII**

1. Anti-Terrorism Policy Review: Before the Senate Committee on the Judiciary (Dec 6, 2001) (statement of John Ashcroft); Anthony Lewis, *Security and Liberty: Preserving the Values of Freedom*, in Richard C. Leone and Greg Anrig Jr., eds, *The War on Our Freedoms: Civil Liberties in an Age of Terrorism* 50 (Century Foundation 2003); Richard C. Leone, *The Quiet Republic: The Missing Debate About Civil Liberties after 9/11*, in Leone and Anrig, *War on our Freedoms* at 8.

2. James Goodby & Kenneth Weisbrode, *Bush's Corrosive Campaign of Fear*, Financial Times (Nov 19, 2003).

3. Leone, *The Quiet Republic* at 5 (cited in note 1).

4. United and Strengthening America by Providing Appropriate Tools Required to Intercept and Obstruct Terrorism Act of 2001, Pub. L. No. 107-56, 115 Stat. 272 (Oct 26, 2001), §§ 201–25, 302, 501–8.

5. Leone, *The Quiet Republic* at 8 (cited in note 1). The PATRIOT Act passed the Senate by a vote of 99 to 1. The only senator to vote against the legislation was Democrat Russ Feingold of Wisconsin. Thereafter, several other senators told him privately that they agreed with him but were afraid to appear to the public as "soft on terrorism." Timothy Lynch, *Breaking the Vicious Cycle: Preserving Our Liberties While Fighting Terrorism*, 443 Policy Analysis 7 (June 26, 2002); Robert E Pierre, "Wisconsin Senator Emerges as a Maverick," Washington Post (Oct 27, 2001). In the House, the vote was 356 to 66. See Nancy Chang, *Silencing Political Dissent: How Post- September 11 Anti-Terrorism Measures Threaten Our Civil Liberties* 43 (Seven Stories 2002).

6. Leone, *The Quiet Republic* at 9–10 (cited in note 1); Kathleen M Sullivan, *Under a Watchful Eye: Incursions on Personal Privacy*, in Leone & Anrig eds, *War on Our Freedoms* 128, 132–33 (cited in note 1); Jonathan Riehl, *Lawmakers Likely to Limit New High-Tech Eavesdropping*, Cong Q 406 (Feb 15, 2003).

7. Jeffrey Rosen, *Why Congress Is Brave and the Courts Aren't*, 228 New Republic 19 (issue 20, 2003).

8. 542 U.S. 466 (2004).

9. 542 U.S. 507 (2004).

10. Id at 536.

11. 542 U.S. 426 (2004).

12. 128 S. Ct. 2749 (2006).

13. Id at 2798

14. 541 U. S. 36 (2004).

15. Id at 44–45.

16. Id at 62.

17. *Senate Approves Detainee Bill Backed by Bush*, Washington Post A1 (Sept 29, 2006).

18. The Attorney General's Guidelines on General Crimes, Racketeering Enterprise and Terrorism Enterprise Investigation, VI(a)-(b) (2002). See http://www.usdoj.gov/olp/generalcrimes2.pdf; see Neil Lewis, *Ashcroft Permits F.B.I. to Monitor Internet and Public Activities*, New York Times A18 (May 31, 2002).

19. See *United States v. Miller*, 425 U.S. 435 (1976) (no "reasonable expectation of privacy" in banking records).

20. See *Katz v. United States*, 389 U.S. 347 (1967).

21. *United States v. United States District Court (Keith)*, 407 U.S. 297, 300 (1972).

22. Id at 297.

23. Id at 310, 314.

24. Id at 316–18.

25. Id at 318–21.

26. Pub. L. 95-511, Title I, 92 Stat. 1796 (Oct 25, 1978), codified as amended at 50 U.S.C. §§ 1801 *et seq.*

27. S. Rep. No. 95-604(1) at 7 (1978).

28. James Risen and Eric Luchtblau, *Bush Lets U.S. Spy on Callers Without Courts*, New York Times 1 (Dec. 16, 2005).

29. Press Release, White House, Press Briefing by Attorney General Alberto Gonzales and General Michael Hayden, Principal Deputy for National Intelligence (Dec 19, 2005), available at http://www.whitehouse.gov/news/releases/2005/12/20051219-1.html.

30. Press Conference of President George W Bush (Dec 19, 2005), available at http://www.whitehouse.gov/news/releases/2005/12/20051219-2.html.

31. James Risen, *State of War: The Secret History of the CIA and the Bush Administration* 44 (Free Press 2006).

32. Several lower courts have suggested that there is a foreign intelligence exemption from the Fourth Amendment. See *In re Sealed Case*, 310 F 3d 717, 742 (U.S. Foreign Intell. Surveillance Ct Rev. 2002); *United States v. Truong Dinh Hung*, 629 F 2d 908, 912–914 (4th Cir 1980).

33. Authorization for Use of Military Force, Pub. L. 107-40, 111 Stat. 224 (2001).

34. See 50 U.S.C. § 1811.

35. *Youngstown Sheet & Tube Co. v. Sawyer*, 343 U.S. 579, 644 (1952) (Jackson, J., concurring)

36. H.R. Rep. No. 95-1283, pt. 1, at 24 (1978) (emphasis added).

37. *Little v. Barreme*, 6 US (2 Cranch) 170 (1804).

38. *Youngstown Sheet & Tube Co. v. Sawyer*, 343 U.S. 579 (1952).

39. Id at 587.

40. Id at 638 (Jackson, J., concurring).

41. 542 U.S. at 536.

42. 128 S. Ct. at 2774 n. 23.

43. See section 314 (a) (2) (B) of Pub. L. 107-108, the Intelligence Authorization Act for Fiscal Year 2002, 115 Stat. 1402 (Dec 28, 2001). Moreover, the administration also amended FISA in the PATRIOT Act, which amended FISA in both sections 215 and 218 of the act.

44. Risen, *State of War* at 46 (cited in note 25).

45. Daniel Klaidman, Stuart Taylor Jr., and Evan Thomas, *Palace Revolt*, Newsweek 34 (Feb. 6, 2006).

46. Press Briefing by Attorney General Alberto Gonzales and General Michael Hayden, Principal Deputy Director for National Intelligence (Dec 19, 2005), available at http://www.whitehouse.gov/news/releases/2005/12/20051219-1html.

47. *Thank You for Wiretapping*, Wall Street Journal A14 (Dec 20, 2005).

48. 18 USC § 793(e). For an example of those outside the Bush administration who have advocated such prosecutions, see Gabriel Schoenfelt, *Has the* New York Times *Violated the Espionage Act?*, Commentary (Mar 2006). After the *New York Times* disclosed the NSA spy program, Senator Pat Roberts of Kansas suggested that he might propose legislation expressly making it unlawful for nongovernment employees to communicate classified information. See Walter Pincus, *Senator May Seek Tougher Law on Leaks*, Washington Post A1 (Feb 17, 2006). President Bill Clinton vetoed similar legislation in 2000. See id.

49. See *Olmstead v. United States*, 277 U.S. 438 (1928).

50. See *Katz v. United States*, 389 US 347 (1967).

51. Richard A. Posner, *Not a Suicide Pact: The Constitution in a Time of National Emergency* 132 (Oxford 2006).

52. John Podesta, *Need to Know: Governing in Secret*, in Leone & Anrig, eds, *War on Our Freedoms* 220, 227 (cited in note 1).

53. Id at 221–25; Leone, *The Quiet Republic* at 9 (cited in note 1); John F Stacks, *Watchdogs on a Leash: Closing Doors on the Media*, in Leone & Anrig, eds, *War on Our Freedoms* 237 (cited in note 1).

54. Stephen J Schulhofer, *No Checks, No Balance: Discarding Bedrock Constitutional Principles*, in Leone and Anrig, eds, *War on our Freedoms* at 91 (cited in note 1). On the secrecy of deportation hearings, compare *Detroit Free Press v. Ashcroft*, 303 F3d 681 (6th Cir 2002) (closed hearing unconstitutional) with *North Jersey Media Group, Inc v. Ashcroft*, 308 F3d 198 (3d Cir 2002) (closed hearing constitutional).

55. Podesta, *Need to Know* at 225 (cited in note 44).
56. Francis Biddle, *In Brief Authority* 216 (Doubleday 1962).

**CONCLUSION**

1. Robert H Jackson, *Wartime Security and Liberty Under Law*, 1 Buff L Rev 103, 116 (1951).
2. John Keane, *Fear and Democracy*, in Kentor Worcester, Sally Avery Birman-sohn, and Mark Ungar, eds, *Violence and Politics: Globalizations' Paradox* 226, 235 (Routledge 2002).
3. Zechariah Chafee Jr., *Free Speech in the United States* 70 (Harvard 1948).
4. 323 U.S., 219.
5. Learned Hand, *The Spirit of Liberty* 189–90 (Knopf 1974). See Larry B Kramer, *The People Themselves: Popular Constitutionalism and Judicial Review* (Oxford 2004).
6. Hand, *Spirit of Liberty* at 190 (cited in note 5).
7. Henry Steele Commager, *To Secure the Blessings of Liberty*, New York Times SM3 (Apr 9, 1939).
8. See Cass R Sunstein, *Why Societies Need Dissent* 8, 11, 27 (Harvard 2003).
9. Jackson, *Wartime Security* at 115 (cited in note 1).
10. Anthony Lewis, *Security and Liberty: Preserving the Values of Freedom*, in Richard C Leone & Greg Anrig, Jr., eds, *The War on Our Freedoms: Civil Liberties in an Age of Terrorism* 47, 67 (Century Foundation 2003).
11. *Terminiello v. City of Chicago*, 337 US 1, 37 (1949) (Jackon, J, dissenting).
12. William Rehnquist, *All the Laws But One: Civil Liberties in Wartime* 221 (Vintage 2000).
13. Biddle, *In Brief Authority* 219 (Doubleday 1962).
14. Rehnquist, *All the Laws But One* at 224 (cited in note 12).
15. Clinton L. Rossiter, *The Supreme Court and the Commander-in-Chief* 54 (Cornell 1951).
16. See *Schneiderman v. United States*, 320 US 118 (1943) (the government cannot constitutionally denaturalize an American citizen because of his membership in the Communist Party unless it can prove by "clear, unequivocal and convincing evidence" that he had personally endorsed the use of "present violent action which creates a clear and present danger of public disorder or other substantive evil); *Baumgartner v. United States*, 322 US 665 (1944) (the government cannot constitutionally denaturalize a former member of the German-American Bund for making "sinister" statements ); *Taylor v. Mississippi*, 319 U.S. 583 (1943) (the government cannot constitutionally punish an individual for stating that "it was wrong for our President to send our boys . . . [to be] shot down for no purpose at all); *Hartzel v. United States*, 322 U.S. 680 (1944) (the government cannot constitutionally

punish an individual for distributing pamphlets that depicted the war as a "gross betrayal of America," denounced "our English allies and the Jews" and assailed the "patriotism of the President"); *Keegan v. United States*, 325 U.S. 478 (1945) (overturning the convictions of twenty-four members of the Bund who had been charged with advocating draft evasion).

17. *West Virginia Board of Education v. Barnette*, 319 US 624 (1943).

18. *Duncan v. Kahanamoku*, 327 US 304 (1946).

19. *Youngstown Sheet & Tube Co. v. Sawyer*, 343 US 579 (1952).

20. See *Yates v. United States*, 354 US 298 (1957); *Sweezy v. New Hampshire*, 354 US 234 (1957); *Konigsberg v. State Bar*, 353 US 252 (1957); *Speiser v. Randall*, 357 US 513); *Elfbrandt v. Russell*, 384 US 11 (1966).

21. *Whitney v California*, 274 US 357, 375 (1927) (Brandeis, J, concurring).

# About the Author

Geoffrey R. Stone is the Harry Kalven, Jr. Distinguished Service Professor of Law at the University of Chicago. He has been a member of the faculty of the University of Chicago Law School since 1973. From 1987 to 1993, he served as Dean of the University of Chicago Law School, and from 1993 to 2002 he served as Provost of the University of Chicago.

Stone received his undergraduate degree in 1968 from the University of Pennsylvania and his law degree in 1971 from the University of Chicago, where he served as editor-in-chief of the *Law Review*. Between 1971 and 1973, he served as a law clerk first to Judge J. Skelly Wright of the U.S. Court of Appeals for the District of Columbia Circuit and then to Justice William J. Brennan, Jr. of the Supreme Court of the United States.

Stone teaches and writes primarily in the field of constitutional law. His most recent book, *Perilous Times: Free Speech in Wartime, From the Sedition Act of 1798 to the War on Terrorism* (W. W. Norton, 2004), received the Robert F. Kennedy Book Award, the Los Angeles Times Book Prize as best book of the year in history, the American Political Science Association's Kammerer Award as best book of the year in political science, Harvard University's Goldsmith Award as best book of the year in public policy, and the Scribes Award as best book of the year in law. It was also one of three finalists for the American Bar Association's Silver Gavel Award and was hailed as among the most notable books of 2004 by the *New York Times*, *Washington Post*, *Los Angeles Times*, *Chicago Tribune*, *Philadelphia Inquirer*, and the *Christian Science Monitor*.

Stone is currently chief editor of a fifteen-volume series, *Inalienable Rights*, which is being published by the Oxford University Press. He is also working on a new book, *Sexing the Constitution*, to be published by W. W. Norton. Stone has more than one hundred publications to his credit and serves as an editor of the *Supreme Court Review*. Among his many public activities, Stone is a member of the national board of directors of the American Constitution Society, a member of the national advisory council of the American Civil Liberties Union, vice president of the American Academy of Arts and Sciences, a member of the American Law Institute, and chair of the board of the Chicago Children's Choir. He lives in Chicago with his wife, Nancy. They have two grown daughters, Julie and Mollie, and two grandchildren, Maddie and Jack.

# Index

207